Rebuilding Yemen:
Political, Economic and
Social Challenges

The Gulf Research Center Book Series at Gerlach Press

The GCC in the Global Economy
Ed. by Richard Youngs
ISBN 9783940924018, 2012

Resources Blessed: Diversification and the Gulf Development Model
Ed. by Giacomo Luciani
ISBN 9783940924025, 2012

GCC Financial Markets: The World's New Money Centers
Ed. by Eckart Woertz
ISBN 9783940924032, 2012

National Employment, Migration and Education in the GCC
Ed. by Steffen Hertog
ISBN 9783940924049, 2012

Asia-Gulf Economic Relations in the 21st Century The Local to Global Transformation
Ed. by Tim Niblock with Monica Malik
ISBN 9783940924100, 2013

A New Gulf Security Architecture Prospects and Challenges for an Asian Role
Ed. by Ranjit Gupta, Abubaker Bagader, Talmiz Ahmad and N. Janardhan
ISBN 9783940924360, 2014

Gulf Charities and Islamic Philanthropy in the 'Age of Terror' and Beyond
Ed. by Robert Lacey and Jonathan Benthall
ISBN 9783940924322, 2014

State-Society Relations in the Arab Gulf States
Ed. by Mazhar Al-Zoby and Birol Baskan
ISBN 9783940924384, 2014

Political Economy of Energy Reform The Clean Energy-Fossil Fuel Balance in the Gulf
Ed. by Giacomo Luciani and Rabia Ferroukhi
ISBN 9783940924407, 2014

Security Dynamics of East Asia in the Gulf Region
Ed. by Tim Niblock with Yang Guang
ISBN 9783940924483, 2014

Islamic Finance Political Economy, Performance and Risk
Ed. by Mehmet Asutay and Abdullah Turkistani
ISBN 9783940924124, 3 vols set, 2015

Employment and Career Motivation in the Arab Gulf States: The Rentier Mentality Revisited
Ed. by Annika Kropf and Mohamed Ramady
ISBN 9783940924605, 2015

The Changing Energy Landscape in the Gulf: Strategic Implications
Ed. by Gawdat Bahgat
ISBN 9783940924643, 2015

Sustainable Development Challenges in the Arab Sates of the Gulf
Ed. by David Bryde, Yusra Mouzughi and Turki Al Rasheed
ISBN 9783940924629, 2015

The United States and the Gulf: Shifting Pressures, Strategies and Alignments
Ed. by Steven W. Hook and Tim Niblock
ISBN 9783940924667, 2015

Africa and the Gulf Region: Blurred Boundaries and Shifting Ties
Ed. by Rogaia Mustafa Abusharaf and Dale F. Eickelman
ISBN 9783940924704, 2015

Rebuilding Yemen: Political, Economic and Social Challenges
Ed. by Noel Brehony and Saud Al-Sarhan
ISBN 9783940924681, 2015

Gulf Research Centre Cambridge
Knowledge for All

Rebuilding Yemen: Political, Economic and Social Challenges

Edited by Noel Brehony and Saud Al-Sarhan

Gerlach Press

First published 2015
by Gerlach Press
Berlin, Germany
www.gerlach-press.de

Cover Design: www.brandnewdesign.de, Hamburg
Printed and bound in Germany by Hubert & Co., Göttingen

British Library Cataloguing in Publication Data.
A catalogue record for this book is available from the British Library.

Bibliographic data available from Deutsche Nationalbibliothek
http://d-nb.info/1072308800

ISBN: 978-3-940924-68-1 (hardcover)
ISBN: 978-3-940924-69-8 (ebook)

Acknowledgements and Note on Transliteration

The chapters in this book were selected from papers presented at the Gulf Research Center's Annual Conference held at Cambridge 24-28 August 2014 and were redrafted taking into account comments made by participants in the Future of Yemen panel. The editors would like to acknowledge the contribution made by participants and to thank the GRC, especially Christian Koch and Elsa Courdier, for their excellent support at the conference and since. They also want to thank Shelagh Weir, John Shipman among others for commenting on some of the chapters in draft. Hanna Siurua of the King Faisal Centre for Research and Islamic Studies provided invaluable help in preparing the text. Above all they are very grateful for Helen Lackner who gave a great deal of time in helping with the editing and collaborating with the editors in writing the introduction.

For transliterating Arabic into English the editors have adopted the approach used by the King Faisal Centre for Research and Islamic Studies. There are no diacriticals. With respect to people, they use the transliteration individuals use for themselves in the case of living personalities, which may lead to some inconsistencies. With respect to place names they have used the same spellings throughout the book in the chapters and maps.

Contents

Introduction

Noel Brehony, Helen Lackner and Saud Al-Sarhan

The chapters in this book are based on papers that were originally presented to a panel on the future of Yemen as part of the Gulf Research Center's annual conference held in Cambridge in August 2014. They were selected for this book (then provisionally entitled *Yemen to 2020*) in late 2014, and the final drafts were completed by February 28, 2015. During this period, the tumultuous changes described in this introduction were taking place: the extraordinary advance of the Huthis who, with the assistance of military units loyal to former president Ali Abdullah Saleh, took over Sanaa in September 2014 and expanded from there to take control of or move into other parts of Yemen; the resignation of President Abd Rabbuh Hadi on January 22, 2015; the Huthis taking power in a coup on February 6; the escape of Hadi to Aden on February 21 and his resumption of the presidency; a military advance by the Huthi-Saleh alliance on Aden in March, provoking Hadi into requesting external military intervention and leaving to Riyadh. On March 26, 2015, Saudi Arabia, with the support of the Gulf Cooperation Council (GCC) states (except Oman), as well as Egypt and several other countries, launched Operation Decisive Storm with logistical and intelligence support from the US and the clear acquiescence of other leading states.

At the time of writing (end April 2015), it appears that the air campaign, the naval blockade, and the fighting on the ground have degraded the military capacity of the Huthi-Saleh alliance but failed to halt their advance. The political objective of the campaign was to force the Huthis to negotiate and persuade them that they had much more to gain by working with other political forces in Yemen than by using violence against them.[1] All Yemenis – and the international community – will have to face the consequences of the conflict, which greatly exacerbated Yemen's already dire humanitarian problems, severely damaged infrastructure and the economy, and led to hundreds of deaths; many more were injured and over 150,000 were displaced by the end of April 2015. When the fighting ends there will be an urgent need not only to reconstruct what has been destroyed but to build an inclusive and stable government that can, with international support, enable Yemen to develop the full potential of its people and resources.

The authors of this book's chapters examined some of the many issues that will have to be tackled by any future Yemeni government. Since then the problems have been exacerbated and finding solutions will be an even greater challenge.

Historical and Political Background

Though Yemen is a geographical entity, albeit without clearly defined borders, it has been governed as a single state only since 1990, when the Yemen Arab Republic (YAR) and the People's Democratic Republic of Yemen (PDRY) were united to form the Republic of Yemen. In pre-Islamic Arabia states such as Saba, Main, Awsan, Qataban, and Hadramawt rose, fell, and left their traces in today's tribal names and places: Saba and Hadramawt were designations for proposed federal regions in 2014.[2] The Marib dam is a famous example from antiquity of an attempt to harness water for agriculture and urban use – the subject of two chapters of this book. Islam arrived in the seventh century, and tradition has it that the tribes of the northwest highlands were early converts. From the ninth century, this region has been dominated by the Zaydis, a distinct branch of Shia Islam whose name derives from Zayd ibn Ali ibn al-Husayn ibn Ali, a direct descendant of the Prophet Muhammad through Muhammad's daughter Fatima and her husband, Ali. They are different from the Twelver Shia of Iran, Iraq, and the GCC states and are usually regarded as close to the Sunni Hanafi school of law.[3] The most recent Zaydi Imamate, that of the Qasimi dynasty, was created at the turn of the sixteenth century and lasted until its overthrow in 1962. The majority of Yemenis are Sunni Muslims adhering to the Shafii school of law.[4] As Stephen Day notes in Chapter 1, "the religious practices of Yemen's two main sectarian groups are relatively compatible because they evolved along conciliatory lines, unlike the differences between northern Sunni and Shia Arabs of Lebanon, Syria, and Iraq.[5] He argues that political differences in Yemen are usually the result of competition between different regions, not between different sects. Thus, Zaydis and Sunnis have lived in relative harmony for centuries. [6]

The Zaydi Qasimi leaders of the Mutawakkilite Imamate based their power in the northwest highlands: the two principal tribal confederations in the region, the Hashid and the Bakil, were known as the "wings of the Imamate."[7] Day notes that the Qasimis, like other regimes before and since in this relatively resource-poor region, sought to extend their rule to richer parts of Yemen – the largely non-tribal Tihama coastal plain with its ports and the populous and highly cultivated regions of al-Janad around Ibb, Taiz, and toward the port of Aden and its hinterland. It was more difficult to penetrate the mountains of Lahij, al-Dhala, al-Bayda, and Abyan and the regions of al-Jawf, Marib, and Shabwa, which intrude into the Empty Quarter. The Imams ruled over Hadramawt only briefly, and Mahra was beyond their reach. Recent regimes have wanted to control the oil and gas resources of Marib, al-Jawf, Shabwa, and Hadramawt.

The British arrived in Aden in 1839 at a time when the Imam's tenuous grip on eastern and southern Yemen was loose and nine of the region's principal tribes were independent. The Ottomans, who had briefly established themselves in northern Yemen in the late sixteenth century, returned in 1871 but never fully subdued the country or tried to rule without the Imams. The British were interested in Aden as a port and reluctantly extended their influence into the hinterland. As they did so, their interests clashed with those of the Ottomans and the Imams. Britain offered protectorate agreements to the nine tribes and in 1904 agreed with Istanbul on what became the border between the Imam's North and Britain's South Arabia. The Turks left in 1918, and in 1934 an independent Imam accepted the arrangement, grudgingly, at a time when the expanding Saudi state was annexing Yemen's most northern provinces. In the late nineteenth century the British extended their "protection" to the sultanates of Hadramawt and Mahra, which later became the Eastern Aden Protectorate – while the nine tribes became the nucleus of the Western Aden Protectorate. Aden was administered from Bombay, not London, until 1927, leaving local matters in the hands of the amirs, sultans, and sheikhs.[8] The Hadrami sultanates had developed comparatively sophisticated administrations before the British arrived and along with Mahra, very distant from Aden, enjoyed a greater autonomy. Hadramawt had long been engaged with South East Asia and India, where large and often wealthy Hadrami communities had established themselves while maintaining strong family and religious links with their homeland. The Hadrami diaspora, then and now, exerts considerable influence in Yemen.

Arab nationalist ideals of the mid-twentieth century inspired the overthrow of the Imamate in 1962 by military officers led by Abdullah Sallal and contributed to the end of British rule and their hopes of handing over power to what had become the South Arabian Federation (which is discussed in Day's chapter). The YAR endured an eight-year civil war between supporters of the new republic, backed up until 1967 by the presence of Egyptian troops, and Royalist supporters of the Imam. In the south, the National Liberation Front (NLF) used the safe base provided by the YAR and the backing of the Egyptians to oust the British and the sultans and to create the People's Republic of South Yemen. It became the PDRY in 1970 after a left-wing faction within the NLF seized control.

The civil war in the YAR ended in 1970 in a compromise that ensured the survival of the republic with former royalist supporters (but not the Imam or his family) sharing power. Ibrahim al-Hamdi, an army officer, overthrew Sallal's successor, Abd al-Rahman al-Iryani, in 1973. Al-Hamdi was then and now regarded as one of Yemen's most successful leaders, but he was assassinated in 1977, as was his successor Ahmed al-Ghashmi in 1978 (when a briefcase carried by an emissary from the PDRY president exploded, killing both al-Ghashmi and the emissary). Al-Ghashmi, in turn, was succeeded by President Ali Abdullah Saleh, who ruled until 2011 and remains a nefarious influence.

The political systems of the YAR and the PDRY developed in radically different directions. A Marxist, centralized state in the south dominated by the Yemeni Socialist Party (YSP) provided its citizens with the rule of law, effective administration, and good government services. Corruption was largely absent. Women had greater rights than they did anywhere else in the Arab region except Tunisia. PDRY leaders sought to eliminate tribalism and treated Islam as a private matter in a secular state. The country became an outer part of the Soviet bloc, which brought in significant defense and security support but not enough money to develop the economy. Aden's pro-Soviet policies and support for revolution in the Gulf alienated its Arab neighbors, which were then enjoying the oil booms of the 1970s and 1980s. The PDRY was very different from the conservative and still largely tribal YAR, whose leadership rejected the explicit secularism of the southern state. Only minimal government services existed in the 1970s in the north, which had good relations with its neighbors in the Arabian Peninsula.[9]

The Saleh Regime in the YAR

In 1978, many observers thought that Saleh would not last long, but they underestimated his abilities and political cunning to forge a durable regime able to exert authority, if not always continually, in most parts of Yemen. By the mid-1980s the YAR was starting to overtake the south in economic performance and benefited indirectly through remittances and economic assistance from the oil boom of the early 1980s. Saleh created a series of interconnecting networks of influence involving leading tribal, military, political, business, and local interests. These networks were maintained through the patronage he was able to provide (boosted by oil revenues after 1985), including posts in the military, security, and civil services; contracts and stipends to sheikhs; and the favors that a government can offer those who help it. Corruption became pervasive. Saleh set up the General People's Congress (GPC) to provide a political party that incorporated the elites, national and local, and was able to deliver a substantial majority in parliamentary elections.

At the heart of the regime were members of Saleh's extended family and his Sanhan tribe, part of the Hashid confederation. Sheikh Abdullah al-Ahmar, paramount leader of the Hashid, cooperated with the system from which he and his relatives benefited, even though in 1991 he set up the Yemeni Congregation for Reform, known as Islah, in opposition to the GPC. The leaders of the GPC and Islah did not allow political differences to interfere with their sharing of the spoils until the later 2000s, when the oil revenues that had fed the patronage systems fell sharply.[10]

Yemeni Unity

The PDRY and the YAR governments spoke constantly of their determination to unite what they called the two parts (*shatrayn*) of Yemen. Despite the rhetoric, there was much ambivalence. One group within the PDRY wanted to work with allies in the north to create a socialist regime for the whole of Yemen. Others saw unity as a long-term aspiration and sought first to build up the strength of the PDRY to prevent its being overwhelmed in a unified state by the four times more populous YAR. In the YAR, which also wanted to focus on internal development, there were concerns about the Marxism and secularism of the PDRY leaders. The two states acted as if they had the right to interfere in each other's affairs, and the losers of power struggles in one state were given refuge by the other. They fought brief border wars in 1972 and 1979, each of which was followed by the signing of a unity agreement. Neither government took these seriously, but they cooperated with each other when it was in their interests to do so.

Though the PDRY leaders set out to destroy tribalism, they built their own support networks from tribal alliances in their home regions. Having used violence to achieve power, they failed to solve their political and personal difficulties through peaceful means and turned their guns on each other in a disastrous quasi-civil war in January 1986. Several thousand people died, the economy was shattered, and part of the YSP, led by President Ali Nasser Muhammad, moved to the YAR. As the PDRY struggled to recover, the collapse of the Soviet Union exposed Aden's failure to build good relations with Saudi Arabia and other neighbors.[11]

The post-1986 southern leadership concluded that it was in the PDRY's interests to form a "confederation" with the YAR, stimulated by the gains that could be made from the exploitation of oil fields straddling their borders. Ali Abdullah Saleh knew that this was the time to press for federation. However, when negotiations took place in November 1989, Saleh and Ali Salem al-Bayd, the southern leader, without consulting their colleagues, agreed to implement full unity within a year, later reduced to six months. Neither wanted to allow time for opposition to unity to grow, particularly in the YAR. But the result was that the two very different systems were hastily glued together and became a model for how not to unite two states.

The unity accords allowed for a two-year transition period during which the GPC and the YSP would share power equally in the new Republic of Yemen despite the disparity in population size. Both parties agreed to a remarkable democratic opening that saw the flourishing of free media and the formation of many new political parties. However, relations deteriorated rapidly. YSP leaders concluded that President Saleh was trying to marginalize them and suspected that a campaign of assassinations of their party leaders was inspired by the Saleh regime. Matters came to a head after elections held in April 1993 gave the YSP only 20% of the parliamentarians, which, Saleh and the northern parties claimed, meant that the YSP could no longer have an equal share in the leadership, especially as the recently formed Islah polled almost the same percentage. The YSP interpreted this claim as an attempt to undermine its role as the representative of the southern people and pointed out that it won a large majority of the southern constituencies. Compromise proved impossible, and the northern armies, supported by Ali Nasser's men, defeated the south in July 1994, forcing its leaders into exile. In May 1994 al-Bayd announced the creation of the Democratic Republic of Yemen (DRY), which some assert still exists. Saleh and his allies believed that the unity accords gave them the authority to rule the south and regarded the 1994 war as the suppression of a coup against the elected authority.

Yemen after 1994

The regime was plagued with the accumulated debts of the YAR and the PDRY, and its situation was made worse by the consequences of the 1994 war and the impact of up to one million Yemenis expelled by Saudi Arabia and other GCC states in response to

Yemen's "support" for the Iraqi occupation of Kuwait.[12] Yemen experienced the travails of IMF structural adjustment despite rising revenues from oil exports. Much of the oil money was used to feed the patronage networks and to consolidate support for the regime. The president and his allies became more authoritarian. Living standards for most Yemenis did not improve, and dissatisfaction with this and the growing insecurity of the late 1990s saw an increase in disaffection exacerbated by the rise of al-Qaeda and by Yemen's support for the United States in the war against terrorism after the 11 September 2001 attacks.[13]

The Saleh regime simply extended its governing style to the south. Tens of thousands of southern military and civil personnel were forcibly retired or sacked after 1994. State land and confiscated property were given or sold to people linked to the patronage networks. Privatization of state-owned companies led to the dismissal of large numbers of workers. Southern private companies were hampered in competing for state contracts. Aden, which had officially been designated the commercial capital after unity, was allowed to languish – although attempts were made to modernize its port with foreign partners. Revenues from southern oilfields were also funneled into the regime's patronage networks. In the late 1990s Saleh acted to weaken Ali Nasser's supporters while retaining southerners in important but lesser positions including those of vice-president and prime minister. Poverty, corruption, a weak judicial system, and land disputes were ubiquitous in Yemen, but there was a growing sense in the south that it was being marginalized and "occupied" by the north.[14]

These frustrations gave rise after 2007 to the Southern Movement, or Hirak, in protests that were initially carried out by former soldiers demanding reinstatement or full pensions but quickly joined by young people demanding an end to a perceived bias against the south in the provision of government jobs, hand-outs, and services. Overreaction by the security forces led only to more determined protests and the emergence of a better organized but divided leadership. The YSP, despite its status as the former ruling party of the PDRY, lost support as it was perceived as bartering for a share of power in Sanaa rather than representing the real interests of the south.

The Huthis

The Huthi movement originated in the early 1990s in an organization called the Believing Youth set up by Hussein Badr al-Din al-Huthi.[15] It is often described as a Zaydi revivalist movement reacting to the encroachment of Wahhabism, Salafism, and Muslim Brotherhood ideology in the Saleh state.[16] The Huthis, as they came to be known after the early 2000s, felt that the republican ethos of the Saleh regime betrayed traditional Zaydi values even though Saleh and the regime's leading figures were notionally Zaydis. Their grievances include economic and social marginalization, corruption in government, the state's close alignment with the United States and Saudi Arabia, and excessive Salafi influence on state policy and schools. Increasing militancy and government reaction led to the first of six rounds of major fighting between the government and the Huthis in 2004, who were supported by tribal allies in Saada and able to exploit the difficult terrain of the area. The last of these mini-wars in 2009–2010 drew in Saudi forces reacting to an intrusion into Saudi territory by the Huthis.

In recent years, the movement has developed, alongside its militia, a political organization known as Ansar Allah, which some see as modeled on the organization of Hezbollah in Lebanon. Since 2011 Ansar Allah has participated in mainstream Yemeni politics. At the same time, the Huthi leaders have sought to build alliances within the Hashid and Bakil confederations.[17] By late 2013 they had an effective political organization, a well-equipped militia (with arms acquired from the Yemeni military), powerful alliances with former president Ali Abdullah Saleh, and indications of Iranian support. Shipments of arms from Iran have been intercepted and Iranian intelligence officials arrested in Yemen.[18] There is suspicion that Iranian and/or Hezbollah expertise has helped strengthen Huthi organizational capacity.[19] Following the Huthi takeover of Sanaa in September 2014 Iran signaled that it was willing to increase its political and economic support. Whatever the importance (or otherwise) of the Iranian connection, there is no doubt that the Huthis have become a formidable force and now seek to use their power to shape the future of Yemen.

The Gradual Disintegration of the Saleh Regime

The economic crisis of the early 2000s, tensions within the Sanhan clan over the conduct of the war against the Huthis, and political difficulties between the GPC and Islah, which in 2005 helped set up the Joint Meeting Parties (JMP) coalition with the YSP and three smaller groups,[20] contributed to the accelerating disintegration of the Saleh system. The death of Abdullah al-Ahmar in December 2007 brought into the open rivalries between, on the one hand, Sheikh Abdullah's sons and, on the other, the sons and nephews of President Saleh, who were appointed to key positions in the defense and security services, including the Special Forces and the Republican Guard. There was growing divergence between Saleh and General Ali Mohsen, Commander of the First Armored Division and long his close Sanhan ally. Ali Mohsen's forces bore the brunt of the fighting against the Huthis, which led some of his allies to suspect that Saleh was deliberately trying to weaken his power.[21]

Impact of the Arab Uprisings

In early January 2011, the Yemeni parliament, dominated by the GPC, discussed changes to the constitution that many feared would enable Saleh to become president for life, retiring only once he was sure that his son Ahmed could succeed him. Not long afterward, the first demonstrations of the Yemen Spring took place and soon escalated, as protesters established tented camps in Sanaa and other cities. Young people were in the vanguard but quickly drew in others from all walks of life and parts of society. From the outset, Islah – including the sons of Abdullah al-Ahmar – supported the protesters, providing tents, food, and protection. The Huthis also took part, establishing their own well-organized tented areas.

On March 18, 2011, demonstrators marching in the center of Sanaa were fired on by plainclothes snipers, who killed at least 50 people in what was widely described as a massacre. This event was a trigger for change in the balance of power. Many allies abandoned Saleh and Ali Mohsen announced that his First Armored Division would henceforth protect the demonstrators against the security forces. This was the most dramatic sign that the regime could be crumbling. The divisions at the top infected Yemen's politicized armed forces.

In May, there were armed clashes between Saleh's forces and militias linked to his opponents, and on June 3 he was injured in an assassination attempt that killed a number of his prominent supporters. When Saleh returned from medical treatment in Riyadh in late September, civil war seemed likely. The prospect galvanized Yemeni and international actors and prompted a weakened Saleh (who was also facing the threat of UN sanctions) to sign a GCC transition deal, which in essence saw him leave office in return for immunity for himself and close associates and the right to stay in the country in a political role as the leader of the GPC. Abd Rabbuh Mansour Hadi, an ex-PDRY army officer who left Aden in 1986 with Ali Nasser and had been the vice-president since 1994, took over as acting president for an interim period of two years – confirmed when he was the only candidate in an election in February 2012.

The Transition Deal

The transition deal was endorsed by the UNSC and the GCC and has two main elements.

Political Element

A coalition government was sworn in with equal participation by the GPC and the JMP. A broadly inclusive National Dialogue Conference (NDC) was set up to make recommendations for a new constitution, which was to pave the way for presidential and parliamentary elections in 2013. Of its members, 30% were to be women and 20% youths. Half of the delegates were southerners, and Hirak had 85 members.

Military and Security Element

The second element was the most crucial: a restructuring of Yemen's defense and security services with the objective of ensuring their loyalty through their commanders to an elected government. This was an attempt to remove the relatives and cronies of Saleh, Ali Mohsen, and Sadiq and Hamid al-Ahmar; to convert those units that were little better than tribal militias in uniform; and to deal with the problem of "ghost soldiers" who were paid (or whose salaries were paid to sheikhs on their behalf) but who did not function as soldiers. President Hadi took some important steps toward these aims, but found that while he might be able to remove generals and colonels from office and break up Ali Mohsen's First Armored Division as well as units under the control of Saleh's relatives, this did not address the depth of soldiers' personal loyalties to their patrons.

In retrospect, the major flaw in the transition deal was that it not only allowed Salah to remain in Yemen as head of the GPC (with Hadi as his deputy) but also failed to prevent him using his wealth and power to undermine the transition and the Hadi regime. The threat of UN sanctions or the withdrawal of immunity proved to be ineffective.

A third strand in the transition deal was the allocation via the Friends of Yemen (which had been set up in January 2010) of more than USD 8 billion to economic development and reform. However, much of the promised assistance has not been disbursed over concerns about stability, the efficacy of Yemen's administration, the corruption within the system, and the security threats to foreigners working in Yemen to implement the development program (see the "Economic Challenges" section below).

Outcomes of the NDC

On the surface, the NDC seemed to fulfill its promises of inclusiveness with regard to women, youth, and organizations representing the civil society serving in its nine working parties alongside politicians from the main political parties, Hirak, and the Huthis, the last two lured into participation by the promise that the NDC would address their grievances. Beneath the surface it encountered many problems. It took months to prepare for its opening, and it lasted for eleven months, instead of the scheduled six. It produced 1,800 recommendations, but the final report, written by a monitoring body and issued in January 2014, edited the recommendations in a way that was perceived especially by the Huthis and Hirak but also by young people and women as distorting the conference's actual outcomes.

The most controversial issues, dealing with the south and future government structure, were handed over to special committees, selected by President Hadi and his advisers. One of these proposed that Yemen should become a federal republic of six regions, four in the north and two in the south. This proposal was passed to the Constitutional Drafting Committee despite strong objections from the Huthis and many southerners. When the draft constitution was published in January 2015 it included this six-region federal structure. In response, the Huthis kidnapped the head of President Hadi's office to prevent him handing over the draft to an oversight committee, mostly because of their opposition to the proposed federal structure.

The Huthis (and the southerners) object not to federalism but to the way the borders of the proposed regions were imposed by Hadi and did not take sufficient account of their interests, as Stephen Day describes in Chapter 1.

Political Challenges

Huthi Ambitions – and Power

While the Huthis participated in all working parties in the NDC, they used their militias and tribal allies to consolidate their power in Saada and to move into neighboring governorates. This process accelerated during 2014 as they overran a Salafi stronghold at Dammaj[22] and took control of Amran governorate, where they attacked military units linked to Ali Mohsen and Islah and the tribal allies of the sons of Abdullah al-Ahmar. Ansar Allah put forward a populist agenda opposing cuts to fuel subsidies announced in July and calling for good governance and an end to corruption. The Huthis increasingly used "popular committees"[23] as fronts for their actions, backed up by armed militias. By September 2014 they were in control of Sanaa and strong enough to force President Hadi's government to sign the Peace and National Partnership Agreement (PNPA), which granted most of their demands in exchange for the withdrawal of Huthi militias from the capital. However, they accused Hadi of bad faith and increased their pressure, occupying government ministries, paralyzing normal government functions, and failing to withdraw their militias from Sanaa. Huthi militias took control of parts of Hodeida and Hajjah, moved into other largely Sunni-majority governorates in middle Yemen and seemed intent on continuing their advance to the south and the east. These actions and their harsh treatment of those opposing or protesting against them attracted severe criticism from Yemeni politicians and the international community. In January 2015, the Huthis challenged the president and the prime minister directly, with militias attacking Hadi's office and residence leading – as described above – to a chain of events that led to the launch of Decisive Storm on 26 March.

Saleh's Influence

The scale and speed of the Huthi advance would not have been possible without the support of military units (and some tribes) loyal to Saleh. The Huthis and Saleh have been co-operating closely since at least the start of 2014 as they sought to undermine their joint enemies associated with Islah, the sons of the late Abdullah al-Ahmar and Ali Mohsen as well as the Hadi government. It is uncertain how this alliance was formed but, as noted above, Saleh is highly skilled at manipulating political groups to his advantage. During 2014, the Saleh-influenced military units usually stood aside as the Huthis advanced and attacked military units associated with Islah. Since early 2015, it has been clear that the co-operation between military units loyal to Saleh and Huthi militias has become much more active, particularly in Taiz, Marib, and the south. The history of the Saleh regime suggests that he, rather than Abd al-Malik al-Huthi, has been the master strategist who would, when necessary, discard the Huthis. This time he may have miscalculated: his military potential is being seriously damaged by the coalition air attacks and his actions are alienating many of his supporters.

Whatever the outcome of the conflict is, the Huthis will have to be a key part of any political settlement. Their opponents at the time of writing were weak and divided and will need to recognize their power – and listen to their demands – but the Huthis will have to understand that they are not strong enough to rule alone and can only make a better Yemen by working with other Yemeni groups and ending their alliance with Saleh. It is difficult to envisage a future role for Saleh but a place will have to be found for those who were still supporting him in early 2015.

Southern Demands

Hirak asserts that southerners want a return to independence, though some might be satisfied by an arrangement in which the south forms a single region in federal Yemen with a referendum after a period of years offering the choice of permanent separation.[24] Divisions over strategy, organization, and leadership have weakened the movement. Many southerners, including those who live and work in the north and occupy leading positions in the civil service, the armed forces, and the business community, want to remain part of a united country. Nonetheless, although there is no reliable test of public opinion, close observers believe that many southerners, possibly a majority, may now favor independence. Part of Hirak participated in the NDC, but all but a rump abandoned the dialogue when the final report called for a federal Yemen with two regions in the south.

The Huthis supported southern demands during the NDC, but southerners opposed their overthrow of President Hadi and have resisted Huthi moves to take over Aden and other parts of the south. The scale and intensity of current fighting suggests that southerners will never want to be part of a Huthi-dominated regime. One of the effects of the rise of the Huthis has been the emergence of local groups throughout Yemen who feel that they must take responsibility for governance and security in their home regions – which may have implications for how Yemen is governed in any post-crisis settlement.

AQAP Terrorism

Al-Qaeda has had a presence in Yemen since the late 1990s (the infamous attack on the USS Cole in Aden harbor took place in 2000), but it was suppressed by the Saleh regime after 9/11.[25] It revived after 2006 when several of its key leaders escaped from prison, and in 2009 it merged with the Saudi branch of al-Qaeda, which had been forced out of the kingdom by the state's effective counter-terrorist program, to form Al-Qaeda in the Arabian Peninsula (AQAP). It has gained strength particularly after 2011. AQAP in the late 2000s seemed to give higher priority to Yemen as a base from which to launch or encourage terrorism in the West and GCC states, notably undertaking an attempt to assassinate the head of the Saudi counterterrorist organization and another to bring down a US airline on December 25, 2009. Anwar al-Awlaki, who was killed in a drone strike in late 2011, was responsible for initiating the AQAP strategy of encouraging lone wolf attacks via the internet, including providing advice on how to produce homemade bombs and to select targets.

In 2011 AQAP created an insurgent group – Ansar al-Sharia – to seize land in Abyan and set up an Islamic emirate, taking advantage of the withdrawal of security forces as Saleh and his opponents confronted each other in Sanaa. Ansar al-Sharia resorted to public executions and violence, which created popular aversion to the group as well as bolstering national support for the Hadi government. In 2012 the military, with the aid of citizen-created popular committees, expelled Ansar al-Sharia from the areas it had taken over.[26]

The AQAP forces were scattered but not destroyed, and the organization dispersed its operations to Sanaa and the eastern and central areas of southern Yemen. Since the rise of the Huthis AQAP has portrayed itself as the defender of Sunni Islam against militant Zaydism, as can be seen in its alliances with tribal groups in al-Bayda and Ibb since late 2014. In April 2015, AQAP was able to take control of parts of Mukalla and other coastal towns in Hadramawt following the withdrawal of the military.

Western governments assess that AQAP is the most dangerous of the al-Qaeda franchises. AQAP has a hard core of a few hundred terrorists but is able to mobilize many more via Ansar al-Sharia, often recruiting members from local tribes. Parts of AQAP have declared their loyalty to Islamic State of Iraq and the Levant (ISIS or Daish in Arabic) and were responsible for two devastating attacks on Huthi mosques in Sanaa in March 2015. Terrorists from both groups will take advantage of the 2015 fighting to expand their operations and try to create new Islamic emirates.

Both the Saleh and Hadi regimes invested heavily in counterterrorism, taking advantage of US and other Western support, which included the use of drone strikes. Up to early 2015 counterterrorist forces were overstretched in trying to cover such a vast country in which AQAP can find plenty of secure hiding places. These forces were part of the elite groups that supported Saleh and their capacity will thus have been affected by the current fighting and will need to be rebuilt. Despite the anti-US rhetoric of the Huthis they share Washington's interest in suppressing AQAP and Ansar al-Sharia.

Building New Governing Systems

Stephen Day in Chapter 1 examines the structure for a federal Yemen that was included in the draft constitution completed in January 2015 based on the proposals of a special committee, which was trying to balance many competing pressures over the make-up of the federal regions. The Huthis were angered that their demand for access to a port and for a share in Yemen's oil resources was disregarded. Day argues that a federal system can only work well if it takes full account of Yemen's physical geography and the distribution of its population and resources. He illustrates this by examining the failures of previous experiments in federation under the British in the 1950s and 1960s and in the Republic of Yemen in the early 1990s. Any new government in Yemen will need to persuade Hirak and its supporters that their demands for a separate state can be accommodated in a new and fairer federal system. Federation will remain on the agenda in any post-2015 settlement, but it can only work if those affected are fully consulted in an open and transparent process.

Under the draft constitution Hadramawt (with Mahra, Shabwa, and Socotra) was to become a single region separate from the rest of the former PDRY, which was to form the Aden region. This seems to have been designed to placate fears in the north that the creation of a single southern region would lead to the eventual secession of the south. Iain Walker in Chapter 2 deals with the Hadrami community in Saudi Arabia and its interaction with its Yemeni homeland. For centuries, Hadramawt has been a distinct – some might argue separate - part of geographical Yemen that became attached to British-protected South Arabia at the end of the nineteenth century and came close to not forming part of independent South Yemen in the 1960s. However, as Walker shows, there is a strong sense among Hadramis that their distinctiveness should be given political recognition in the form of a region. Some prefer an independent Hadramawt and few want a return to being dominated by Aden or Sanaa – or a regime in any part of Yemen dominated by the Huthis. Political attitudes in Hadramawt have long been influenced by the Hadrami diaspora, particularly in recent years by the Hadramis in Saudi Arabia, but there are also many Hadramis who have played important roles in the Yemeni political, economic, and cultural life and want to do so within a united Yemen.

The GCC transition deal of 2011 failed to curb the influence of ex-President Saleh and his patronage networks. Peter Salisbury in Chapter 3 exposes how these networks operated to distort the governing system and the functioning of the economy. He shows that President Hadi set out with "noble aims" to reform the system and its corruption but found that Saleh's control was too strong, despite threats of UN sanctions to curb the impact of what it called "spoilers." Hadi was compelled by his circumstances to try to work with, not against, the networks with the result that they remained in place. The Huthis during 2014 exploited the deep resentment among Yemenis against corruption to appeal for support, but they, too, decided to co-operate with the Saleh networks in the armed forces. As Salisbury concludes "With the Huthis now in control of Sanaa, meaningful reform of the kind required to prevent Yemen from economic collapse and a political quagmire is just as much of a distant possibility as it was under Hadi and Saleh before him."

Any future governing arrangements will require well-trained and motivated services, free of political and tribal influences and led by professional officers who take orders from an elected government. As Joana Cook discusses in Chapter 7, it is important that more women be recruited into military roles.

Economic Challenges

The country's economic situation is at least as grave and represents an even greater challenge to its longer-term future and very existence. With about 26 million people in 2015, Yemen still has a population growth rate of about 3% per annum, meaning that the population will double within 20 years or so, causing additional strain on its limited natural resources and increased demands on its weak social welfare structures. Charles Schmitz, in Chapter 4, provides an interesting critical analysis of the country's macroeconomic problems, but here we focus on those that are less comprehensively discussed in his chapter.

Water

The description of Yemen as "Arabia Felix" in the Roman period reflects its much higher rainfall compared to the rest of the peninsula thanks to the escarpments near the Red Sea that allow rainfed agriculture and occasionally lush landscapes. However, east of the escarpments, the main part of the country is largely arid, as reflected in the fact that, for centuries, its people relied on outmigration and remittances in one form or another to increase their income.

Water is the main constraint on Yemen's future. The country's annual usage of 3.5 billion m^3 exceeds its renewable resources of 2.1 billion m^3, so a third of the water used annually is mined from non-renewable deep aquifers. Per capita annual water availability has dropped to 84 m^3, well under 10% of the WHO estimate of 1,000 m^3 per capita requirement for acceptable living conditions. About 90% of Yemen's water is used for agriculture, 2% for industry, and the rest for domestic uses. Moreover, water sources are distributed unevenly within the country, with the largest aquifers located mostly under areas with low population density in Hadramawt, Shabwa, and al-Mahra governorates. Other areas are under greater pressure, particularly the densely populated western highlands, which have little in the way of deep aquifers and are mainly dependent on renewable resources: first, climate change is making rainfall patterns in these areas more irregular and problematic for agriculture, and second, the daily task of water collection is particularly onerous in terms of time and energy consumed for the women and children who spend many hours waiting for and carrying water from wells, springs, and streams. This situation has already forced the evacuation of some villages that have completely run out of water, as without water life is no longer possible. In other areas, such as the coastal villages of al-Mahra, all water has to be trucked in from distant wells. It is often saline and polluted and therefore unsuitable for drinking without purification. The cost of water is a major and unavoidable expense for all households and particularly problematic for the poor.

While Sanaa is estimated to become the first capital to run out of water in the coming decades, the urgency of the situation has already been apparent for decades in Taiz, as explained by James Firebrace in Chapter 6, which also addresses the constraints affecting the first desalination project in the country. Urban water supply problems are part of the daily life of Yemenis: those connected to the water distribution network also have to stock water in tanks and other containers as the supply is erratic and delivery frequency varies from the extreme of once every eight weeks or so in Taiz to a couple of times a week in Sanaa. Most people also have to buy water from private suppliers, even though this water is rarely potable as a result of pollution during transport and the infiltration of waste water in the urban water tables. Retail-level water purification plants play an important role in providing reasonably cheap, clean drinking water and are also profitable microenterprises.

The water situation has implications at many levels and is one of numerous causes of conflict in the country. Nor is this likely to change, given that water basins and sources appear to be completely left out of the political debates and struggles that are currently taking place.

Agriculture

With only 3% of the country's land arable, only 0.05 ha of arable land per capita, and given that 70% of the population still lives in rural areas, it is unsurprising that more than 11 million rural people are poor. Although agriculture produces only about 19% of the country's GDP,[27] it is the main economic activity for the majority of the population, despite the fact that it is no longer the main source of income for most rural households, which have to supplement the income derived from crop production and livestock through the casual labor of male household members in towns and cities. The lack of water is clearly a major constraint on agricultural development, which would otherwise be one of Yemenis' main mechanisms to get out of their worsening poverty. A major contributor to the water crisis has been the considerable increase in irrigated agriculture (which accounts for close to 40% of the total cultivated area). In some areas it is responsible for the mining of deep aquifers, and it also penalizes smallholders dependent on shallow wells as the wealthier larger landowners deepen their boreholes, thus draining the upper water-bearing layers. Almost everywhere irrigation is responsible for increasing salinity, which damages soils and reduces their fertility.

Until the turn of the century, agricultural policies in Yemen were deeply influenced by mainstream Washington Consensus strategies, which focus on the development of export-oriented crops, mainly mangoes and bananas, which typically require irrigation. In addition, agricultural research concentrated on irrigated cash crops. As a result, the country's traditional staple crops, which had previously enabled many households to be self-sufficient in food, received little attention from policy makers and researchers. Since the 1970s and with high levels of labor migration to the GCC states, the terraces that had earlier produced much of the rainfed staple crops were abandoned and left to deteriorate. The impact of the combination of neoliberal agricultural strategies and neglect of traditional crops is discussed in detail by Martha Mundy and Frédéric Pelat in Chapter 5. While there is no doubt that the considerable and rapid increase in population has played a major role in reducing Yemen's ability to feed its population, Mundy and Pelat argue that the country could have a much higher level of self-sufficiency in basic grain crops if its traditional diet of sorghum and millet had been maintained and favored over the promotion of imports that now constitute 90% of the wheat consumed in the country.

Recent years have seen some weak attempts to correct this bias through small projects supporting the development of drought-resistant staple crops (sorghum, millet, and wheat), which would directly reduce poverty and improve nutrition levels for poor rural households and bring them closer to food self-sufficiency. However, support for rainfed crops is still significantly below what would be needed to have any real impact either on food security or on the exhaustion of water supplies.

In discussions of agriculture as well as of poverty in Yemen, it is rare that qat remains unmentioned. A mild stimulant, widely cultivated in the highlands (it grows best at altitudes between 800 m and 2,000 m above sea level) and consumed everywhere in the country, qat is widely blamed, mostly by foreigners, for using up vast quantities of water and curtailing the income available for basic necessities, including food, as well as reducing the productivity of Yemenis. Although it accounts for only about 12% of cultivated land, it does consume about 30% of water, almost exclusively through irrigation. However, it plays a major role in the economy and in poverty reduction, as it is mostly cultivated by smallholders and provides employment for one-seventh of the workforce.[28] Not only does it feed the smallholders who cultivate it, but it also provides employment to casual laborers in picking and packing, drivers in transporting, and a large network of wholesale and retail traders. Without it, rural poverty would be even worse than it is. At the very least, qat can be credited with retaining a significant number of people in rural areas rather than sending them to fill urban slums.

Oil and Gas

While, as mentioned, agriculture occupies most of the population, the bulk of the country's income comes from the export of oil and gas. As elsewhere, this sector produces very little in the way of employment, and most of its income is in the form of royalties, which go into state coffers. Even in this decade, despite the multiplicity of problems, it still formed 63% of government revenues[29] and 89% of export revenues. At the height of production in 2001 the country extracted 440,000 barrels per day (bpd); this dropped to a mere 164,000 bpd in 2014 for two main reasons: First, exhaustion of the very limited reserves, and second, frequent sabotage of the pipelines by local people protesting the lack of development investments in exchange for letting their oil fill state coffers. With respect to long-term income, it is also extremely relevant to note that local consumption is already almost at the level of total production, which means that the country will not only lose export income in the future, but will also have to finance imports. The graphs in Chapter 3 illustrate the problem.

Many hoped that income from the export of gas would compensate for the expected drop in oil income. However, this is far from likely. While reserves are estimated at 16.9 trillion cubic feet, exports started in 2009 and rose to 330 billion cubic feet in 2013. Initial investment in gas exports amounted to USD 4.5 billion. The prices agreed on in the original gas export contracts have been challenged after the replacement of President Saleh. Many people have complained that these contracts did not benefit Yemen, and in 2012 the transitional government started to renegotiate them. By mid-2014, only one of the purchasing companies had agreed to a higher price. Yemen LNG is the country's largest company and its main shareholder is the French oil giant Total, followed by Hunt Oil and a Yemeni conglomerate. While there is little doubt that the earlier contracts were unsatisfactory, given the interruptions in supply due to persistent attacks, and the vast scale of the investments made by the company as well as some vested interests in Yemen (Yemenis own over 21% of the capital), it may be some time before a solution satisfying all parties is reached. Peter Salisbury discusses some of the issues around gas contracts in Chapter 3. Moreover, the drop in world prices since the summer of 2014 suggests that further successful renegotiation is unlikely in the immediate future.

Other Economic Sectors

Although industry produces 15% of Yemen's GDP, its role in employment is still far from sufficient to absorb the available labor. Industry is mainly controlled by a small number of major local companies, which primarily produce processed foods for the local market, in many cases using imported raw materials. Trade represents 9% of GDP and certainly is a very important sector. As Schmitz points out, one of the main constraints on economic development is the low skill and education level of the vast majority of the country's labor force. Much of the non-agricultural sector is under the control of a small group of large investors who focus on high and rapid returns from services investments rather than on what would be long-term development through investments in manufacturing and the transformation of produce, which would create more employment.

While employment figures for Yemen range so widely that it would be unwise to provide any specific numbers, it is often estimated that well over half of youth are unemployed and that the adult unemployment rate is also extremely high. The rate of job creation lags far behind the 400,000 or so new entrants into the labor market annually, most of whom remain un- or underemployed in rural areas. This explains in part Yemen's ongoing efforts to increase the number of its citizens working in the neighboring GCC states, the vast majority of whose labor force is imported from further east in Asia.

The country's overall poverty rate is over 54%, and the current political instability can only worsen the situation and living conditions of its people. In 2011 GDP growth was negative to the tune of 12.7% and since then has shown only very limited recovery. No investment or new jobs are likely to be created in the current uncertain situation; most existing development projects and other activities are operating at a minimal level at best and most of those under design have been put on hold.

Social Development, Gender, and Humanitarian Issues

Yemen ranks 154th in the UNDP's Human Development Index, and although its score has improved over the years, the situation is still grave with weak social sector indicators. In the long run, the general social conditions prevailing in Yemen have a significant impact on people's living conditions and their ability to improve them.

Education

Although education expenditure amounts to 5% of the country's GDP, an increasing share of this is household financing in the private sector, and indicators remain unimpressive. Illiteracy is very high, with an overall adult literacy rate of 65% and only 48.5% of women being literate. Despite improvements in school enrollment, dropout rates remain high, which means that the illiteracy rate will continue to be significant. Moreover, the number of Yemenis with secondary or tertiary education is still comparatively small, with only 16% of adults over 25 having had any secondary education. Current enrollment in secondary education includes less than half of the relevant age group (47%), while only 10% of the population of tertiary school age is enrolled in education. This still means thousands of graduates annually, but the quality of their education is generally considered much lower than that found in other countries, thus reducing their employability outside Yemen as well as preventing the emergence of innovative industries in Yemen itself.

Health

Health expenditure represents 5.5% of GDP, and here, too, increasing amounts are self-financed medical expenses in the private sector. Despite widespread complaints about the medical services, it is certainly worth noting that some indicators have improved significantly in recent decades. The infant mortality rate is now 46 per 1,000 births, and levels of immunization are much higher than they were a decade or two ago. These improvements have taken place mainly through public-sector coverage of preventative measures, while curative services have suffered considerably from a lack of state financing and the introduction of "cost recovery," which has discouraged people from seeking medical help, often till it is too late. However, should the current level of internal strife continue, both health and education indicators will deteriorate.

Gender

The position of women is worldwide considered an important indicator of overall well-being, and it strongly affects social development. Health and other gender-related data clearly indicate that much remains to be done to improve women's conditions and to achieve gender equity in Yemen. Maternal mortality rates are very high at 200 per 100,000 live births, and there is a high rate of adolescent births. While less than 8% of adult women have had at least some secondary education, the rate for men is over 24%. Girls are often withdrawn from schools at puberty, and their access to secondary and higher education is also severely limited by restrictions on their movements beyond the village or the neighborhood.

The current political struggles also focus on the situation of women. On the one hand, the NDC agreed that in the future women should hold 30% of the positions in all major political institutions; on the other, there is continued retrograde pressure from fundamentalist political forces, whether Sunni or Shia, to restrict women's autonomy. With future parliamentary elections uncertain, the recent death of the only woman member of the elected lower house of parliament leaves the body without any female representation.

Yemeni women's conditions are frequently deplored, and the country ranks at the bottom of the World Economic Forum's gender gap index. However, despite being widely used, this index is extremely biased because it focuses almost exclusively on political representation and public presence. It does not take into account "women's considerable involvement in economic and decision-making roles in the household economy, especially in rural areas, nor their rights in local contexts."[30] Women are extremely active in agriculture, where they carry out over 70% of the work (almost all livestock husbandry and most crop production activities), but their involvement in formal employment is substantially lower, and mostly in the traditional female sectors of health and education. Cook's Chapter 7 is particularly interesting for this reason, as it discusses women's participation and involvement in a sector usually primarily associated with men, namely, security.

Many problems remain, including a high rate of child and adolescent marriage. However, although far from satisfactory, women's position and circumstances in Yemen are certainly better than they are in a number of other countries. Supporters of gender equality still have much work ahead of them, particularly with the increased political role of Huthi fundamentalists since 2014.

Humanitarian Situation

Concurrently with the political and economic crises, Yemen's humanitarian situation has been worsening since 2011 to the point that in 2015, prior to the full-scale war which started in March, 16 million people were estimated to be in need of humanitarian assistance of one kind or another, including 10.5 million food insecure. Child malnutrition is the most reliable and effective indicator of severe humanitarian crisis: in Yemen it has now reached emergency proportions, with 13% of children under five wasted and 41% stunted! Despite this, only 67% of the UN's Humanitarian Strategic Response Plan for 2014 was funded, leaving many emergency programs unfunded and people wondering why. The situation in 2015 is deteriorating by the day as fighting and the blockades are vastly increasing the number of people without access to water and food, and prices are rocketing as a result of shortages of fuel.

Conclusion

Whatever the outcome of the tumultuous events of early 2015, Yemeni politicians will have to find a new way to live with each other and form a stable system of government. No single group, however powerful, can rule alone. The aspirations of women, youth, and many other groups who took part in the Yemen Spring and the NDC cannot be ignored or marginalized without serious implications for Yemen' s long-term stability.

Yemen cannot deal with its many formidable challenges without massive support from its neighbors in the GCC and the wider international community. The GCC played a crucial role in the 2011 transition deal and has since been attempting, by peaceful and then military means, to deal with the aftermath of the 2011 uprising, the emergence of the Huthis, and the residual influence of Saleh and those loyal to him. Whatever now happens, Yemen will require the international community to invest resources in reconstruction after the destruction caused by the fighting and work with Yemenis to build a better future that will provide the stability that Yemenis and their neighbors dream of. That will require all parties and states to take into consideration the interests of others and Yemeni and international political realities. If they fail, then the events of 2015 could be just the beginning of a long period of instability with a worsening humanitarian crisis, and new opportunities for AQAP and ISIS.

When considering future funding for Yemen, the international community will need to acknowledge that its failure to support the transitional regime was one of the causes of its collapse. With USD 8.49 billion pledged by the international community by mid-2014, little was visible on the ground. Delays were explained away with reference to lack of transparency and the low absorptive capacity of state institutions. The September 2012 donor conference had agreed on a "Mutual Accountability Framework," which would ensure transparency both from the Yemeni side and from funders financing the projects of the Transitional Development Plan. The plan was to be managed by an Executive Bureau, which became operational only in March 2014 because of disagreements regarding its management between the Yemeni government and the funders. Since then there has been some progress, with 70% of all funds approved for specific projects and 39% of the pledges disbursed. One-third came from Saudi Arabia, an amount almost equal to the contribution of all OECD funders put together. Most approved projects focus on long-term infrastructure, and some are of questionable value. They fail to provide solutions to long-term economic development, which needs the creation of lasting employment to provide real economic independence to poor and ordinary people. The Bureau ceased to function in April 2015 due to the absence of a recognized government.

It is clear that the current fighting will inflict severe damage on Yemen's people and economy. The situation was already dire in early 2015 and urgent assistance will be needed to meet the humanitarian crisis and reconstruct the infrastructure and the economy. After the first emergency phase, which could be prolonged, Yemen with the support of its international friends will resume the task of the rebuilding of the country so that it can sustain its people over the long term. We have examined in this book some of key issues, of which the future availability of water for agricultural and domestic use is the most critical. No action will be possible until there are viable solutions to Yemen's political problems which will require painful compromises and the commitment of all to the central goal of implementing sustainable development policies. The alternative of prolonged conflict, suffering and poverty would have the severest consequences for Yemen, its neighbors and the international community.

Notes

1 Adel Jubeir, the Saudi ambassador to the US, said, "The objective is limited to defending and protecting the legitimate government of Yemen and preventing its collapse to the Huthis, and we hope that the

wisdom will prevail among the Huthis and that they will become part of the political process rather than continue their radical approach to try to take over Yemen and destroy it." http://susris.com/2015/03/26/statement-by-saudi-ambassador-al-jubeir-on-military-operations-in-yemen-transcript/

2 Klaus Schippmann, *Ancient South Arabia: From the Queen of Sheba to the Advent of Islam* (Princeton, NJ: Markus Wiener, 2001).

3 Muhammad Zahid al-Kawthari, *Muqaddimat al-Imam al-Kawthari* (Damascus and Beirut: Dar al-Thurayya, 1997), 412.

4 Most estimates of the size of the Zaydi population vary from 25% to 30% (some are as high as 40%), reflecting the difficulty in distinguishing between the two groups. Scholars such as Bernard Haykel and Shelagh Weir have documented the spread of Sunni Islam into Zaydi areas. For most ordinary Yemenis there is little difference between the two sects and their practices.

5 A small minority of Yemenis are Ismailis.

6 For further background see Gabriele Vom Bruck, *Islam, Memory and Morality in Yemen: Ruling Families in Transition* (London: Palgrave Macmillan, 2005).

7 See Paul Dresch, *A History of Modern Yemen* (Cambridge: Cambridge University Press, 2000) and *Tribes, Government, and History in Yemen* (Oxford: Clarendon Press, 1989).

8 For a good account of the British period in the south, see R. J. Gavin, *Aden under British Rule, 1839–1967* (London: Hurst, 1975).

9 For a detailed account of the PDRY, see Noel Brehony, *Yemen Divided: The Story of a Failed State in South Arabia* (London: I. B. Tauris, 2011) and Helen Lackner, *P.D.R. Yemen: Outpost of Socialist Development in Arabia* (London: Ithaca, 1985).

10 For a good account of how the Saleh regime operated, see Sarah Phillips, *Yemen's Democracy Experiment in Regional Perspective: Patronage and Pluralized Authoritarianism* (London. Palgrave Macmillan, 2008).

11 See Brehony, *Yemen Divided.*

12 Estimates of the number expelled range from 800,000 to 1.2 million.

13 The Saleh regime expelled suspected foreign extremists, closed some religious institutes and increased its counter-terrorist activities in the country

14 For an account of this period, see Stephen Day, *Regionalism and Rebellion in Yemen: A Troubled National Union* (New York: Cambridge University Press, 2012).

15 For a detailed description of the origins and rise of the Huthis, see Barak Salmoni, Bryce Loidolt, and Madeleine Wells, *Regime and Periphery in Northern Yemen: The Huthi Phenomenon* (Santa Monica, CA: Rand Corporation, 2010).

16 There is some evidence that Saleh may have encouraged the development of the Believing Youth in an attempt to counter the growing influence of Salafism. See: Al-Jazeera interview with Muhammad Yahya Azzan: http://j.mp/Aljazeraa

17 For an analysis of tribal grievances developed during the Huthi wars, see Marieke Brandt, "The Irregulars of the Sa'ada War: 'Colonel Sheikhs' and Tribal Militias in Yemen's Huthi Conflicts (2005–2010)," in *Why Yemen Matters: A Society in Transition*, ed. Helen Lackner (London: Saqi, 2014).

18 Iran has been supplying arms to the Huthis since 2009. See for example: https://www.middleeastmonitor.com/news/americas/18380-un-report-iran-arming-houthis-since-2009

19 See Peter Salisbury, *Yemen and the Saudi-Iranian "Cold War"* (London: Chatham House, 2015).

20 The JMP consists of Islah, the Yemeni Socialist Party, the Popular Nasserist Unity Organization, the Union of Popular Forces, and al-Haqq.

21 A number of sources claim that Saleh deliberately used the First Armoured Division, commanded by Ali Mohsen, in the wars against the Huthis in order to weaken a powerful figure who might aspire to become president.

22 For an account and analysis of Salafism in Yemen see Laurent Bonnefoy, *Salafism in Yemen: Transnationalism and Religious Identity* (London: Hurst, 2011).

23 The Huthi popular committees should not be confused with the popular committees set up by the army in southern provinces, especially Abyan, to enable local communities to defend themselves against

AQAP. Members of these committees have moved to Aden to fight the Huthi-Saleh forces since March 2015.

24 Proponents of this solution refer to it as the "Sudanese" model, as applied to southern Sudan.

25 For a detailed examination of the rise, fall, and resurgence of AQAP, see Gregory Johnsen, *The Last Refuge: Yemen, al-Qaeda, and America's War in Arabia* (New York: W. W. Norton, 2013).

26 See note 20 above.

27 There are various estimates of the contribution of agriculture to GDP; Schmitz gives a lower figure in Chapter 4.

28 Christopher Ward, *The Water Crisis in Yemen: Managing Extreme Water Scarcity in the Middle East* (London: I. B. Tauris, 2015), 82.

29 For the years 2010–2012, US Energy Information Administration, Annual Country Report, September 25, 2014.

30 Dan Varisco, personal communication, November 2014.

References

Each author provides a list of references for his or her chapter. The following books are of more general interest and expand on the themes discussed in this introduction.

Bonnefoy, Laurent. *Salafism in Yemen: Transnationalism and Religious Identity*. London: Hurst, 2011.

Boucek, Christopher, and Marina Ottaway, eds. *Yemen on the Brink*. Washington, DC: Carnegie Endowment for International Peace, 2010.

Brehony, Noel. *Yemen Divided: The Story of a Failed State in South Arabia*. London: I. B. Tauris, 2011.

Burrowes, Robert D. *The Yemen Arab Republic: The Politics of Development, 1962–1986*. Boulder, CO: Westview Press, 1987.

Carapico, Sheila. *Civil Society in Yemen: A Political Economy of Activism in Modern Arabia*. Cambridge: Cambridge University Press, 1998.

Dahlgren, Susanne. *Contesting Realities: The Public Sphere and Morality in Southern Yemen*. Syracuse, NY: Syracuse University Press, 2010.

Day, Stephen W. *Regionalism and Rebellion in Yemen: A Troubled National Union*. New York: Cambridge University Press, 2012.

Dresch, Paul. *A History of Modern Yemen*. Cambridge: Cambridge University Press, 2000.

Dresch, Paul. *Tribes, Government, and History in Yemen*. Oxford: Clarendon Press, 1993.

Gavin, R. J. *Aden under British Rule, 1939–1967*. London: Hurst, 1975.

Halliday, Fred. *Arabia without Sultans*. London: Penguin, 1974.

Hill, Ginny, Peter Salisbury, Leonie Northedge, and Jane Kinninmont. *Yemen: Corruption, Capital Flight and Global Drivers of Conflict*. London: Chatham House, 2013.

Johnsen, Gregory D. *The Last Refuge: Yemen, al-Qaeda, and America's War in Arabia*. New York: W. W. Norton, 2013.

Lackner, Helen. *P.D.R. Yemen: Outpost of Socialist Development in Arabia*. London: Ithaca, 1985.

Lackner, Helen, ed. *Why Yemen Matters: A Society in Transition*. London: Saqi, 2014.

Makhlouf, Carla. *Changing Veils: Women and Modernisation in North Yemen*. Austin: University of Texas Press, 1979.

Peterson, J. E. *Yemen, the Search for a Modern State*. London: Croom Helm, 1982.

Phillips, Sarah. *Yemen's Democracy Experiment in Regional Perspective: Patronage and Pluralized Authoritarianism*. London: Palgrave Macmillan, 2008.

Phillips, Sarah. *Yemen and the Politics of Permanent Crisis*. New York: Routledge, 2011.

Philbrick-Yadav, Stacey. *Islamists and the State: Legitimacy and Institutions in Yemen and Lebanon*. London: I. B. Tauris, 2013.

Vom Bruck, Gabriele. *Islam, Memory, and Morality in Yemen: Ruling Families in Transition*. New York: Palgrave Macmillan, 2005.

Ward, Christopher. *The Water Crisis in Yemen: Managing Extreme Water Scarcity in the Middle East.* London: I. B. Tauris, 2015.

Wedeen, Lisa. *Peripheral Visions: Publics, Power, and Performance in Yemen.* Chicago: University of Chicago Press, 2008.

Weir, Shelagh. *A Tribal Order: Politics and Law in the Mountains of Yemen.* Austin: University of Texas Press, 2007.

Willis, J. *Unmaking North and South: Cartographies of the Yemeni Past.* New York: Columbia University Press, 2012.

1

The Federal Plan in Yemen: History of an Idea and Its Current Development

Stephen W. Day

At the conclusion of Yemen's National Dialogue Conference (NDC) on 25 January 2014, the most significant outcome of its broad-ranging debates was a proposal to adopt federal structures of government. As a topic of debate, federalism also proved to be the NDC's most divisive issue because delegates failed to reach consensus on the number of federal regions.[1] The topic was first placed on the conference agenda by representatives of the southern protest movement, known as Hirak, who served on two working groups dealing with "the southern issue" and "state building." The majority of Hirak leaders had earlier boycotted the NDC because they refused to negotiate over their demand for southern independence. In the end, conference organizers recruited most Hirak delegates to act in the group's name.[2] These individuals decided to demand a two-region federal division between populations of the old northern and southern territories that had originally merged in 1990. Meanwhile, northern delegates pressed for a greater number of federal regions because they did not want to enable Hirak to recreate the country's pre-1990 division. Two weeks after the NDC concluded, interim president Abd Rabbuh Mansour Hadi unveiled the decision of a special presidential committee to adopt a six-region federation, including four regions in the former north and two regions in the former south.

Because the choice of a six-region federal system was taken outside the NDC's rules for consensual decision making, it remained under dispute throughout 2014 as members of a separate presidential committee drafted a new constitution reflecting outcomes of the National Dialogue. When the first draft of the NDC constitution was presented to the public in early January 2015, its call for a six-region federation led to sharp conflict between President Hadi and leaders of the northern Zaydi/Shia religious movement, known as the Huthis, with a political organization called Ansar Allah, "Partisans of God." During the year when the country had waited for the draft constitution to be written, Huthi leaders and commanders of battle-hardened militia took advantage of the delay to defeat domestic enemies between their home base in Saada governorate and the capital

Sanaa. In September 2014, the group's commanders surprised most observers by fighting their way into the capital. Thereafter, President Hadi fell under increased pressure from Huthi leaders who successfully negotiated an end to fighting via the Peace and National Partnership Agreement (PNPA). The PNPA increased the Huthi's political power, allowing them to demand the appointment of a new prime minister and cabinet, while influencing the "National Authority" tasked to ensure the draft constitution did not contradict NDC outcomes.

As a matter of principle, Huthi leaders saw the six-region federal plan as a contradiction of NDC outcomes because of the irregular way it was originally proposed following the NDC's closing ceremony. As a matter of power politics, however, they also objected to three of the proposed regional boundaries cutting across northern territories which they hoped to control: namely, areas of Tihama along the Red Sea coast in Hajja and al-Hodeida governorates, which the group coveted for access to seaports; and areas of Saba in the desert interior of al-Jawf and Marib provinces, which hold valuable petroleum and water resources, as well as electricity generation stations. When President Hadi resisted Huthi demands to cancel the six-region federal plan, Huthi gunmen kidnapped the president's chief of staff, Ahmed bin Mubarak, on 17 January 2015. Kidnapping is a common practice in Yemen's northern mountains where heavily armed tribesmen often use it without causing personal harm, in order to increase bargaining leverage over the head of state. In this case, it led to a tense standoff in the capital that erupted two days later in deadly armed conflict around the presidential palace and Hadi's personal residence. It is widely suspected that Huthi militia had support from military commanders loyal to deposed President Saleh, who still maintained considerable behind-the-scenes influence due to an amnesty granted to himself, his sons, and other close family members.

When President Hadi and his appointed prime minister, Khaled Bahah, submitted their resignations on 22 January, while held captive inside their homes, it left Yemen's entire post-2011 political transition in doubt. Not only was the six-region federal plan likely to be abandoned, but the draft constitution was in jeopardy of being scrapped. Even more ominously, it seemed possible that Yemen's national unity would not survive because many regions chose to break away from Sanaa rather than live under Huthi rule. In particular, people in southern and eastern regions rallied in greater numbers to Hirak's original call for secession, while provincial administrators of these regions announced they would not follow orders coming from Sanaa. Soon administrators and popular committees in some northern governorates like al-Hodeida, Taiz, al-Bayda, Marib, and al-Jawf expressed interest in joining southern secession. Between 30 January and 1 February, Huthi leaders organized an expanded National Conference in Sanaa, which was modeled on the NDC, in an attempt to unite groups across the country. In the following weeks, they arranged a five-person presidential council to replace Hadi, and began to create a National Council as an expanded version of the old parliament. Then on 21 February, Hadi turned the tables on Huthi leaders when he and his family managed to escape house arrest in Sanaa. Hadi fled with his family to the former southern capital Aden where he denounced "the Huthi coup in Sanaa," sought to reclaim his role as president, and pledged to implement the NDC outcomes.

This chapter examines the sharply contested debates over Yemeni federalism, and growing doubts surrounding the NDC six-region plan, by analyzing the history of federal ideas inside the country. Federalism was twice previously proposed in Yemen. The first instance came at the end of the 1950s in the former British-ruled south Arabia. Although the British plan was never fully implemented, the idea remained an active subject of political debate as recently as the 1990s at the time of unification between north and south Yemen. By reviewing Yemeni history, it is hoped that lessons from the past might serve three functions: first, to inform about the dynamics underlying recent events in the country; second, to examine what the future might hold, whether or not Yemen actually becomes a federal state; and third, to offer suggestions of how federalism could help strengthen Yemen's representative government, while improving the country's prospects of economic development. The federal plan that arose from the NDC did not suddenly appear in a vacuum, as if it were detached from all prior experiences in the country. Rather it is rooted in much older developments prior to Yemen's national unification in 1990, and long before its recent participation in the Arab Spring. In reality, Yemeni unity never rested on a firm foundation due to multiple regional divisions that have shaped and defined its politics for centuries.

The analysis presented in this chapter derives partly from the author's book, "Regionalism and Rebellion in Yemen: A Troubled National Union," which was published by Cambridge University Press in 2012. The book develops its line of analysis based upon a set of theories about nation building, state development, and identity formation among citizens of countries divided along regional lines. According to these theories, political unity and social stability depend upon how governments manage relations between members of regional groups that compete over political and economic resources, such as ministerial portfolios in government cabinets, and the distribution of state revenues generated from taxes and valuable natural resources. Failure to manage resource competition in regionally divided countries increases intra-group solidarities and inter-group rivalries. In other words, citizens from different regions are likely to adopt stronger regional identities that undermine a common sense of national unity. This clearly happened in Yemen after its 1990 unification, leading to a brief civil war in 1994. Thereafter, various regional opposition movements undermined a single national identity because President Saleh failed to manage resource competition in constructive ways before being overthrown in 2011. The flawed policies of his regime, and its well-documented corruption, abuse of human rights, and discrimination against citizens from outlying regions, generated fierce opposition from groups like the Huthis after 2003, and Hirak after 2006.

Throughout Yemen's three millennia history, it has no record of being governed as a federation of regional states. Indeed the population has rarely been united under a single authority. More often Yemenis were divided into regions ruled by separate authorities. For this reason, the experience of national unity during the past two and a half decades is an exception to the rule, while the NDC-proposed federal system of government would, if implemented, create something entirely new. Federalism will always have some relevance in Yemen because its social and political geography is unlike other parts of the Middle East more famous for dynastic rule under a single authority, such as the Nile river basin governed by a long succession of pharaohs; lands of the ancient Sumerians and Babylonians between the Tigris and Euphrates Rivers; or the high plateau of ancient Persia. In ancient Egypt and Iraq, fertile plains around lengthy rivers created environments capable of sustaining large-scale, centralized rule for centuries. This is not true of Yemen, where there are no major rivers or permanent bodies of fresh water.

Throughout history, Yemen's remarkably diverse mountain and desert terrain made it possible for ruling groups to remain relatively isolated in different regions, where group members developed distinct ethnic-cultural traits. Regional identities persisted for three millennia because rugged mountains and deep canyons made travel difficult prior to the widespread introduction of car and air transportation in the 1960s. Today it is still common for Yemenis to marry within their regional and tribal groups. Thus group structures are fairly static in the 21st century. In pre-Islamic times, there were at least two rival civilizations, and occasionally as many as four: first, in the interior desert at Marib; second, near Dhamar in the mountains south of Sanaa; third, along the Red Sea coast in Tihama; and fourth, near the interior canyons of Hadramawt. Among the ancient civilizations, rivalries existed between rulers who sought to acquire lands and markets of neighbors. Sometimes two rulers formed an alliance to fight a third in battle. Occasionally, one group unified larger territories, as Himyarite rulers briefly did in the first centuries C.E., by controlling the Red Sea and Gulf of Aden coasts. But decades later, they were inevitably forced out because of difficulties holding such rugged terrain.

During the time of Islam's prophet and his early successors, who ruled from the Hejaz region north of Yemen, the land was divided into three regions: Asir in the northwest, which included the southwestern part of modern Saudi Arabia, as well as the highlands around Sanaa; al-Janad in the southwest, which included lands between Aden and the fertile valleys of Taiz and Ibb; and the vast region of Hadramawt in the east. Each of these regions evolved differently under Muslim rule, adopting variations of Islamic laws and customs. The Rasulid Dynasty based in Tihama and Taiz (early 13th - middle 15th centuries C.E.) briefly expanded control as far north as Mecca, and as far east as Oman. Yet it originated as a Turkish sultanate commissioned by an Abbasid caliph in the north, and only later adopted a local Yemeni Arab identity. The only time a local ruler initiated political unification of territory from Tihama to Hadramawt was during the Qasimi dynasty of Zaydi imams in the mid-17th century. Yet after a few decades, the Zaydi imam's highland tribal forces were thrown out of lowland Shafii areas to the south and east, where populations rejected Zaydi rule.[3]

The Shafii-Zaydi division is less a matter of religious sectarianism than a reflection of millennia-old divisions between highland and lowland/coastal regions of Yemen.[4] Zaydis have long predominated in the highland mountain plain between Saada and Sanaa, while Shafii customs prevailed in other regions. Just as Yemen's ancient civilizations were divided across mountain and desert terrain before the rise of Islam, so the division between Zaydi and Shafii reflected geography, too. In other words, the Zaydi arrival in Yemen during the late 9th century C.E., roughly one century after the founding of the Shafii legal school, did not dramatically alter the prevailing regional divisions among the population. Likewise, the end of the Zaydi imamate in 1962, more than one millennium later, did not eliminate the political relevance of Yemeni regionalism. Indeed, the division between highland and lowland regions, and the question of who rules the country, remained relevant after unification in 1990. Even the Zaydi revival by Huthi leaders in the 2000s, and their slow advance south of Saada to overthrow the government in Sanaa in 2015, reflects greater regional than sectarian divisions.

Throughout Yemeni history, the primary determinant of politics is the tendency of highland mountain people (*jabali*, in Arabic), who are members of two large tribal federations called Hashid and Bakil, to seek control over midland/lowland regions. There are two reasons why inter-regional dynamics between highland and midland/lowland people are more important than inter-sectarian dynamics. First, the religious practices of Yemen's two main sectarian groups are relatively compatible because they evolved along conciliatory lines, unlike the differences between northern Sunni and Shia Arabs of Lebanon, Syria, and Iraq. Second, the highlands are a resource-poor region, which motivated tribesmen of Hashid and Bakil to gain power over relatively resource-rich midland and lowland areas that produce higher tax revenues for governments based in the mountains.[5] The latter point remains true in the era of rent allocation from petroleum resources because Yemen's highland mountains contain no oil and gas fields. At the time of Yemeni unity, it became clear that the richest petroleum resources are located in Marib, Shabwa, and Hadramawt provinces in central and eastern regions. Former President Saleh's regime (whose most influential members came from a subdivision of the Hashid tribe, called Sanhan, located near the capital Sanaa) expended great effort to control oil and gas wealth drawn from these regions against the interests of local populations.

The contest between people of different regions, competing over scarce resources, is undoubtedly a more significant factor in the country's recent unrest and instability than inter-sectarian rivalries. Thus, it is a mistake to blame Yemeni sectarianism. This remains true despite the revival of Zaydism, first by the Huthi in Saada after 2003, and second by Ansar Allah's gradual seizure of political control in Sanaa during the fall and winter of 2014/2015. After entering Sanaa in September 2014, Huthi military forces moved outside the traditional Zaydi region to Shafii/Sunni areas of the western midlands around Ibb and Taiz, and the neighboring western coastal region of al-Hodeida. If they persist in this direction, eventually invading Shafii/Sunni areas of southern and eastern provinces, then this will definitely risk greater sectarian conflict with rival Sunni militant groups such as al-Qaeda. More likely, however, it will reflect the continuing historical pattern of highland people in Yemen seeking control over more valuable resources in midland and lowland regions.

The remainder of this chapter examines three episodes in modern history when the idea of federalism was introduced to Yemen: 1959-1967; 1989-1994; and 2011 to the present. These episodes are discussed through an analysis of three main features of federalism: 1) the choice of regional units and boundaries; 2) the definition of central and regional government powers; and 3) the arrangement of revenue-sharing between regions and the central government.

The Choice of Regional Units and Boundaries

In February 1959, the Federation of South Arabian Emirates was announced at a time of rapid decolonization when Britain sought to reduce its role in, and eventually abandon, one of its last colonies.[6] Britain first colonized the harbor town of Aden in 1839, in order to use it as a coaling station for ships traveling to India and beyond. Aden colony gained particular importance after the opening of Egypt's Suez Canal to commercial and passenger shipping in 1869. By the middle 20th century, Aden had become one of the busiest free ports in the world. At this time, British officials managed two large "protectorates" in south Yemen, one in the sparsely populated eastern region of Hadramawt, and the other in a smaller western region around Aden. Yet the British had always operated in south Yemen with commercial eyes turned to the outside world, showing a relative lack of interest in the interior's development. Until the end of British rule in 1967, their primary interest was to guarantee the unobstructed flow of goods into and out of Aden. This meant signing "protectorate" treaties with tribal leaders in the interior, in order to strengthen security in Aden, because Ottoman officials (pre-1918), and Zaydi Imams (post-1918), looked at southern tribes as part of their own political heritage. Both Ottoman and Zaydi states in north Yemen felt free to interfere in south Yemen despite accepting the British border drawn in the early 1900s.

It was only after World War II that the British planned broader political and economic development on southern lands, working in coordination with interior rulers of tribal areas. Yet the sums of money spent were meager and largely inconsequential, except for a few irrigation and agricultural projects close to Aden. The more advanced plan for a federation of southern states in 1959 came in response to threats posed by revolutionary pan-Arab movements in the 1950s, like Nasserism in Egypt. Gamal Abdul Nasser's broad appeal to non-aligned interests in Arab countries, as well as pro-Soviet communist and socialist trends in Syria and Iraq, stirred local dissent against British rule in south Arabia. Britain's federal plan was an attempt to avoid fragmentation of the hinterland, while maintaining Aden's security as a colony. It involved the improbable transformation of more than twenty separate sultanate, emirate, and tribal sheikh authorities into roughly an equal number of federal units. The first problem was that these "authorities" had widely varying degrees of administrative power and capability. Even the designation of some as "sultans" and "emirs" was a pretense maintained by British governors in Aden, who failed to realize that local rulers were often little more than mediators among disgruntled tribes and sub-tribes that rarely obeyed orders.[7] The second problem was that local rulers typically did not trust each other, and had no experience working together.[8] The influential sultan of Quayti in Hadramawt refused to join the federation, along with two other eastern sultans of al-Kathiri and al-Mahra, because of rivalries and disinterest in affairs of western lands near Aden. Meanwhile, a few western leaders from rugged hill country in upper Yafi, northeast of Aden, boycotted the plan because they had never accepted British influence.

The third and final problem with the British federal plan was its unpopularity in Aden, especially among members of labor unions and opposition parties who viewed it with deep suspicion. The latter commonly regarded federalism as the creation of an imperial power accustomed to using "divide-and-rule" tactics to serve secret, ulterior motives. In reality, the plan was a hurried, clumsy attempt to maintain British political and military interests, while forcing Aden into formal political and economic union with more numerous, undeveloped "federal states" of the interior. The plan had little chance of success because Britain no longer wanted to be involved with restless interior regions (especially after Nasser's Egyptian armed forces assisted north Yemen's revolution in September 1962, and south Yemen had commenced its own revolution by October 1963), yet it was prepared to entangle Aden in those interior regions by granting leaders of the interior more leverage over the port city, while inhibiting Aden's government from dominating the federal union. As the spirit of armed revolution rose during the middle 1960s, British military and security officers fought an increasingly violent counterinsurgency campaign inside Aden. Under these circumstances, it was nearly impossible to make the federal plan work.

Following Britain's 1964 election, a new Labor Party government in London announced that the South Arabian Federation would become fully independent by 1968, although it still hoped to maintain military basing privileges in the country. Less than two years later, amidst financial difficulties at home and an inability to afford rising costs in Aden, Britain accelerated South Arabian independence before the end of 1967, while deciding to abandon all of its army, navy, and air bases. Independence came on 30 November 1967, after British officials handed power to leaders of the southern National Liberation Front (NLF) in Aden. To some extent, the NLF benefited by adapting administrative structures of the Federation. Although the NLF removed traditional local rulers from power, it absorbed the British-trained Federal South Arabian Army and Police Force. Then in the summer of 1969, a "corrective movement" was launched by younger Marxist-inspired leaders of the NLF. They overturned remnants of the former system, removed many of the British-trained Arab officers, concentrated political power, and created a centrally planned economy modeled on Eastern Bloc states.

The plan for a Federation of South Arabia died with the British withdrawal from Aden. Yet even if the British had stayed, there is reason to doubt they could have made it work. Forever after, the idea of federalism would be tainted in both halves of Yemen by its unpopular association with western colonialism. To some extent, this association persists today in the minds of Yemenis who debate the merits of the UN-sponsored NDC six-region federal plan, particularly in light of the disastrous consequences of federalism implemented in Iraq's 2005 constitution following the invasion by US and British forces in 2003. Deposed President Saleh, his closest associates, and other individuals of influence in Yemen's highland mountains have often depicted the NDC's federal plan as a western plot to destroy the country as a unified nation. When Ansar Allah pressured President Hadi in January 2015 to remove the six-region federal plan from the draft constitution, the group's leader Abd al-Malik al-Huthi gave a widely watched speech on television condemning federalism as a foreign plot that Hadi and his associates were implementing on behalf of western governments.

Despite the association of federalism with "western plots" against Yemen, public attitudes have generally changed since the 1960s, so more citizens (especially in areas outside the highland mountains) are able to understand how federalism might help resolve problems in their country. This was revealed in a 2014 public opinion survey conducted by the Arab Center for Research and Policy Studies.[9] Following the conclusion of the NDC, the survey found twice as many respondents supported the new federal plan as those opposed to it. Approximately 75% of all respondents understood the basic meaning of federalism; and when supporters of federalism were asked the reason for their support, 56% said the results of the NDC "provided the country with a way out of a crisis, avoiding potential strife and civil war." An additional 17% said it "provides a foundation for a modern, democratic state," and 11% felt it "maintained the unity of Yemen." Compared to public opinion in the 1960s and 1970s, these poll results are a positive sign. Yet circumstances in Yemen today are much closer to the early years of national unity in the 1990s, so there are better lessons to draw from the second occasion when the idea of federalism surfaced in political debates.

In late 1993 and early 1994, Yemenis across the country participated in a series of "national dialogue" conferences that ultimately proved a futile attempt to avoid civil war in late spring 1994. The concluding document of this earlier "national dialogue" became known as the "Document of Pledge and Accord" (DPA), which was signed by President Saleh and Vice President Ali Salem al-Bayd, former head of south Yemen, at a ceremony hosted in Amman, Jordan, by King Hussein. The reason for the DPA was a political stalemate in forming a new government after Yemen's first elections one year earlier in April 1993. From the first year of unification in 1990-91, Saleh, al-Bayd, and their associates engaged in escalating disputes. Before the end of 1991, there was a mysterious campaign of attacks targeting southern politicians for assassination. Al-Bayd blamed the attacks on Saleh and his military strongman, General Ali Mohsen al-Ahmar, who was allied with al-Bayd's main domestic enemies among Arab-Afghan mujahedeen veterans of the anti-Soviet jihad in the 1980s. Twice al-Bayd and his colleagues in the old Soviet-allied Yemeni Socialist Party withdrew from Sanaa and returned to Aden. Their second withdrawal in the fall 1992 led to a six-month postponement of the first election.

When voting finally took place on the basis of proportional representation, no party won an outright majority in parliament. Saleh's party gained the most seats in April 1993, followed by the Islamic "Reform" (Islah) party, and al-Bayd's Socialists. Despite coming third, al-Bayd insisted on continuing to share power on roughly equal terms with Saleh. Yet Saleh intended to form a new governing coalition with Islah as a minority partner equal in weight to al-Bayd's party, while Saleh's party would hold majority control. As the stalemate continued through the summer of 1993, al-Bayd's deputy pushed for government reform along federal lines. Federalism would allow al-Bayd's party to exercise regional autonomy in the former south, where it had won the election by a landslide margin. Saleh and his associates accused al-Bayd and other members of the Socialist party of using federalism to secede from the union. The charge of treason dramatically raised political temperatures threatening to unleash civil war. Saleh reminded al-Bayd that the two leaders had agreed on a unitary model of government in late 1989, despite the fact politicians on both sides of the border had originally suggested unification on the basis of a federal or confederal design. In 1989, members of both ruling parties felt a loose confederation was the best option. Even a majority of leaders in al-Bayd's party favored confederation, so al-Bayd largely acted alone when he signed the agreement to join Saleh in a Sanaa-based unitary state.[10]

At nationwide dialogue conferences in the fall 1993, it became clear the most important reconciliation effort, which was later inscribed in the DPA, would require a devolution of political power to locally elected bodies at provincial and district levels.[11] During this time, a map circulated in newspapers depicting a potential five-region federal state. Yet there was nothing in the DPA stipulating a specific number of regional units. Nonetheless, as early as 1993, it was recognized that some degree of decentralization outside the capital Sanaa was necessary in order to save national unity from the mistakes made in 1989-1990 when a simple unitary state had been formed. Unfortunately, the DPA was never implemented in the spring of 1994 because Saleh continued accusing al-Bayd and associates of plotting to secede, eventually provoking a costly civil war that ended two and a half months later on 7 July 1994. Weeks before the war ended, the UN Security Council passed two resolutions, 924 and 931, recognizing Yemen's DPA as a helpful blueprint for fixing the problems of national unification.

The main lesson of this second occasion when ideas of federalism surfaced in Yemen is that influential actors can derail any devolution of political power by instigating violence or wider conflict. This is especially true of actors inside the highland mountains who are interested in exercising power from the capital Sanaa. These actors exploit conditions of insecurity because it helps justify their own rule over a centralized state. In early 2014, there was clearly a need to check disruptive behavior of certain individuals suspected of wanting to derail Yemen's transition process. For this reason, the UN Security Council passed resolution 2140 on 26 February, creating a "Sanctions Committee" to block the finances and travel of anyone obstructing NDC outcomes.[12] In the following summer, the Security Council's advisory body on Yemen released a statement naming deposed president

Saleh and two Huthi military commanders as individuals acting against Yemen's transition. Yet the Security Council never imposed sufficient penalties, even after September 2014 when Huthi leaders moved aggressively against President Hadi inside Sanaa, presumably with assistance from troops acting on secret orders of Saleh. By the time Hadi was forced to resign in January 2015, it was largely too late for the UN Security Council to prevent damage done to the transition process.

There is an important principle about the number of regional units in a federal system of government. Generally speaking, the greater number of federal units in a fixed territory increases the ability of central government officials to hold more power, while the lesser number of units increases the power of regional officials. This is counter-intuitive because increasing the number of federal units would seem to make the central government's task more difficult. Yet most central governments in federal systems find it easier to control regional governments that are relatively small and weak. Meanwhile, regional governments tend to have greater power relative to the central government when each region represents a larger territory with a higher percentage of the population. This generally explains the difference between southern Hirak's demand at the NDC for a two-region federal state on the one hand, and the preference of northern politicians for a six-region federation on the other hand. During President Saleh's rule before 2011, he occasionally attempted to break up the largest provinces of Yemen by creating two or more local administrative units. For example, he created two new provinces, al-Dhala and Amran in 1998, while attempting to divide Hadramawt between its coastline and interior canyon. He failed in Hadramawt due to massive public protests in the eastern region. One year later, opposition forces in al-Dhala launched an armed revolt against Saleh's government.

Today, Saleh and close associates in the General People's Congress (GPC), the political party he set up, and over which he still exercises control, favor the current local administrative system with more than twenty provinces. By contrast, the young leader of Ansar Allah, Abd al-Malik al-Huthi, had earlier expressed sympathy with Hirak's vision of a federation between northern and southern regions. Thus, there is a chance that greater Huthi influence over government policy in Sanaa could reopen the federal question in favor of Hirak's preference. In reality, if the federal question is reopened or remains unsolved, it could equally redirect Yemen toward a multi-sided breakdown of the state because of the existence of multiple regional groups. The strongest regional group identity in Yemen is undoubtedly the Hadramis. After Huthi forces entered Sanaa in September 2014, a former eastern sultan, Ghaleb bin Awadh al-Quayti, called for the formation of an independent state of Hadramawt, as local tribal militia demanded the removal of all Yemeni armed forces.[13] Meanwhile, on Hadramawt's eastern edge along the border with Oman, citizens of al-Mahra province sought an independent state backed by their former sultan.

After the six-region federal plan was unveiled in February 2014, street leaders of Hirak in Aden and other southern provinces vowed to continue pressing for complete national independence of a united South Arabia. This had also been true of some government-appointed NDC representatives of Hirak. In June 2014, President Hadi appeared to persuade local Hirak to support the six-region federal plan when he received an endorsement from retired General Nasser al-Nuba, who helped initiate southern protests in spring 2007 by organizing sit-ins by retired southern military officers in Aden. In addition, a prominent international lawyer and supporter of southern interests, Dr. Muhammad Ali al-Saqqaf, wrote an online article encouraging Hirak to work with President Hadi. Dr. al-Saqqaf cautioned that the likely alternatives to Hadi's leadership could be far worse for southern interests. The vast majority of Hirak supporters have long sought a public referendum to determine whether citizens of southern and eastern regions want to remain part of Yemen, or quit to form an independent "South Arabia." This idea was floated by Hirak delegates at early sessions of the NDC in 2013, when some suggested a referendum might be held five years after the NDC outcomes are implemented, in order to give Yemeni unity one last chance of success.

The Definition of Central and Regional Powers

Outside the brief moments in time when the idea of federalism surfaced in modern Yemeni politics, government centralization of political and economic affairs has been the norm. As a result, most historical lessons concern the problem of excessive centralized rule. Following Yemen's revolutions in the 1960s, both northern and southern governments opted for strong centralization. Yet each side progressed toward this goal at different speeds. South Yemen moved more rapidly after June 1969, when younger Marxist members of the NLF aligned the country with the USSR. The economic resources of the once flourishing port city of Aden allowed government officials to centralize state revenues more easily for redistribution at provincial and district levels. By the middle 1970s, leaders in Aden also formed a viable ruling party that never lost control prior to unification in 1990. Yet the centralization of state revenues fed a struggle for power among rivals inside the ruling Socialist party. This culminated in a destructive intra-regime battle inside the capital in January 1986, during which thousands were killed and the destruction of buildings left Aden a shell of its former self. President Ali Nasser Muhammad and his allies from a middle region of the country had previously tried to implement liberal reforms designed to decentralize the political and economic systems. They lost the battle of 1986, and were forced into exile, while an alliance of opponents from western and eastern regions took control under the leadership of Ali Salem al-Bayd, who is originally from Hadramawt.

The process of centralization in north Yemen was the opposite of south Yemen. After the 1960s, once republican rule had successfully replaced the centralized order of the Zaydi imamate, the main centers of economic and political activity existed outside the capital. Unlike Aden, Sanaa was not the site of north Yemen's greatest resources, which largely existed in western midland and coastal regions of Taiz and Tihama, respectively. Once the last Zaydi imam fell from power, Shafii citizens in Taiz, Tihama, and other areas, realized greater economic and political opportunities in local cooperatives. The government in Sanaa, which had been a small town at the start of the northern revolution in 1962, gradually attempted to gain central control over cooperative revenues. A few years after Saleh came to power in 1978, he accomplished this goal when he founded the north's first ruling party, the GPC, in 1982. Thereafter, the city of Sanaa expanded rapidly, especially once oil was discovered in Marib and the central government received a flood of new revenues after 1985. On the eve of national unity in 1990, Sanaa had become a sprawling metropolis of one million people, while the once thriving port city of Aden was weary from conflict in a centralized socialist state. In short, politics in the two capitals were mirror reflections of each other.

Once north and south Yemen agreed to unite in late 1989, it was clear that both heads of state were in a rush to achieve what other Yemeni leaders had failed to accomplish. What Saleh and al-Bayd initiated in 1990 amounted to the complete merger of two distinctly different government administrations. Saleh and al-Bayd agreed that their ruling parties would share power in the capital Sanaa until pluralist national elections could be held. Saleh served as president and al-Bayd as vice president on a five-person presidential council composed of three members from the north and two from the south. Saleh was granted majority control because the north's population (roughly twelve million) was more than four times the population of the south. Seats on a thirty-nine member cabinet were split along nearly even lines with the north holding a one person majority. The prime minister was a southerner, and another southern politician served as speaker of parliament. The only power sharing at a local level involved a few provincial governors who exchanged posts across the former border. These governors remained tokens of national unity because real authority remained in Sanaa.

Within the first full year of unity, the northern minister of finance began appointing deputies in southern provincial and district offices. In nearly every case, these deputies came from the highland region around Sanaa because they could be trusted to ensure all revenues flowed back to the capital.[14] Except for the campaign of assassinations against southern politicians in late 1991 and 1992, the seizure of southern finances caused the greatest north-south tensions because it directly challenged southern autonomy. In late 1992, the southern governor of Aden stopped sending local revenues to the finance ministry in Sanaa, choosing instead to distribute funds for local development projects. In addition, southern leaders in Sanaa elevated provincial staff in Aden to the rank of deputy ministers. It was shortly afterward, when the 1993 election resulted in a stalemate, that al-Bayd's deputy first brokered the idea of federalism. Northern politicians have long claimed that southerners pressed a federal agenda only after losing the first parliamentary election in April 1993. Yet this is inaccurate because al-Bayd's party campaigned in early 1993 on a pledge to give local governments "total powers ... (with) financial and administrative independence."[15] Thus, southern party officials clearly viewed the centralization of government power as a problem prior to the first election.

Once civil war broke out in the spring of 1994, northern forces quickly pursued siege warfare on the city of Aden. The UN Security Council intervened with calls for a ceasefire and political reconciliation on the basis of the DPA, which had been negotiated the preceding winter and signed in February 1994. During June 1994, President Saleh dispatched a top member of his ruling party on a diplomatic mission to Cairo, Egypt, where he met Egyptian president Hosni Mubarak. Saleh's personal representative pledged the Yemeni government would observe the DPA and protect the interests of all southern citizens in a united, free, and democratic country.[16] Two days after the civil war ended, Yemen's acting prime minister sent a letter to the UN Secretary General spelling out the Yemeni government's "continuation of the national dialogue ... and compliance with the provisions of pledge and accord (DPA) as a basis for building the modern Yemeni state."[17] In following months, Saleh made more pledges about political decentralization, including a promise to respect southern regional rights. When a new prime minister submitted the government's program to parliament on 31 October 1994, it specifically called for local elections within a year.[18]

Throughout 1995, Saleh delayed taking the necessary steps to hold local elections. After amending the unity constitution to grant himself powers of decree, he demonstrated a clear intent to continue ruling through the central government by appointing all provincial staff in the country. It took more than a decade for Saleh to allow the first provincial governors to take office by means of election in 2008. Yet he was forced to do so by Hirak's massive street protests in southern governorates. The voting in 2008 occurred by indirect means among elected members of powerless consultative councils that were first created in 2001. These consultative councils arose from divisive cabinet debates in 1998 about a draft law regulating central-local government relations. Southern cabinet members had favored holding direct local elections, while granting genuine decision making power to elected provincial governors. But they were opposed by a larger number of northern ministers on the cabinet, who accused the southerners of being "separatists." When the draft law was finally submitted and passed by parliament two years later in 2000, it only permitted consultative councils minimal rights to advise governors, all of whom Saleh continued to appoint. After Hirak's protests forced Saleh to allow the indirect election of governors in 2008, he quickly mobilized armed forces to crush the southern protest movement. By the end of the next year, he fought an undeclared war in the south that resembled earlier wars against Huthi rebels in the north.

The Arrangement of Revenue-Sharing

When seeking to understand the potential for Yemeni federalism based on lessons from the past, the greatest lesson may concern revenue-sharing. The entire balance of central and regional powers depends upon how a federal state sets the percentage of regional government revenues drawn from a variety of sources. The higher percentage of revenues kept by regional governments, the more power they will have. For example, any elected officials in Hadramawt will have more power if they maintain a higher percentage of revenues drawn from oil and gas on their territory. Yet history reveals a long tradition of religious and tribal ruling classes in the highland region seeking to control virtually all state revenues drawn from lowland and coastal regions. This is the main reason Saleh and his allies refused a genuine devolution of power in the 1990s and 2000s. After the 1994 civil war, when Saleh created a more heavily centralized system with tighter controls on government revenues and expenditures, he acted much like Zaydi imams of the past. If Ansar Allah now seeks to run government in Sanaa, then the same dynamics may compel it to deny regional power to groups outside the highlands. In other words, despite making past statements in support of federalism, Ansar Allah's leader could become the latest example of mountain highland leaders exercising strict control over outlying regions of the country.

In reality, political decentralization has never been in the political and economic interests of groups in the highland mountains. If Hadramawt and other resource-rich regions like Marib and Shabwa are granted a favorable share of revenues drawn from their territory, along with coastal ports in Aden and Tihama, then there will likely be great resistance from influential actors in Sanaa and surrounding areas. Highland ruling classes are generally aware that people in outlying regions are more capable of making independent economic progress, so they typically look for ways to constrain development in other regions by keeping them weak and divided. By denying efficient utilization of resources, they limit Yemen's overall progress. Yet they often claim that if people in other regions were allowed self-rule, it would create jealousies and divisions threatening national unity. In truth, members of the highland ruling class are most envious of economic potentials in other regions, so they create their own sense of entitlement to rule non-highland regions. In their minds, residents of the highland region are best able to lead Yemen and defend its national unity. People from other regions are considered "too weak or untrustworthy."

After the 1994 civil war, the families of President Saleh and other influential northerners, particularly the top tribal sheikhs of Hashid, believed that their ownership of economic enterprises in the south assisted national unity by bringing north and south Yemenis together. The resources of Aden and Hadramawt offered the greatest prize, and during the second half of 1994 and following years, there was a rush to grab what could be purchased at low prices, or simply taken without compensation. Saleh and other leaders in Sanaa used post-Cold War language of "capitalism triumphing over communism," in order to justify their actions. Yet they were hardly representatives of western capitalism, just as post-1990 Aden was no substitute for the Soviet Union. When northern officials eliminated southern institutions like the "financial audit and control" office at Aden's central treasury, they destroyed relics of British rule, not Soviet and East Bloc rule. Back in the 1970s, south Yemenis consulted East German advisors to decide whether or not to keep Aden's "audit and control" office. The East Germans recommended preserving the system because it was more efficient than their own at preventing corrupt spending back in East Berlin. Thus officials in Sanaa wiped out what even the East Germans dared not touch. As a result, greater levels of financial corruption seeped into the Yemeni government.

After 1994, citizens in southern regions of the country perceived their land and resources being exploited by outsiders from the north. One critic, Dr. Abu Bakr al-Saqqaf, a well-known philosophy professor at Sanaa University, accused the regime of conducting a policy of "internal colonialism" in southern provinces. After making these remarks, Dr. al-Saqqaf was kidnapped and brutally beaten in December 1995 by secret police wielding electronic batons. In the last half of the 1990s, nearly all top military commanders in southern and eastern regions had family and tribal connections to President Saleh. The heavy post-war military presence, often camped inside major southern cities and on the periphery of smaller towns, was regarded as an extension of Saleh's highland tribal group. For years, northern soldiers operated roadside checkpoints between southern cities and towns, demanding bribes from passing drivers. Local residents sensed they were living under military occupation by forces sent across the former border. In addition to the northern military presence, there was a heavy concentration of government officials from the highland region working in civil administration.

The author's survey of local administration in Yemen between 1985 and 1997 documents that President Saleh appointed top officials from his highland region to carry out the most sensitive work in southern provinces. Before national unity in 1990, the same was true of non-highland regions in the former north Yemen. Only highland officials had high levels of representation in pre-unity provincial government posts. Meanwhile in the former south Yemen, no regional group dominated pre-unity provincial government in the same way. Thus, the history of the highland group's domination is unique. Influential actors from other regions of the country do not seek the same control outside their home regions. Moreover, between 1991 and 1997, the average citizen of the highland region paid tax rates between one-quarter and one-fourteenth the rate of citizens living in other regions. Thus elites from the highland region held the most power in government, and benefited most from revenues drawn from other regions, while highland citizens contributed less in taxes. Government corruption and other abuses of power are systemic in Yemen because they are deeply rooted in traditions of control exercised by highland ruling classes.

This last lesson of history provides ample reason to be wary of what will happen in Yemen if there is continued central government control of revenues drawn from local and regional sources. At the NDC conference in Sanaa, northern delegates often claimed the new federal plan should preserve central control, in order to "keep the government operating smoothly." This expression was particularly common among delegates with past government experience. In June 2013, the author attended sessions of the NDC where debate focused on southern demands for more regional autonomy. At this time, northern delegates stated that they expected Yemen's new federal system would allow each region to keep a maximum of 15 percent of local taxes, as well as 15 percent of income from resources like oil and gas. The remaining 85 percent would be sent to the central government in Sanaa, which would then redistribute funds along demographic lines. Yet such a disproportionate revenue-sharing formula is unlikely to find approval among populations outside the highland region. In 2013, northern NDC delegates also favored adopting a UN formula for "3-Tier" government, where the central government distributes funds to municipal and district governments below the regional level. The rationale is that the central government can best work in coordination with city and town mayors, who are greater in number, rather than heads of regional governments, who are fewer in number. The "3-Tier" formula appeared in Yemen's 2015 draft constitution, specifically chapters three and seven which granted financial and taxation powers to municipal authorities, but not regional authorities. The six regional governments would apparently be disallowed financial autonomy from the central government, thus greatly weakening the role they could play. In fact, it was misleading to call this a "six-region federal plan" because the regional governments were weakened by constitutional design.

Conclusion

Across Yemeni history, the pattern of regional divisions inside the country largely explains the difficulty of maintaining national unity and building effective government at central and local levels. In particular, competition to control scarce valuable resources in regions of unequal size, power, and wealth tends to foment conflicts. There is clearly reason to think a federal structure of government could help manage and resolve conflicts when they occur. Yet federalism in Yemen has long faced opposition for a variety of reasons, perhaps none greater than the fact it too becomes entangled in regional rivalries. This is witnessed by the difficulty of implementing the proposed draft constitution resulting from Yemen's NDC in 2013-2014. Violent armed conflict in Sanaa during late 2014 and early 2015 indicates the NDC plan may be destined to fail, just like earlier attempts to develop federalism in the country.

The greatest lesson of Yemeni history is that powerful tribal groups in the country's resource-poor highland region seek to dominate outlying regions where more valuable resources are located. Thus, one of the keys to making any federal plan successful in Yemen is to devise checks on the systemic abuse of power by influential actors in the highland region. It is a mistake to empower the central government in Sanaa by allowing it to control the lion's share of state revenues drawn from sources around the country. Even if rulers in Sanaa have good intentions in the short term, they may change their intentions over time, or later be replaced by others who revert to old patterns of highland dominance over midland and lowland regions. In the past three decades, the population of Sanaa has nearly tripled in size, despite warnings that the capital may soon run out of water. It makes little sense to continue encouraging massive growth in Sanaa by making it the center of political and economic life. Instead, other regions of Yemen need to be given the means to develop without interference from Sanaa.

Among Yemenis who participated in the country's NDC, the vast majority supported the overthrow of the old pre-2011 regime. They entered national dialogue with hopes of better years ahead. Many of these individuals held strong convictions that if a new Yemeni constitution could be drafted "the right way" with a federal structure of government, then the early promise of national unity in 1990 might be restored, as citizens learned to coexist in peace, and eventually began to prosper. Yet in reality, there are no miracle cures through constitutional design for countries like Yemen. There are only better and worse constitutional designs to manage a unique sets of problems. At present, Yemen faces a set of problems greater than any time in its modern era. The combination of political, economic, and environmental difficulties is nearly impossible to solve in the short term, so the probability of success for any new government is already very low. If Yemen's NDC federal plan had been adopted at the beginning of unity in 1990, or perhaps late 1993, then it would have stood a greater chance of success. Unfortunately, regional divisions within the population have hardened since the 1990s. Whatever level of success the NDC plan finds, Yemen will endure as a divided land just as it has for centuries.

Notes

1 Stephen W. Day, "The Non-Conclusion of Yemen's National Dialogue," *Foreign Policy*, January 27, 2014. During the NDC, the first southern director of the conference's "southern issue" working group resigned his post due to excessive northern influence behind the scenes. The second southern director ended up boycotting the working group's final meetings because northern delegates had assumed control of its agenda.

2 Stephen W. Day, "Can Yemen Become A Nation United?," *Foreign Policy*, March 14, 2013.

3 Robert W. Stookey, *Yemen: The Politics of the Yemen Arab Republic* (Boulder, CO: Westview Press, 1978), 146–47.

4 Stephen W. Day, *Regionalism and Rebellion in Yemen: A Troubled National Union* (New York: Cambridge University Press, 2012), 34 and 94–97.

5 Kiren Chaudhry, *The Price of Wealth: Economies and Institutions in the Middle East* (Ithaca, NY: Cornell University Press, 1997).

6 R. J. Gavin, *Aden Under British Rule, 1839-1967* (London: C. Hurst, 1975), 340.

7 Noel Brehony, "Explaining the Triumph of the NLF," *Middle East Studies*, forthcoming.

8 Helen Lackner, *People's Democratic Republic of Yemen: Outpost of Socialist Development in Arabia* (Reading, England: Ithaca Press, 1986), 19–24.

9 "Trends in Yemeni Public Opinion: Attitudes Toward the National Dialogue Conference Document," ACRPS, Doha, Qatar, 2014. The polling process involved face-to-face interviews with 1500 respondents between 4-27 February 2014. The ACRPS report states that interviews were conducted in urban and rural areas, although it is not clear if these areas were distributed across regions of the country.

10 Noel Brehony, *Yemen Divided: Story of a Failed State in South Arabia* (London: I. B. Tauris, 2011), 173–81.

11 Ahmad al-Bishari, the late editor of the Sanaa-based political journal, *al-Thawabit*, referred to the DPA's plan for local government as the document's "principal element." Al-Bishari, *The Future of Local Government in Yemen* [in Arabic] (Sanaa: Thawabit Press, 1996), ii. The document was originally published in Arabic on January 18, 1994 by the "national dialogue" committee. It was reprinted in English by *Yemen Times*, January 23, 1994.

12 "Security Council Adopts Resolution 2140 (2014), Welcoming Yemen's Peaceful Transition towards New Constitution, General Elections." Item 19 of the resolution addresses the formation of the "Sanctions Committee": http://www.un.org/News/Press/docs/2014/sc11296.doc.htm

13 Feras al-Yaf'i, "The Qu'ayti Sultan Implores the Regional and International Communities to Declare the State of Hadhramaut," *Mukalla Star*, September 26, 2014: http://mukallastar.com/news/2014/177364.html

14 The author's survey of changes in local administrative personnel between 1985 and 1997 showed that most northern and southern personnel continued to serve in their same local positions during the first three years of unity, 1990-1993. Yet by the end of unity's first full year in May 1991, there were new northern directors of finance in Lahij, customs in Hadramawt, taxation in Hadramawt and Shabwa, and central bank branches in Lahij and Abyan. The biggest changes occurred in Aden, where new northern directors were appointed to the offices of finance, customs, taxation, and the central bank. Day, *Regionalism and Rebellion in Yemen*, 138–47.

15 Ahmad al-Bishari, *The Election Programs of Political Parties and Organizations* [in Arabic] (Sanaa: Thawabit Press, 1993), 103. The platform of former president Saleh's ruling party talked in vague terms of giving local authorities "the necessary powers...to supervise and monitor" local affairs, p. 62; and the Islamist third party's platform referred to the need to minimize government centralization, p. 83.

16 David Warburton, "The Conventional War in Yemen," *Arab Studies Journal*, Spring 1995, 37–38.

17 Quoted from a copy of Mohammed al-Attar's July 9, 1994 letter to UN Secretary General Boutros Ghali, which was reprinted by the exiled Yemeni opposition group, MOWJ, based in London, England.

18 Al-Bishari, *Future of Local Government,* v.

References

Anderson, Benedict. *Imagined Communities: Reflections on the Origins and Spread of Nationalism.* London: Verso, 1983.

al-Bishari, Ahmad, ed. *Mustaqbal al-Hukm al-Mahalli fi al-Jumhuriyya al-Yamaniyya* [The future of local government in the Republic of Yemen]. Sanaa: Thawabit Press, 1996.

Boucek, Christopher, and Marina Ottaway, eds. *Yemen on the Brink.* Washington, DC: Carnegie Endowment for International Peace, 2010.

Brehony, Noel. *Divided Yemen: The Story of a Failed State in South Arabia.* London: I. B. Tauris, 2011.

Chaudhry, Kiren. *The Price of Wealth: Economies and Institutions in the Middle East.* Ithaca, NY: Cornell University Press, 1997.

Day, Stephen W. *Regionalism and Rebellion in Yemen: A Troubled National Union.* New York: Cambridge University Press, 2012.

Dresch, Paul. *Tribes, Government and History in Yemen.* Oxford: Oxford University Press, 1994.

al-Mikhlafi, Muhammad Ahmad Ali. *Qadiyat Dawlat al-Qanun fi al-Azma al-Yamaniyya* [The issue of the rule of law in the Yemeni crisis]. Beirut: Dar al-Kunuz al-Arabiyya, 1999.

al-Suwaidi, Jamal, ed. *The Yemeni War of 1994: Causes and Consequences.* Abu Dhabi: Saqi Books, 1995.

Wedeen, Lisa. *Peripheral Visions: Publics, Power, and Performance in Yemen.* Chicago: University of Chicago Press, 2008.

2

Hadrami Identities in Saudi Arabia

Iain Walker

Although the future of Yemen is increasingly unclear, the National Dialogue that ended in early 2014 put forward propositions for a federal system that, rather than attenuating regional identities, seemed to reveal their tenacity. Different groups (Hadramis, Huthis) attempted to ensure that they would be granted their own province, or a province that met their expectations, both politically and geographically, in the new formation. The proposed six-province format that emerged from the National Dialogue seemed to satisfy Hadramis, but there remain those who support full independence for the region, both within Yemen and elsewhere, particularly in Saudi Arabia. The Hadrami community in Saudi Arabia is not only important (both numerically and economically), it has specific characteristics that distinguish it from other communities of the Hadrami diaspora. In this chapter I look at Hadrami identity from an anthropological perspective, considering the personal, subjective and affective aspects of Hadrami identity in Saudi Arabia in the context of, on the one hand, (hypothetical) political possibilities that range from a unitary Yemeni state to an independent Hadramawt within the GCC, and on the other, the criteria for belonging, both formal and social, for Hadramis in the kingdom. I begin by establishing a theoretical framework that will permit an analysis of Hadrami identities in the kingdom.

The Self and Identity

Contemporary thinking in the anthropology of migration and mobilities has led to significant changes in the way issues of identity and belonging are conceptualised, and to a reflection upon the ways people negotiate relationships with each other, with groups, and with (and within) states.[1] However, as Glick Schiller observes,[2] much work remains focused on difference and negotiations thereof, in contexts where difference are perceived to be already existing, rather than being created by the social interactions under consideration. This is unfortunate since questions of identity and belonging become particularly interesting, and more complex, if similarities are considered to be more salient than differences, either by the actors themselves or by observers. However, it is also understandable: the negotiation of differences when they appear to be evident – Catholic Filipino migrant labourers in Riyadh – is a reasonably straightforward problematic; an analysis of differences between individuals and groups who do not appear to be different – members of the Tamim tribe in the Arabian Peninsula – requires a prior problematisation of otherness before any analysis of difference is possible. This is not a particularly new idea in anthropology (one might cite Barth's 1969 book *Ethnic Groups and Boundaries*) but was often neglected in writings produced within the late 20th century fascination with cosmopolitanism, hybridity and difference.[3]

In an ethnographic context in which mobility (be it of nomads or urban migrants) is common and cultures are not discrete (if indeed, they ever were), my analytical point of departure is the proposition that all people have a self[4] much as all people have a body; and while I do not suggest that all cultural constructs of the self are the same, I maintain that all individuals in all cultures and all societies have a self, whether or not it is recognised as such. The self is manifested, partly consciously, partly unconsciously, in personae, performances of specific aspects of the self, based on available identities and usually context-dependent.[5] Personae are brought into play contextually, expressing the variety of interests, aims, desires and constraints that are embedded in an equal variety of intersecting and superimposed fields (political, religious, economic, kin):[6] a mother, a son, a doctor, an imam, a Hadrami, a Saudi, and so on. Personae are socially evaluated, judged on how successful they are, both by the actor and by others, and may be reformulated within certain parameters (established by the self according to the socio-cultural toolkit at its disposition – effectively its habitus) or may be abandoned for another persona, again, habitus permitting. However, while the self may switch personae fairly rapidly, often consciously according to context – adopting the comportment and practices of a mother when her child enters the room, for example – changes to the self are generally not conscious processes, even though there may be self-awareness of changes to the self after the event – the mother becomes aware that she is now "a mother" at some point subsequent to the birth of her child.

One of the characteristics of personae – indeed, one of the reasons for them, since different personae allow individuals to negotiate different relationships – is that they are often incompatible, insofar as they cannot be simultaneously engaged. The work of resolving incompatibilities between personae is undertaken by the self, either explicitly (consciously) or implicitly (unconsciously); however, most incompatibilities are not problematic and it is well-recognised, even expected, that an individual may have different personae and different ways of presenting himself (father, doctor) that are not (or rarely) contradictory. However, incompatibilities may occasionally become conflictual, in which case the task of reconciling them becomes more complex. Consider, for example, an individual in Jeddah whose claims to Saudi identity are challenged by other Saudis, obliging him to adopt a Hadrami identity instead. This may be successful in Saudi Arabia, but in Hadramawt his Hadrami identity may be judged "inauthentic", and he will be compelled to resume the Saudi identity that has been judged defective in Saudi Arabia. In managing these personae the self is concerned with maintaining a degree of coherence (not truth or accuracy) in personal narratives and social interactions that are sometimes difficult to reconcile; if the conflict remains personal then potential problems will likewise remain personal, giving rise perhaps to a little cognitive dissonance; but if conflicting personae are expressed publicly in social contexts then the problems become more acute.

In this example, we may ask why different personae are invoked at all: why should an individual be Hadrami in one context and a Saudi in another? In one sense the answer is intuitive: the individual's expressions of identity are, in a sense, liminal; but this does not answer why the individual chooses different personae rather than accepting that even though his Saudi identity is somehow deficient, he is nevertheless Saudi and must restrict himself to that persona. As we shall see, the answers to this question are largely political in character and it is the context that prompts individuals to strategically engage different personae to achieve their objectives.

What are the criteria for being Hadrami? Inclusive definitions of Hadrami refer above all to genealogy or tribe:[7] this allows a Hadrami in Saudi Arabia to identify his Indian migrant driver as a Hadrami, even if "he didn't know it": he bears the tribal name. More restrictive definitions of Hadrami refer to other cultural practices such as language, food and dress (Hadramis in Saudi Arabia dress like "Saudis", for example, which is a particularly explicit statement on the part of a Saudi Hadrami who returns thus dressed to Hadramawt), but also to more subtle criteria such as codes of honour and personal comportment. However, many of these criteria intersect with criteria for belonging among other groups – the tribes of Abu Dhabi or the Nejd – rendering essentialist constructions of cultural identity difficult if not impossible.

Why, then, if there is little difference between a Hadrami and a Nejdi, are these categories seized upon and developed? The most obvious answer returns us to the point of departure: the politics of identities. Nejdis are Saudi citizens, enjoying all the advantages that such a status confers. Hadramis are Yemeni citizens, a less appealing status, to them at least. However, as already observed, some Hadramis are also Saudi citizens, and so the question becomes more nuanced than one of simple citizenship, returning us again to the strategic aspects of identity and the access to power that identities afford or deny. Identities of all kinds – be they spatial or ethnic, religious, economic or tribal – are all crucially and differentially important in providing the self with tools to construct personae. Social constraints that fix individuals in Hadramawt are mitigated in Saudi Arabia and vice versa: and differential hierarchies of power operate in different social fields as well as in different spatial fields. In Tarim, religious identities are paramount: power is held by the *sada*, religious leaders descended from the Prophet. In Abu Dhabi, tribal identities are key: the values of nomadic culture emphasise kinship above other attributes, even in the contemporary capitalist economy of the UAE. In Saudi Arabia, some Hadramis of low status origin – many of them from the low-status *maskin* caste – are enormously wealthy and wield great economic power. In each of these three examples, political power acquired in a particular field dominates; and hence the wealthy Hadrami businessmen of Saudi Arabia were able to sponsor large numbers of Hadrami Yemenis in the 1990s, thus transforming the community, consolidating their identity as a group and providing cultural tools for individuals to create "Saudi" personae. However, movement between different places in the region implies corresponding shifts in fields: the religious leader who travels to Jeddah may not be accorded the respect he is accustomed to receiving in Hadramawt; the Saudi businessman may see his authority and his power diminished in Tarim. These differential power relationships perturb the networks that sustain them: power may only be exercised within the field that sustains it.

Belonging depends on place and a recognition of the importance of both space and place is essential.[8] There are radical differences between the ways belonging is shared and enacted in a small village in Wadi Hadramawt, and in Jeddah, a city of more than three million inhabitants. Despite changes, of multiple origins but including the influences of members of the diaspora, social structures in rural Hadramawt remain largely based on the systems of stratification as described by Bujra,[9] as well as by kin-group (tribe), place of residence and political affiliation. In Jeddah, in contrast, these categories are subverted and renegotiated by and in the urban milieu: individuals of different origins, social and geographic, meet regularly in the workplace, in restaurants, in markets, in mosques. Similarly, if spatial movement prompts shifts in practice and reveals differences in culture, movement thorough time does likewise and conceptualisations of identity change: in 1930 the identity "Hadrami" in Saudi Arabia may have been similar to that in Hadramawt; today it is somewhat different, and neither are today the same as they were then.

The Hadrami Diaspora

Largely due to the typically harsh conditions in this part of Yemen, where rain-fed agriculture in the wadis frequently fails to provide, Hadramawt has long been a region of out-migration: migration is deeply embedded in the collective consciousness both in the homeland and, perhaps obviously, in diaspora. Hadramis migrated by both land and sea across the Indian Ocean. There are communities of Hadrami of origin in India and in both insular and mainland southeast Asia; in east and northeast Africa there are Hadramis in scattered locations from Sudan to Mozambique and Madagascar and inland to the Ethiopian highlands and the great lakes, with a particularly significant presence in Kenya, Zanzibar and the Comoro Islands; and Hadramis have also migrated north to destinations elsewhere in the Arabian peninsula, notably the Hejaz (Jeddah and Mecca), Kuwait and Abu Dhabi, either overland or by coasting vessels.[10] Although specific destinations seem to have depended on serendipity as much as on strategy, place of origin influenced destinations in a general sense. Those from the coast, not surprisingly, tended to travel by sea, and those from the eastern wadi – the area around Tarim and Seiyun, possibly because of the proximity to the caravan routes to the coast, also tended to head for the coast and thence to Asia and East Africa. Families from Wadi Duan, however, a branch of the western wadi, are more likely to be found elsewhere in the Arabian peninsula, and particularly in Saudi Arabia. Ho has suggested that this is due to the exiguity of life in Wadi Duan: unlike the eastern wadi, where there are large expanses of flat land and properties can be substantial and families wealthy, villages in Wadi Duan are clustered on the hillsides and the valley floors are narrow and crowded.[11] Poorer, more likely to emigrate, and without the means to pay for lengthy sea passages, the families of Wadi Duan, from all social strata, headed north. One of my informants – now one of the wealthiest men in Saudi Arabia – indeed confirmed that his father was so poor he walked to Jeddah.

The chronic character of diasporic practice has profoundly affected Hadrami identity. Emigration was, and remains, essential to the well-being of the homeland and its people: not only does the simple fact of emigration permit individual survival, but emigrants, once established elsewhere, support families who remained behind; and there was always someone who remained behind, "to look after the house and the dates". In addition to an economic dependence on remittances, Hadramawt has been deeply shaped, culturally and socially, by the influences of returnees. Food, clothing and architecture are obvious cultural contributions from the diaspora, but the role of Hadramawt as a center of religious learning is also due to the activities of emigrants, many of who emigrated for proselytization (*dawa*). Indeed, the act of emigration itself is socially imbued. The word used by Hadramis to refer to the diaspora, *al-mahjar*, is not generally used by other emigrants, such as the Lebanese or Palestinian diasporas, who refer instead to *al-shatat*. The etymology of *shatat* is linked to scattering and dispersal: it is an abstract noun that is concerned with a physical scattering, the process of going to different places, of no longer being together: it refers to the place of origin. *Mahjar*, on the other hand, refers to the act of migration itself, to a departure, certainly: a separation, a relinquishment, a suggestion of a lack of choice; but, crucially, it also refers (as indicated by the *ma-* prefix) to the diaspora as emplaced. *Shatat* is an abstract collection of dispersed people; *mahjar* is community emplaced in the world: it has a concrete existence there where it is. Furthermore there is a morality to *mahjar* that is not associated with *shatat* and that sees it inscribed within Islamic mobilities: the root of the word is the same as that of Hijra, the original emigration of the Prophet Muhammad to Medina. There is a symbolic aspect to the Hadrami *mahjar* that accords it a cohesion that encourages the maintenance of Hadrami identity in diaspora despite intermarriage and what might appear to be assimilation by the host communities. Emigration was a regular feature of life and memories (both individual and social) shape perceptions emigration generally and of the harshness as well as the ideal of life in the homeland among emigrant communities in particular.

Although united by a diasporic consciousness, there are differences in the profiles of the communities in these different places, a result of the identities of those who left, the identities subsequently constructed in diaspora and the relationships maintained with the homeland. The lower costs of the passage to East Africa means (or is remembered as meaning) that lower status families tended to migrate southwards, while higher status sailed east. In East Africa large numbers of lower status Hadramis found work as laborers and in small businesses, many eventually succeeding in establishing their own enterprises. Only in the Comoro Islands, untouched by colonial prosperity, were the majority of Hadramis of high status, *sada*, descendants of the Prophet. In Indonesia many Hadramis were successful in business: a number of wealthy families of both Singapore and Jakarta were (and remain) of Hadrami origin, while in India the profile seems to have been more akin to that of East Africa. In destinations where Islam is practised the Shafii school of thought (*madhhab*) is generally dominant as it is in Hadramawt and Hadramis, particularly the *sada*, provided religious leadership throughout the ocean. Differences in status, place of origin and tribal affiliation did not preclude links between different places in the diaspora: there are families who can boast members in several different locations and although emigrants tended to prefer to follow members of the same tribe who had previously migrated there is a broad similarity both in the profiles of Hadrami diasporic communities in Africa and Indonesia and in their relationships with the homeland. These diasporic communities are characterised both as maintaining a strong sense of community identity and as being integrated locally, largely through intermarriage since Hadrami women rarely travelled. "They take the shape of the people who live there", said one informant, explaining that Hadramis mix with the community in which they live, "but they don't forget their roots".

There is, however, a significant difference between the profiles of the Hadrami diaspora in transoceanic destinations and that in the Arabian peninsula, particularly with respect to their relationships both with the host community and with the homeland. While there are Hadramis in the Gulf (notably in Dubai)[12] who have arrived from other parts of the diaspora, most Hadramis in the region have arrived directly from Hadramawt over a period that ranges from centuries (in Jeddah and Mecca) to the past 50 years (Abu Dhabi) to the present (various locations but Saudi Arabia and the UAE in particular). There are several distinguishing characteristics of the Hadrami diaspora in the Gulf. Most obviously, Hadramis arriving in Saudi Arabia found co-religionists. The Hadrami diaspora elsewhere was marked by proselytization and Hadrami religious leadership was a distinguishing characteristic of the diaspora: "Business and religion, just like the Prophet," is a widespread characterisation of Hadrami migrants. Saudi Arabia, in contrast, and the Hejaz in particular, was a source of religious authenticity and there was (and remains) no call for proselytization and little scope either for the teaching of Shafii jurisprudence or, particularly, for the dissemination and practice of sufism that was the cornerstone of *dawa* elsewhere in the Indian Ocean but anathema to the Wahhabi of the kingdom. Indeed, and perhaps paradoxically given the cultural similarities that otherwise exist between Hadramawt and the Hejaz, characteristically Hadrami practices such as sufism and respect for the *sada* are engaged with great discretion.

Similarly, linguistic differences are minimal: Saudis, like Hadramis, speak Arabic. There are dialectical variations which are often accorded prominence precisely as part of a process of asserting Hadrami identity (or, alternatively, downplayed as part of the process of claiming local belonging), but generally there is no barrier to intercomprehensibility between the versions of Arabic spoken across the peninsula. Again, this is in contrast to the Indonesian or East African context where Hadrami immigrants were required to learn Indonesian or Swahili. Conversely, Saudi-born Hadramis face no linguistic obstacles when they return to Hadramawt; their East African or Indonesians counterparts, locally born who may have little or no Arabic beyond a knowledge of the Koran, often have great difficulty communicating with kin when they visit the homeland. A shared language is indicative of wider socio-cultural compatibilities: there is little to physically distinguish Hadramis from other Arabs and in the Gulf there is a corresponding lack of the type of racial conflict that has and occasionally continues to characterise relationships between both groups and individuals in East Africa. Finally, and perhaps crucially for the maintenance both of a cohesive community identity and of links with the homeland, there was no need for intermarriage in the Gulf states. Hadrami emigrants to East Africa and Indonesia were almost invariably men, and usually single men; but even if married, for cultural reasons wives and families usually remained in Hadramawt: Hadrami women were not encouraged to travel. This accorded the Hadrami diaspora two characteristics. First, there were significant levels of intermarriage between Hadrami men and local women[13] throughout the Indian Ocean thus creating a community of locally born Hadramis (those who "take the shape of the people who live there") known as *muwalladin*; and second, both in Indonesia and, particularly, in East Africa, from where it was easier to return to Hadramawt, a significant incidence of uxorilocal polygyny: it is common to find men, married in Hadramawt, who emigrated to East Africa and took a second wife locally without divorcing the first, periodically returning to spend time with the first family in the homeland.

This latter practice is anathema to Hadramis in Saudi Arabia[14] precisely because marriage with Hadrami women from the homeland is both possible and common. Residence after marriage in Hadramawt is virilocal and there is therefore no obstacle to a woman changing residence (leaving her father's household to take up residence in her husband's house) upon marriage, quite the contrary; but the removal of women to culturally undesirable environments and subsequent exposure to undesirable influences – the twin evils of promiscuity and alcohol in East Africa, for example – was to be avoided at all costs, even if those costs were marriage to a Swahili woman and the birth of children of mixed ancestry.[15] This, coupled with the physical distance involved, and subsequent separation of the woman from her kin (a woman is expected to return to her mother's house for the birth of her first child, in the days of sea travel close to impossible if she lived in Mombasa and the mother in Seiyun), was a further reason for Hadrami women to remain at home. On the other hand, the movement of a woman to take up residence with her husband in Jeddah posed no such problems; indeed, residence in the Hejaz, and particularly in Mecca, was often seen as desirable: the Hejaz was similar to the homeland, physically and culturally, and from a spiritual perspective residence in Mecca was even more meritorious than Hadramawt. Hadrami men were therefore able to continue to practice preferential (endogamous) marriages, not only socially acceptable but logistically practical given the physical proximity of Hadramawt.[16]

These characteristics of the Hadrami community thus present two general and opposing tendencies. On the one hand, the socio-cultural proximity of Hadramawt and Saudi Arabia rendered integration and even assimilation not only possible but desirable (within certain limits); on the other hand, the closer ties to Hadramawt (through marriage, a maintenance of parallel cultural and linguistic practices, and the greater ease of returns) facilitated the maintenance of a cohesive and identifiable community with a distinctive identity. In particular, relationships with the homeland are less ambiguous than those between African-born *muwalladin* and their kin in Hadramawt since, crucially, Saudi-born Hadramis are not considered to be *muwalladin* since they were not born "abroad" – Saudi Arabia, like Oman and the UAE, is conceptually assimilated to "greater Hadramawt", the homeland – thus allowing for (potentially) greater social acceptance in Hadramawt. This does not mean that ascribed identities were without ambiguity: many Hadrami Saudis are identified in Hadramawt (and even more so in Yemen generally) as "Saudis", even if Hadrami origins are acknowledged; but they are less likely to face the problems of re-integration that East African or Indonesian *muwalladin* often encounter.

The Hadrami Community of Saudi Arabia

There has long been a Hadrami community in Saudi Arabia, particularly in the Hejaz where Hadrami merchants established in Jeddah and Mecca were influential in the mid-19th century (and undoubtedly earlier: there were Hadramis in Jeddah in the 17th century) and constituted the core, and the leadership, of what appears to have been a particularly cohesive community; as elsewhere in the Indian Ocean, the community was composed of Hadramis of all classes, and not all were wealthy;[17] whereas community leadership in other areas was in the hands of the religious elite, and particularly the *sada*, this does not seem to have been true in the Hejaz even prior to the arrival of Ibn Saud and the Wahhabis.

The state of Saudi Arabia was formed in 1932 through the merging of the two kingdoms of the Hejaz and the Nejd but until formal frameworks governing citizenship and immigration were elaborated in the 1950s there were few controls on the movement of individuals in the region. Hadramis arriving in the early 20th century were free to settle and the fathers and grandfathers of many of today's community arrived during this period. Perhaps paradoxically, it was the poor recent arrivals who were to make their fortune under the house of Saud, for while many members of the older, established families regarded the Saudis with ambivalence, those who had arrived from Hadramawt in the 1920s and 1930s had no qualms about undertaking menial tasks in the royal households and chose, much to their advantage as it turned out, to support the new regime. Many worked as servants or book-keepers, or undertook various laboring or administrative tasks. Thus Salem bin Mahfouz lent the king money and would go on to found Saudi Arabia's first bank, the National Commercial Bank (NCB), while Muhammad bin Laden built the king's new palaces and founded what is now one of the largest construction companies in the kingdom. These "narratives of origin" are particularly common among the newer families and follow a similar pattern: the poor father or grandfather makes his way from Hadramawt to Jeddah, finds a job, often with the help of kin already in place, and through thrift, honesty and hard work slowly establishes a place in society. In time, he sends home for a wife, or returns to Hadramawt to marry, and founds a family.

Controls on mobility followed the establishment of formal states in the Western image in the Arabian peninsula. The end of the Ottoman Empire paved the way for the independence of the Imamate of Yemen while further east the Kathiri and Quayti sultanates of Hadramawt were British protectorates (politically and culturally quite distinct from Yemen) until they were incorporated into the newly independent South Yemen in 1967. In the 1950s, as oil-driven economic growth led to a rise in the number of immigrants arriving in the kingdom, Saudi Arabia established the *kafala* system, under which immigrants were required to obtain a sponsor (*kafil*) in order to be granted a residence permit (*iqama*). However, in recognition both of the esteem in which the royal family held the Hadrami community, and, post-1969, of the status of many Hadramis as refugees from the marxist regime in South Yemen, they were, exceptionally, permitted to be collectively sponsored by a Saudi citizen who could vouch for them.[18] Other immigrants were required to be sponsored by their employer, and subsequently work for their sponsor. Consequently, several prominent Hadramis who possessed Saudi citizenship proceeded to sponsor large numbers of Hadramis; most notably, this included Ali Abdullah Bugshan, who is said to have sponsored thousands of his fellow countrymen – indeed, his company maintained an office dedicated to processing Hadrami *iqama* applications free of charge. It is indicative of the cohesive character of the community and the social structures that enforced codes of behavior (that, amongst other things, generally prevented Hadramis from behaving in such a way that they would bring shame upon their sponsor) that this was a possible and successful system. Until 1990 therefore Hadramis were free to travel to, reside and work in the kingdom (under the collective sponsorship system), and although they were not allowed to own land or businesses, these restrictions could usually be circumvented by coming to an arrangement with kin who were Saudi citizens.

Many Hadramis in Saudi Arabia were indeed citizens. Saudi citizenship was formally established on 6 December, 1938;[19] in its current form it dates from 1954, with amendments. Regardless of the letter of the law, obtaining citizenship seems to have been relatively uncomplicated until the 1980s when stricter interpretations were applied, although even as late as the 1990s naturalization does not seem to have been particularly difficult, if costly: one Saudi-born informant, regretting his lack of a Saudi passport, explained that a cousin had managed to obtain Saudi citizenship in the early 1990s at a cost of some 100,000 riyals but added, "You can't do that now, no matter how much money you have." For many Hadramis, as for Yemenis, Saudi citizenship was of course not necessary; for others it was undesirable. Another informant explained that his father refused to apply for citizenship since not only did he not need it, he did not want people to think he was a Saudi since "Saudi Arabia wasn't a civilized country, the Saudis are Bedouin". In this case, remaining a South Yemeni was an explicit statement of identity. As the conditions for acquiring Saudi citizenship were tightened, and the advantages of acquiring it more significant, many who might have once have been eligible to apply either no longer qualified or lacked the means. By the time citizenship became essential it was too late.

1990 was a pivotal year in Hadrami-Saudi relations for two reasons. In May, the two independent Yemeni states were unified into a single Republic of Yemen; and in August, Iraq invaded Kuwait. The first event implied that Hadramis were now citizens of Yemen and thus (albeit, as we shall see, briefly) subject to the immigration regulations (or lack thereof) applicable to Yemenis. Yemeni status in Saudi Arabia was governed by the 1934 Treaty of Taif, which provisionally fixed the border between the new Saudi state and the Imamate of Yemen. The terms of the treaty were effectively imposed upon Yemen, but in return for the concessions "granted" to Saudi Arabia by the Imam (which included renouncing his claims over Najran and the Idrisi emirate of Asir) Yemenis were granted full freedoms in Saudi Arabia on what was in theory an equal footing with Saudis: under Article 16 of the treaty the two nations were considered one ("*umma wahida*"). Yemeni citizens were granted entry into the kingdom without a visa and, following the introduction of the *kafala* system, this exemption was formalized, if restricted somewhat; but they were nevertheless given a four-year renewable *iqama* without the need for a sponsor.[20] This effectively permitted them to enter, reside, work and own businesses in Saudi Arabia freely and permanently and without the restrictions imposed upon other nationalities, including Hadramis. They were also, uniquely among non-citizens, entitled to free healthcare and education. These concessions applied equally to all Yemeni citizens, a category that, after Yemeni unification in 1990, included Hadramis. The requirement that Hadramis be collectively sponsored was therefore redundant.

In August in the same year, however, Iraq invaded Kuwait. Alone among the Arab states, Yemen declined to support calls for foreign intervention, preferring to remain neutral and believing instead that the matter was an Arab affair and could be resolved within the Arab community.[21] The rest of the Arab League, including Yemen's powerful neighbor, were calling for Western intervention, and in retaliation for Yemen's stance Saudi Arabia's reprisals were swift and radical, as it withdrew the privileges hitherto accorded to Yemenis in the kingdom, giving them three months to regularize their status (which required finding an employer who would then sponsor them) and sell their businesses. This prompted a well-documented mass return of Yemenis who were either unable to find the requisite sponsors or refused to accept their new status, referring to their rights to be in Saudi Arabia as members of the *umma wahida*.[22] Some 800,000 Yemenis therefore returned to Yemen, disproportionately to the north, the former Yemen Arab Republic); the number of Hadramis who returned was notably small, both because Hadramis did not maintain the same historical relationship with Saudi Arabia, and, since they were well integrated, because they were able to find individual sponsors among the Hadrami Saudi community – if they had married a Saudi citizen of Hadrami origin this might even be a spouse –, thus permitting them to remain.[23]

Even if the changes to the requirements imposed upon Hadramis were less disruptive than might have been anticipated, the wider effects of these events on the Hadrami community have been significant. Immigration to Saudi Arabia has not, until recently, been particularly difficult for those able to find a sponsor, and many Hadramis have confirmed that it had long been practice to arrive in the kingdom on an *umra* visa, seek out Hadrami kin and apply (generally successfully) for an *iqama* – drawing on Hadrami networks much the way they have always done, even if the formalities are more cumbersome than they might have been in the past. However, the withdrawal of privileges from their northern compatriots had led to a criminalization and subsequent marginalization of northern Yemenis (known in Hadramawt as *Shimalis*) in Saudi Arabia and has had unexpected repercussions on the status of Hadramis. Until 1967, Hadramis were not and never had been described as Yemeni; between 1967 and 1990, despite their homeland being known as "South Yemen", they were nevertheless distinguished from northern Yemenis. After 1990, however, those who were not Saudi citizens were now Yemenis with status (both in terms of citizenship and residency) that, for the first time, was now identical to that of their *Shimali* neighbors; and while older Saudis were (and remain) well aware of the differences between Hadramis and Yemenis, many younger Saudis are less well-informed. Assertions of identity therefore became more important: one informant, an Indian of Hadrami origin living in Jeddah, recounted how his father, an immigrant from Hyderabad, gave up his Yemeni passport for an Indian one following the first Gulf War because he didn't want people to think he was Yemeni.

To those who know them, and to the community itself, Hadramis have a particular reputation. Thrifty, honest, trustworthy, astute, miserly, clannish, these are all adjectives that, for better or for worse, have been applied to them. What is certain is that the cohesive character of the community is widely recognized; and that while not all Hadramis have been successful in business, even the poorest have a reputation for honesty and discretion. *Shimalis*, on the other hand, are characterised as hot-tempered, dishonest and unruly, if hard-working. Again, regardless of the truth of these epithets, the latter were ubiquitous on the streets of the cities of the Hejaz, hawking fruit, begging or, if fortunate, engaged as manual laborers (and if even more fortunate, with an *iqama*). The porous character of the border and the extreme (both absolute and comparative) poverty of Yemen suggests that this is not likely to change in the near future: despite the efforts of Saudi border patrols and the resumption of the construction of a border fence, the number of illegal crossings, and the number of deportations from the border areas to Yemen, only continue to increase.[24] For those already in Saudi Arabia, or who succeed in avoiding the border patrols, recent changes in Saudi policy and practice – the implementation of *nitaqat* (Saudization) and an accompanying clampdown on residents who are working for employers other than their sponsors – will undoubtedly see northern Yemenis further marginalized. In contrast, the consensus among the community is that few Hadramis were in an irregular position and those that were will undoubtedly manage to regularize their status. Differentiating themselves from Yemenis is therefore crucial to many Hadramis.

These differences are further exacerbated by the situation within Yemen itself. Unification was not an untroubled process. Conflict between south and north broke out into civil war in 1994, and although peace was re-established and the political relationship between north and south has been relatively stable if not entirely harmonious during the subsequent twenty years, the social and cultural consequences of unification have been otherwise. A variety of issues, from the central (northern) government's grants of southern land to members of the military, the arrival of internal immigrants from the north (begging, hawking and taking jobs), the perceived (and undoubtedly real) appropriation by Sanaa of the revenues from Hadrami oil production, the lack of investment in Hadramawt and the lack of Hadramis in positions of real power have all contributed to an increasing disenchantment with the union and a growing hostility towards *Shimalis* in Hadramawt itself. Conflicts in the homeland have shaped relationships between Yemenis of all origins in the diaspora and Hadramawt is sufficiently close, both physically and socially, for these conflicts to be of real importance to Hadramis in Saudi Arabia.

An Independent Hadramawt?

As in other parts of the former South Yemen there has been significant popular support in Hadramawt for expressions of southern identity, and over the past decade, a growing dissatisfaction with the union and a parallel growth in support for southern autonomy, if not independence.[25] In 2011, however, as demonstrations broke out across Yemen, talk of southern independence in Hadramawt was surprisingly muted, particularly in view of the sentiments that had been expressed over the preceding few years. What was being expressed in its place, as the political circumstances changed and the break-up of the Yemeni state began to seem possible, was a desire for Hadrami independence, not only from the north, but also from the south. Calls for Hadrami independence from the north as part of a new southern Yemeni state are understandable in view of the reasons evoked above, generally the effects of the perceived northern domination. Hadrami independence from the south, however, is based on historical and affective arguments and appears to be supported by a growing number of Hadramis in Hadramawt as well as a significant group in Saudi Arabia.

This reconstruction of Hadrami identity has three components: a foregrounding of the uniqueness of Hadrami culture; the identification of other parts of southern Yemen, and particularly Aden and the governorates of Lahij and Abyan, as being culturally Yemeni and thus more like the north; and a rejection of southern claims over Hadramawt, invoking the illegitimacy of the process by which the Hadrami sultanates were incorporated into South

Yemen in 1967, seen by many as the beginning of an insidious process by which Hadramawt "became" Yemeni. During first half of the 20th century the two principal sultanates in Hadramawt, the Kathiri (by then reduced to the wadi towns of Seiyun and Tarim and the surrounding areas) and the Quayti (most of the rest of Hadramawt including the western wadi and the coastal towns of Mukalla and Shihr), together with the Mahra sultanate based in Suqutra, formed the British Eastern Aden Protectorate, distinct not only from the colony of Aden but from the sultanates of the Western Protectorate. As independence loomed, the British administration managed to persuade most of the rulers of the Western Protectorate[26] to form the Federation of South Arabia as a first step towards independence; but the three eastern sultanates remained apart and constituted the Protectorate of South Arabia which, it was assumed, would also be granted independence, but not as part of the state that would emerge from the Federation. Whether they would be granted independence as three states or as some sort of federation had not been decided when deliberations were overtaken by events as the Aden-based National Liberation Front extended its control over the Federation and moved into the protectorates. The British fled, the NLF annexed the protectorate states, deposing the sultans (who sought exile in Saudi Arabia), and the entire Protectorate became part of the independent People's Republic of South Yemen on 30 November 1967.

During the existence of South Yemen there appears to have been muted resistance to the incorporation of Hadramawt into the republic; likewise, following unification, and until well into the first decade of the 21st century, discourse on the pre-unification period was more concerned with the state as a whole and the contrast with the post-unification period. Policies of the Marxist government were viewed with ambivalence as perspectives shifted from criticisms of the repressive character of the government to nostalgia for a time when things were cheap and plentiful, citizens enjoyed greater equality, life was secure if not luxurious, and there were no *Shimalis* to contend with. Hadramawt shared these discourses with other regions of the south: the perceived injustices suffered by the south at the hands of northerners serving as a unifying factor. More recently, however, and as part of the process of a "rediscovery" of Hadrami identity (which I will come to in a moment), and a parallel growing fear that Hadramawt would not be any less marginalized within an independent southern state, British responsibility for the loss of independence is increasingly invoked in an attempt both to delegitimize the incorporation of Hadramawt into the south and to attempt to recruit wider (specifically British but by extension international) support for Hadrami independence. This was expressed particularly clearly in a letter addressed to the British Ambassador in Cairo on the occasion of a meeting he facilitated on the Southern Question on 11th June 2012 which called for British support for Hadrami independence. Continued Hadrami insistence on British responsibility for Hadramawt was seen by many observers to have finally borne fruit when the British ambassador to Yemen visited the governorate – for the first time – in May 2013.[27]

Dissatisfaction with the leaders of the southern movement (Hirak) based in Aden is also increasingly vocal. This is based partly on a belief that Hadramis are being excluded from the negotiation process that is intended to reconcile differences between south and north, and partly in fear that Aden will reach an accommodation with the northern leaders that will not satisfy the demands of Hadramawt. Informants frequently point out that Hadramis in the former independent South Yemen government "forgot" Hadramawt and pursued their own personal agendas as members of an Aden-based ruling clique. Finally, there is a fear that replacing Sanaa with Aden would be no solution and that Hadramawt would continue to see its resources being appropriated by the elite of a distant government.

Indeed, economic arguments are at the forefront of independentist discourses, particularly among the Hadrami community in Saudi Arabia who claim that, shorn of a populous but resource-poor Aden and hinterland, never mind the north, an oil-rich Hadramawt would be able to grow rapidly and achieve a level of development that would make membership of the GCC perfectly feasible, something that would not be offered to a unified Yemen in a foreseeable future despite promises made in 2006.[28] Economic growth would be even more rapid following GCC membership, and the accompanying freedom of movement of both capital and people between the GCC and Hadramawt would return the region to the greater Arab fold where it properly belongs. This would not necessarily see non-Saudi Hadramis granted access to facilities currently denied to them in Saudi Arabia (education, health and so on), but it would ideally see Hadramawt itself develop economically to the point where facilities of a commensurate level would be available in the homeland.

On a more symbolic level, Hadrami voices have become particularly audible over the past decade for several reasons. First, the Yemeni government has permitted the return of the deposed sultans of the Hadramawt and Mahra sultanates. Sultan Ghaleb al-Quayti returned to Hadramawt in 1996 for the first time since 1967, to be welcomed by large crowds at the airport. Members of the Kathiri royal family have also returned, as did, most recently, the Mahra Sultan Abdullah al-Afrar, who returned to Suqutra to a tumultuous welcome in February 2013. These highly symbolic returns have provided a focal point for expressions of identity that invoke pre-independence autonomy, regardless of whether or not an envisaged independent state (or states) would be monarchy or republic.

A second event that appears to have been instrumental in awakening Hadrami diasporic consciousness and which is regularly invoked by Hadramis across the region, was the transmission by the Saudi-owned satellite television channel al-Arabiya in 2008 of a four-part, two and a quarter hour documentary on the Hadrami diaspora financed by Abdullah bin Mahfouz, another prominent Saudi of Hadrami origin. The history of Hadramawt within South Yemen was strongly shaped by Marxist doctrine while in post-unification Yemen, the unifying discourse of the central government placed its emphasis on Yemen, often to the exclusion of regional variations,[29] and this lengthy celebration of the influence wielded across the Indian Ocean by Hadramis was, for many, the first time that they became aware of their own history and the extent of their (collective) activities. I have been advised on countless occasions by Hadramis both in Hadramawt itself and in the diaspora to see this documentary as testimony to their influence and prestige across the Indian Ocean.

Another phenomenon is linked to rather particular individual. In 2000 the Jeddah Treaty between Saudi Arabia and Yemen fixed the border between the two countries, conclusively recognizing Yemen's relinquishment of all claims over the southern Saudi provinces of Najran, Jizan and Asir but in return granting to Yemen a significant tract of hitherto unclaimed territory between Yemen and Saudi Arabia. For at least one Saudi of Hadrami origin, this removed a long-standing obstacle to a personal reconciliation of his different identities and allegiances. In March 2002 Abdullah Ahmed Bugshan, a member of one of Saudi Arabia's more prominent Hadrami families and who had hitherto not felt able to visit Yemen, made his first visit to his homeland since 1967. Since then he has invested significantly in Hadramawt, funding hospitals, roads and schools and running a charitable foundation that funds education and healthcare for Hadramis as well as engaging in business ventures. On a more personal level, over the past decade he has organized visits to Hadramawt for Hadramis living in Saudi Arabia. These all-expenses-paid trips are common knowledge among the community and those who take advantage of them range from personal friends, to homesick exiles, young men in a quest for their identity and, simply, the curious. Abdullah Bugshan's activities in this sphere contribute significantly to the construction of a diasporic identity among the Hadramis of Saudi Arabia – even among those who do not avail themselves of the opportunity to visit the homeland – and a recognition in Hadramawt of the important of the community over the border.

Visits to the homeland are not always straightforwardly unambiguous. Reactions of those who "return" range from bemusement to joy. One young man whose first visit to Hadramawt, aged in his mid-20s, was with Abdullah Bugshan told me he felt nothing in particular. "It was interesting," he said, "but just a visit to another country. I wouldn't go again. It's very poor." Others are more appreciative, and more expressive. Another man, who first returned when he was in his 40s, said "When I went to Hadramawt I saw people like me and I felt I was like them. I inherited it in my genes, I felt I belonged there." Another informant repeated the genetic link: his father had died when he was very young and his mother was Saudi, so he couldn't have been socialized as a Hadrami, he could only have acquired his sense of Hadrami genetically: "We are unique. We have certain ingredients in our personality, honesty and hard work, that we have inherited from our parents." Yet another told me "I went back to the village and I visited my grandparents' homes. I smelt the history." This discourse of belonging is accompanied by an assertion of difference and an exceptional identity; it is part of distinguishing themselves from Yemenis – "Whenever anyone calls me a Yemeni I say, I am not a Yemeni, I am a Hadrami" – but it also part of distinguishing themselves from Saudis.

Conclusion: Hadrami or Saudi?

Hadramis who are Saudi citizens have a liminal status. Unlike Hadramis in East Africa (for example), many retain close links with Hadramawt, returning particularly to marry, thus reinforcing a sentiment of Hadrami identity in a way that East Africans, marrying locally and no longer speaking Arabic, do not. There is an emphasis on differentiation from other Saudis, a sense of pride in their identity: "a Hadrami will always say he's a Hadrami, even if he's a third generation Saudi" is a common refrain in Saudi Arabia; "Call me '*ba*' not '*abuya*'", a father tells his son, "or people will think you are Saudi." Yet at the same time, Hadrami men in Saudi Arabia wear the thobe and the ghutra, performing their Saudi personae outwardly even while expressing Hadrami personae in private. The performance of these different personae are recognized as strategies that are required in Saudi Arabia: outward belonging that marks their status in the kingdom, while social and cultural practices undermine this very identity because it has already been undermined by their liminality.

Although formal identities in Saudi Arabia are not exclusive to the extent that they are in some of the other GCC states, Hadramis, both those who are Yemeni and those who are Saudi citizens, are particularly sensitive to their identity. Hadramis who are not Saudi citizens are excluded on a number of levels. In addition to the requirement that they possess *iqama*s (at some expense), they are not permitted to own businesses and are denied access to public health services, schools and universities, often being obliged to obliged to "return" to Yemen if they wish to pursue higher education. Despite a recent relaxation of the rules – public universities are now permitted to enrol non-citizens up to a ceiling of 10% of admissions – private hospitals and schools are effectively the only option for many. Perhaps most frustratingly for "divided" families, that is, those who count both Saudi and Yemen citizens, is the difficulty of marrying a Saudi citizen.[30] Not only are "Saudi" Saudis thus excluded, but a man intending to marry a Hadrami kinswoman who has Saudi citizenship faces similar constraints. The formal status of Hadramis who are Yemeni citizens is therefore a significant barrier to integration in the kingdom and an incitement to the maintenance of community identity.

However, Hadramis are not simply excluded by virtue of not being Saudi citizens, they are further assimilated to a category which many find even less desirable, that of "Yemeni". The renewed sense of a Hadrami collective identity, concurrent with anti-Yemeni sentiments in the homeland leave many Hadramis with no formal identity at all, or at least, none that is satisfactory. Neither Yemeni nor Saudi, their only option is to voice support for an independent homeland which would both grant them an acceptable formal status and, ideally, allow both for their formal incorporation into the GCC, where many of them feel they correctly belong, and for the subsequent possibility of being "at home" in Saudi Arabia. This, for many, is the only solution which will permit them to remain where they are while at the same time ceasing to be outsiders.

Notes

1 See, e.g., R. Brubaker, "Migration, Membership, and the Modern Nation-State: Internal and External Dimensions of the Politics of Belonging," *Journal of Interdisciplinary History* 41, no. 1 (2010): 61–78; L. Pries, "Ambiguities of Global and Transnational Collective Identities," *Global Networks* 13, no. 1 (2013): 22–40.

2 N. Glick Schiller, "Situating Identities: Towards an Identities Studies without Binaries of Difference," *Identities: Global Studies in Culture and Power* 19, no. 4 (2012): 520–32.

3 E.g., J. Pieterse, "Globalization as Hybridization," in *Global Modernities*, ed. M. Featherstone, S. Lash, and R. Robertson (London: Sage, 1995); S. Vertovec and and R. Cohen, eds., *Conceiving Cosmopolitanism: Theory, Context, Practice* (Oxford: Oxford University Press, 2002); P. Werbner, ed., *Anthropology and the New Cosmopolitanism* (Oxford: Berg Press, 2008).

4 M. Sökefeld, "Debating Self, Identity and Culture in Anthropology," *Current Anthropology* 40, no. 4 (1999): 417–47; N. Quinn, "The Self," *Anthropological Theory* 6, no. 3 (2006): 362–84.

5 Cf. M. Mauss, "Une categorie de l'esprit humain: La notion de personne, celle de "moi'," *Journal of the Royal Anthropological Institute of Great Britain and Ireland* 68 (1938): 263–81.

6 See P. Bourdieu, *Distinction: A Social Critique of the Judgement of Taste* (Cambridge, MA: Harvard University Press, 1984).

7 E. Ho, *The Graves of Tarim: Genealogy and Mobility across the Indian Ocean* (Berkeley: University of California Press, 2006).

8 E.g., J. Willis, *Unmaking North and South: Cartographies of the Yemeni Past* (New York: Columbia University Press, 2012).

9 A. Bujra, *The Politics of Stratification: A Study of Political Change in a South Arabian Town* (Oxford: Clarendon Press, 1971); see also S. Camelin, "'Shihr une grandissime cité…': Quartiers et organisation dans une ville du Hadramaout (sud-Yémen)" (PhD thesis, Université Paris Ouest Nanterre La Défense, 2000); M. A. Rodionov, *The Western Ḥaḍramawt: Ethnographic Field Research, 1983–91* (Halle: Orientwissenschaftliches Zentrum der Martin-Luther-Universität, 2007).

10 On the Hadrami diaspora in the Indian Ocean, see, for example, U. Freitag and W. G. Clarence-Smith, eds., *Hadhrami Traders, Scholars and Statesmen in the Indian Ocean, 1750s–1960s* (Leiden: Brill, 1997) and L. Manger, *The Hadrami Diaspora: Community-Building on the Indian Ocean Rim* (Oxford: Berghahn, 2010); in Saudi Arabia, see T. Pritzkat, "The Hadhrami Community in Saudi Arabia and the Rationale of Investing in the Homeland," in *Le Yémen contemporain*, ed. R. Leveau, F. Mermier, and U. Steinbach (Paris: Karthala, 1999) and P. Pétriat, "Notables et rebelles," *Arabian Humanities* [Online] 1 (2013): http://cy.revues.org/1923

11 Ho, *Graves of Tarim.*

12 I use the term "Gulf" here to refer to the GCC states.

13 Some of whom would be the daughters of previous marriages between Hadrami men and local women and thus at least partly Hadrami.

14 Indeed, my suggestion that it does occur is met with denial: I must be mistaken. Note that men are also brought from the homeland to marry Hadrami daughters born in diaspora, but this is acceptable and common practice everywhere.

15 The cultural problems attendant upon having children raised by Swahili mothers were solved by sending boys back to Hadramawt for an education. The (cultural) loss of girls was less of an issue.

16 Note also that the restrictions on non-citizens marrying Saudi women also encourages marriage with women from Hadramawt, thus reinforcing community identity.

17 Pétriat, "Notables et rebelles."

18 Under the provisions of Article 44 of the Residence Regulations, which allowed for *iqama*s to be granted to those likely to contribute to the kingdom irrespective of their employment status (Kingdom of Saudi Arabia, *The Residence Regulations. These Regulations by the Supreme Royal Order No. 17/2/25/1337 on 11/09/1371H (4/6/1952G)*, www.refworld.org/pdfid/3fb9f0d44.pdf, downloaded 30/07/2012). Article 44 has not to my knowledge been revoked, but it is now extremely difficult to obtain an *iqama* under its provisions.

19 13 Shawwal 1357.
20 Note that, following the 1962 revolution, Saudi Arabia remained well-disposed towards royalists fleeing the new Yemeni republic.
21 Yemen's stance was popularly expressed as support for Iraq; however, the trigger for Saudi retaliation was Yemen's public neutrality, calling for negotiations between Iraq and Kuwait, and, as the only Arab member of the UN Security Council at the time, abstaining from the subsequent vote on Resolution 660.
22 On the return, see N. A. Colton, "Homeward Bound: Yemeni Return Migration," *International Migration Review* 27, no. 4 (1993): 870–82; G. Okruhlik and P. Conge, "National Autonomy, Labor Migration and Political Crisis: Yemen and Saudi Arabia," *Middle East Journal*, 51, no. 4 (1997): 554–65; N. Van Hear, "The Socio-economic Impact of the Involuntary Mass Return to Yemen in 1990," *Journal of Refugee Studies* 7, no. 1 (1994): 18–38. Many Yemenis, never particularly happy with the Treaty of Taif, continued to see it as temporary and, indeed, since one of its terms was periodic renewal, in abeyance. Technically it would indeed have appear to have expired, since most Yemeni republican governments had rejected it and under Article 22 ("If not renewed or modified by that date [six months prior to expiry of each 20 year term], it shall remain in force until 6 months after such time as one party has given notice to the other party of his desire to modify it.") this is sufficient for abrogation. See A. H. Al-Enazy, "'The International Boundary Treaty' (Treaty of Jeddah) Concluded between the Kingdom of Saudi Arabia and the Yemeni Republic on June 12, 2000," *American Journal of International Law* 96, no. 1 (2002): 161–73.
23 Not surprisingly, northern Yemenis were less likely to have acquired Saudi citizenship since it conferred no particular advantages and, generally, were less well integrated in Saudi Arabia, exception made for the border areas.
24 "Border Guards Report Spike in Infiltrations from Yemen," *Saudi Gazette*, July 14, 2011, http://www.saudigazette.com.sa/index.cfm?method=home.regcon&contentid=20110714105200; "Crackdown to Flush out Infiltrators Continues," *Saudi Gazette*, March 3, 2013: http://www.saudigazette.com.sa/index.cfm?method=home.regcon&contentid=20130303155204
25 On the southern question see S. Day, *Yemen on The Brink: The Political challenge of Yemen's Southern Movement*, Middle East Program 108 (Washington: Carnegie Endowment for International Peace, 2010); ICG, *Yemen's Southern Question: Avoiding a Breakdown*, Middle East Report 145 (Brussels: International Crisis Group, 2013); N. Stracke and N. S. Haidar, *The Southern Movement in Yemen* (Dubai: Gulf Research Center, 2010).
26 With the exception of Upper Yafa. The Wahidi sultanates in western Hadramawt joined the Federation: their territory is today part of the Shabwa governorate, not Hadramawt.
27 This was not of course anything more than a regular visit which the ambassador had long held a desire to do before the expiry of his term.
28 In 2006 the GCC set a target date of 2015 for Yemeni membership, but no progress has been made and the prospect is now quite fanciful.
29 Even the use of the word "Hadrami" was discouraged. Abdullah Ba Haj's thesis was called "Yemenis in Saudi Arabia," although it dealt almost exclusively with Hadramis.
30 Permission is required from the ministry of the interior and there are a number of restrictions bases on age, income and employment status.

References

Barth, F. *Ethnic Groups and Boundaries: The Social Organization of Culture Difference*. Boston: Little, Brown, 1969.

Bourdieu, P. *Distinction: A Social Critique of the Judgement of Taste*. Cambridge, MA: Harvard University Press, 1984.

Brehony, N. *Yemen Divided: The Story of a Failed State in South Arabia*. London: I. B. Tauris, 2011.

Brubaker, R. "Migration, Membership, and the Modern Nation-State: Internal and External Dimensions of the Politics of Belonging." *Journal of Interdisciplinary History* 41, no. 1 (2010): 61–78.

Bujra, A. *The Politics of Stratification: A Study of Political Change in a South Arabian Town*. Oxford: Clarendon Press, 1971.

Camelin, S. "'Shihr une grandissime cité…': Quartiers et organisation dans une ville du Hadramaout (sud-Yémen)." PhD thesis, Université Paris Ouest Nanterre La Défense, 2000.

Colton, N. A. "Homeward Bound: Yemeni Return Migration." *International Migration Review* 27, no. 4 (1993): 870–82.

Day, S. *Yemen on The Brink: The Political challenge of Yemen's Southern Movement*. Middle East Program 108. Washington: Carnegie Endowment for International Peace, 2010.

Al-Enazy, A. H. "'The International Boundary Treaty' (Treaty of Jeddah) Concluded between the Kingdom of Saudi Arabia and the Yemeni Republic on June 12, 2000." *American Journal of International Law* 96, no. 1 (2002): 161–73.

Freitag, U., and W. G. Clarence-Smith, eds. *Hadhrami Traders, Scholars and Statesmen in the Indian Ocean, 1750s–1960s*. Leiden: Brill, 1997.

Glick Schiller, N. "Situating Identities: Towards an Identities Studies without Binaries of Difference." *Identities: Global Studies in Culture and Power* 19, no. 4 (2012): 520–32.

Hill, G., and G. Nonneman. *Yemen, Saudi Arabia and the Gulf States: Elite Politics, Street Protests and Regional Diplomacy*. London: Chatham House, 2011.

Ho, E. *The Graves of Tarim: Genealogy and Mobility across the Indian Ocean*. Berkeley: University of California Press, 2006.

ICG. *Yemen's Southern Question: Avoiding a Breakdown*. Middle East Report 145. Brussels: International Crisis Group, 2013.

Manger, L. *The Hadrami Diaspora: Community-Building on the Indian Ocean Rim*. Oxford: Berghahn, 2010.

Mauss, M. "Une categorie de l'esprit humain: La notion de personne, celle de "moi'." *Journal of the Royal Anthropological Institute of Great Britain and Ireland* 68 (1938): 263–81.

Okruhlik, G., and P. Conge. "National Autonomy, Labor Migration and Political Crisis: Yemen and Saudi Arabia." *Middle East Journal*, 51, no. 4 (1997): 554–65.

Pétriat, P. "Notables et rebelles." *Arabian Humanities* [Online] 1 (2013): http://cy.revues.org/1923

Pieterse, J. "Globalization as Hybridization." In *Global Modernities*, edited by M. Featherstone, S. Lash, and R. Robertson. London: Sage, 1995.

Pries, L. "Ambiguities of Global and Transnational Collective Identities." *Global Networks* 13, no. 1 (2013): 22–40.

Pritzkat, T. "The Hadhrami Community in Saudi Arabia and the Rationale of Investing in the Homeland." In *Le Yémen contemporain*, edited by R. Leveau, F. Mermier, and U. Steinbach. Paris: Karthala, 1999.

Quinn, N. "The Self." *Anthropological Theory* 6, no. 3 (2006): 362–84.

Rodionov, M. A. *The Western Ḥadramawt: Ethnographic Field Research, 1983–91*. Halle: Orientwissenschaftliches Zentrum der Martin-Luther-Universität, 2007.

Sökefeld, M. "Debating Self, Identity and Culture in Anthropology." *Current Anthropology* 40, no. 4 (1999): 417–47.

Stracke, N., and M. S. Haidar. *The Southern Movement in Yemen*. Dubai: Gulf Research Center, 2010.

Van Hear, N. "The Socio-economic Impact of the Involuntary Mass Return to Yemen in 1990." *Journal of Refugee Studies* 7, no. 1 (1994): 18–38.

Vertovec, S., and R. Cohen, eds. *Conceiving Cosmopolitanism: Theory, Context, Practice*. Oxford: Oxford University Press, 2002.

Werbner, P., ed. *Anthropology and the New Cosmopolitanism*. Oxford: Berg Press, 2008.

Willis, J. *Unmaking North and South: Cartographies of the Yemeni Past*. New York: Columbia University Press, 2012.

3

Corruption in Yemen: Maintaining the Status Quo?

Peter Salisbury

Introduction

For at least the past decade, corruption and the use of corrupt practices to distribute patronage in Yemen have been at the heart of discourse on Yemen's political economy and the country's many policy and developmental failures. Since a 2011 uprising that displaced longtime president Ali Abdullah Saleh, accusations of corruption between different political factions and disputes over high-profile Saleh-era deals have increasingly been used as political tools to bolster the anti-establishment and reformist credentials of key Yemeni political players.

Corruption was one of the key issues raised during Yemen's 2011 uprising: the protest movement was primarily focused on "corruption, limited access to basic services, and the extreme centralization of power",[1] particularly with respect to former president Saleh who is alleged to have amassed a fortune of billions of dollars. Since then, corruption has been central to the rhetoric of Yemeni groups presenting themselves as anti-establishment movements, including protestors who took part in the uprising, and members of the country's leading political parties attempting to reposition themselves as opposition groups. Yemen's transitional president until January 2015, Abd Rabbuh Mansour Hadi, vowed to combat malfeasance, as did the government he appointed in December 2011. Anti-corruption rhetoric was also an important part of the messaging issued by the Huthis, a Zaydi Shia rebel group that seized Sanaa in September 2014 and displaced Hadi four months later. They partially justified their actions by claiming that the Hadi administration had marked a continuation of, rather than a break from, historically corrupt practices. And indeed, by most measures, including the annual Transparency International Corruption Perception Index, corruption has worsened rather than improved since Saleh's ouster[2] despite public messaging around anti-corruption reform.

Yet, in most cases, those who have criticized high levels of corruption have done so in order to bolster their image and position themselves as being outside of the status quo rather than out of a genuine concern with the impact corrupt practices have on the efficacy of government and on development; most anticorruption rhetoric has focused on symbolic deals rather than the pervasive culture of corruption that undermines governance in Yemen.

In February 2014, for example, Hadi took a publicly hardline stance on what is widely perceived in Yemen as being one of the highest profile cases of economic mismanagement in the country's recent history, framing the maneuver as a push towards greater transparency and as an attempt to mitigate past missteps and corrupt practices. The president demanded that the French company Total, the biggest single investor in Yemen's oil and gas industry, renegotiate the price it pays for liquefied natural gas (LNG) supplied by Yemen LNG, a Yemeni-international joint venture in which Total holds a stake of just under 40 per cent. In February 2014, the office of the public prosecutor announced that it was investigating allegations of malfeasance during the negotiations that led to the series of contracts that underpin the scheme.[3]

If the price renegotiations, ongoing at the time of writing, were to be successful, it would mark the second time in as many years that governments under Hadi have overturned a major deal struck under Saleh, who stepped down from the presidency in November 2011 after a year of popular protest and elite infighting. In September 2012, a Yemeni-Dubai joint venture led by the ports company DP World agreed to cancel a concessionary deal to run Aden port for 25 years after repeated government accusations of malpractice.[4] The government presented DP World's departure as a victory for the anticorruption agenda, despite the fact that they paid a fine to the Dubai firm for breach of contract.

But the way in which conversations around malpractice and corruption were framed by the Hadi administration – the gap between that conversation and the reality of government action – reflected a continued failure to address the intricate networks of patronage and corrupt practices that have been a barrier to economic growth and development. The focus of debates around the Yemen LNG scheme, for example, has been on the way gas sales prices were negotiated rather than a deal struck between the government and YLNG - a private company - for gas supply at source at an extremely low rate; or on construction, maintenance and security deals awarded by YLNG to key facilitators of the initial YLNG. Corruption investigations have been aimed at denting the economic interests of a few key players while building public support for the government. As such, they marked a continuation of, rather than a break from, Saleh-era practices.

As this chapter was being written, the Huthis were consolidating their control over the apparatus of the state in Sanaa. The group's leader, the cleric Abd al-Malik al-Huthi, was maintaining his own critical stance on corruption. But again, it would appear that the group is both limited in its willingness and ability to take on the culture of patronage that has maintained an unsteady peace in the north of Yemen for more than three decades.

Aims

This chapter aims to do several things. First, it gives a broad definition of corruption and explains the impact of corruption on development in poor countries like Yemen. Using a political economy approach it then attempts to provide a general taxonomy of corruption in Yemen, unpacking malfeasance in the context of patronage networks and the 'rules of the game' in Yemen. Finally, the paper asks whether corruption has worsened or improved since the transitional government took over in December 2011 and whether successive 'reformists' have actually stepped outside of the bounds of accepted norms in Yemen.

Using past behavior to highlight continuing trends, the author argues that the YLNG and DP World cases were emblematic of a continuation, if not an intensification, of business as usual in Yemen under Hadi rather than any meaningful change in the way that the government approaches corruption - a particularly worrisome trend given Yemen's economic instability. Rather than make actual attempts to combat malfeasance, the state instead attempts to create the perception that it is doing so, using the maneuver to improve its own political position and weaken its rivals'.

Methodology

Political economy analysis is concerned "with the interaction of political and economic processes in a society: the distribution of power and wealth between different groups and individuals; and the processes that create, sustain and transform these relationships over time."[5] Analysis of the kind practiced by the author looks at the interactions between, and relative strength of formal and informal institutions in the hope of uncovering "isomorphic mimicry"[6] where physically visible government bodies and paper polities are undermined or entirely subverted by vested interests whose influence is not immediately visible; where informal institutions – "sanctions, taboos, customs, traditions, and codes of conduct" outweigh formal rules – "constitutions, laws, property rights."[7] Only by understanding the rules and incentives at play among the groups and networks who practice them can barriers to reform be assessed and overcome.

To build an analytical framework, this chapter draws on the work of Sue Unsworth and the Netherlands' Conflict Research Unit, particularly the 2007 *paper Framework for Strategic Governance And Corruption Analysis: Designing Strategic Responses Towards Good Governance; USAID's 2006 Corruption Assessment Handbook: Final Report;* and the OECD's International Drivers of Corruption: A Tool for Analysis. Unsworth et al. argue that in order to assess 'Power and Change Analysis', as they describe political economy studies, discussion should revolve around:

1. 'Foundational Factors' – *assessing "whether government controls the territory, and embedded social and economic factors that significantly shape the political system"*
2. 'The Rules of the Game' – *analyzing formal and informal institutions of the state, civil society and the private sector, that shapes how business is conducted and relationships managed'* and
3. 'The Here and Now' – providing an overview of *"key actors' capacities and interests, and the events and pressures (context) to which they are responding"*[8]

The paper combines analysis of foundational factors and the rules of the game into a single section before introducing another section, the Here and Now, which focuses on the DP World and YLNG deals. The author limits his discussion of foundational factors to more fully discuss changes in the political economy since 2011.

Political Economy, Corruption and the Rules of the Game

Developing countries, we are told, almost without "exception suffer from high levels of corruption". Corruption "impacts on development outcomes... It undermines accountable and effective institutions, prevents access to basic public services and holds back economic growth."[9] If corrupt practices are not addressed in poor countries, the potential for development and inclusive growth will be limited.

But what, exactly, is meant by corruption? The OECD defines corruption as the "abuse of entrusted authority for illicit gain."[10] As the organization notes, "public officials can break different laws in different ways with different implications for the public good". The causes and effects of corruption vary widely and are often linked to a wider set of informal norms and institutions - 'rules of the game' - that may not even be viewed as corrupt by beneficiaries.

In 2013 *Transparency International* ranked Yemen at 167 out of 177 countries assessed for perceived levels of corruption.[11] Despite rising inflows of aid, considerable input from international development agencies and a reform agenda that included the creation of a new anti-corruption body launched in the mid-2000s, levels of poverty increased in each successive year between 2006 and 2010. Since 2011, when a popular uprising descended into inter-elite violence, the poverty rate has been above 50 per cent.[12]

Corruption does not necessarily lead to weak economic growth or development, as the (largely unique) case of South Korea shows, and has not by any means been the sole factor in weak development in Yemen. But as my Chatham House colleagues and I noted in 2013, it has been a barrier to the implementation of government policy genuinely aimed at promoting broad inclusive growth, the provision of basic services and the construction of important infrastructure - in no small part because of the resistance of key political players to reforms that might challenge corrupt practices and the flow of patronage to non-state actors.[13] With more and more state resources being directed towards maintaining a fragile peace and barriers to reform increasingly insurmountable, the Saleh-era political economy dragged on the state and hurt development.

Yemen in Context: Foundational Factors

The February 2012 accession of Abd Rabbuh Mansour Hadi to the presidency of Yemen marked a formal end to an elite compact that had lasted for more than three decades between a clique of powerful tribal and military leaders mainly from the north west of Yemen. The man he replaced, Ali Abdullah Saleh, had been president of north Yemen since 1978 and of the unified Yemen – created by a 1990 merger of the socialist south and republican north – for more than two decades. The Saleh regime was built around members of Saleh's Sanhan tribe, who held or assumed top military positions, and the leadership of the powerful Hashid tribal confederation (of which the Sanhan is a part), most notably sheikh Abdullah al-Ahmar, at that time, and until his death in 2007, the paramount sheikh of the confederation.

When Saleh became president, he inherited a state in the making that had been ostensibly ruled by a succession of religious ruling elites for much of the previous millennium, in which the state "acted as a mediator in local disputes rather than as a central authority that imposed a set rule of law uniformly across the country."[14] Along with his partners, Saleh worked over the following three decades to centralize power, wealth, and the management of natural resources in a manner that was almost entirely new to Yemen. After the 1990 unification of the north and south and a subsequent 1994 north-south civil war, the regime built a monopoly over land and natural resources, most significantly oil and gas, income from which were to form the bulk of state revenues for the next 20 years.

Although often described as an autocracy, the Saleh regime was more "neopatrimonial" than "sultanistic", and relied on wide participation and consequently wide distribution of patronage.[15] "Far from restricting illicit wealth to small circles of kin or colleagues, the government proved ecumenical."[16] Participation in the regime was extended to anyone who was powerful enough to pose a threat to the status quo; inclusion came on the condition that participants did not cross certain 'red lines', and who did not object to the inclusion of other participants. Refusal of patronage, however, was frowned upon. The ultimate aim of patronage and co-option was to make elite players as dependent on the regime as possible. The incentive at an elite level was to participate in, rather than to act against, corruption - and at the very least to turn a blind eye to corrupt practices in their own jurisdictions. Only when it was clear that potential rivals for power and legitimacy could not be co-opted or gently coerced did the regime use all-out violence to impose its authority.

Patronage networks were underpinned by oil revenues and the regime's control of key economic levers, particularly business licenses from imports to telecommunications, and land, with patronage distributed by formal and informal routes. The Department of Tribal Affairs, for example, paid stipends to an estimated 6,000 tribal sheikhs, while tribal leaders and senior regime officials were handed control of the operations and budget for military units.[17] Tens of thousands of bogus 'ghost' jobs were allocated to regime-affiliated groups and individuals giving them a steady stream of income. Military leaders were given broad autonomy to produce their own budgets, as were government ministries, through which further patronage was distributed in the shape of jobs and lucrative project contracts which were poorly enforced. Sheikhs and military officers were also handed ownership of vast swathes of land in the south, and important regime players were handed big business licenses, from telecommunications operatorships to fishing rights for huge stretches of the coastline.[18]

Foreign companies hoping to secure contracts and deals to extract resources or work in the lucrative oil sector were often forced to use regime-approved intermediaries to broker deals and construction and service contractors owned by regime intimates. Companies and individuals were allocated volumes of fuel far in excess of their needs that they either sold on to foreign firms or into east Africa. Security firms owned by regime players earned lucrative deals to protect oil and gas production facilities and the interests of foreign firms operating in Yemen.[19]

The cost to the state of this broad nexus of cooperative corruption is impossible to calculate but ran into the billions of dollars, and accounted for a rising share of the state budget. In 2008, Daniel Egel calculated that 'ghost workers' in the education sector accounted for up to 6 per cent of the state budget that year.[20] . In 2009, Sarah Phillips estimated that about a third of the budget of fuel subsidies, around US$3 billion, that year, went to diesel smuggling networks.[21] More recently, international observers have come to believe that as much as a third of the government's 1.2 million employees are 'ghost workers' or simply do not turn up for work.[22] Senior executives at state-run oil firms believe that the cost of using regime-approved contractors in the sector increased overall development costs by up to 20 per cent compared to the regional average.[23]

"This patronage system is one of the most important forms of corruption in Yemen and, as such, has likely contributed to Yemen's weak economic growth and development," Egel wrote.[24]

The system strongly resembled a 'limited access order' of the kind described[25] as a system in which a small group of actors dominates control over state resources, using these resources to provide patronage to potential rivals, mitigating the potential for conflict and challenges to the regime, at the cost of producing meaningful development outcomes or building durable state institutions.

"Rather than building up the formal institutions of the nascent state, Saleh co-opted local leaders and powerful rivals into a patronage network based on oil rents and access to licit and illicit business opportunities, gradually divorcing these figures from increasingly marginalized local constituencies and using divide-and-rule tactics to ensure that the power of the central leadership could not be challenged," my Chatham House colleagues and I wrote in 2013.[26] "This strategy maintained a fragile peace, but limited reform options, particularly when the state was the main conduit for patronage."

The state struggled to cover its costs in the late 2000s, yet little effort was made to ease the pressure of these networks of patronage. Doing so would have meant dismantling the foundations of the cooperative structure of the regime. "Grand corruption is not a tangential problem in Yemen. Rather, it is the glue that keeps things in place," wrote the authors of a 2006 USAID report on corruption.[27]

Competition and Censure

While the regime was highly inclusive, there were 'red lines' for participants. Crossing these informally codified lines was heavily penalized. Attempting to supplant Saleh, or denying his authority, constituted a clear breach of the elite compact. So too did public political challenges to the regime and refusal to comply with its demands. Non-cooperation with the economic structures built up by the regime was also a punishable offence.

To enforce discipline, the regime also made use of state institutions including the court system and Yemen's anti-corruption body, the Central Organization for Control and Auditing (COCA), accusing businesses of corrupt practices when they stepped out of line, or when their practices had become too obvious.[28] A former Saleh associate describes COCA as acting as "the president's black box; it was there to make sure he had dirt on everyone so he had all the chips in his hands; it had zero to do with stopping corruption."[29]

In 2006, for example, the government demanded that Tawfiq Abd al-Rahim al-Mutahhar, an alleged Saleh crony who acted as the sole distributor of fuel to the Public Electricity Corporation, pay YR2 billion in back taxes.[30] Two years earlier, Saleh had ordered that al-Mutahhar's contracts be cancelled and for COCA to investigate his business activities. Yet the contract was not cancelled, the taxes were not paid, and, although al-Mutahhar was taken to court, no action was ultimately taken against him.

Officials with knowledge of the various suits brought against al-Mutahhar described the cases, and the publicity around them, as being in equal parts a bargaining technique aimed at getting a better deal not for the state but for the regime, specifically Saleh, and as a warning shot aimed at Ali Mohsen al-Ahmar, a key regime intimate who from the late 1990s onwards had been increasingly at odds with Saleh and was said to play an important role in al-Mutahhar's operations. As the relationship slowly deteriorated - Mohsen would defect from the regime during the 2011 uprising - Saleh, according to these officials, began to apply pressure to Mohsen's business interests, but stopped short of cutting off his access to patronage, perhaps the ultimate red line among leading members of the regime.[31] Outside of these public spats, few cases were brought to court by COCA and fewer still were successful. It benefited no one to have the wider Yemeni public understand the regime's internal workings, and until 2011 the regime was largely successful in maintaining internal discipline.

Some cases did become public knowledge, largely because they were heard in foreign courts; for example, a dispute in 2004 with an Oman-registered, Yemeni-run firm company, Desert Line. Desert Line refused to hand part of the contract over to a regime-affiliated group, and the government refused to honor contracted payments. The dispute "was exacerbated by harassment, threats and thefts committed by Yemeni armed forces and non-State armed groups and by the incarceration of some of Desert Line's personnel", and the case ended with Desert Line being awarded $23 million in damages by a Yemeni court in 2004. The government refused to honor the decision, and Desert Line took the case to the International Centre for Settlement of Investment Disputes in Washington, DC. The court again found in Desert Line's favor in 2008, and added an extra US$1 million for 'moral damages'.[32]

In 2010, meanwhile, the *Wall Street Journal* announced that the US Department of Justice was investigating allegations of corrupt practices at the oil services company

Schlumberger. In order to secure a 2002 deal to develop an oil-sector databank, the *Journal* said, the company had contracted Zonic Investments, a firm run by Tawfiq Saleh, President Saleh's nephew, paying the firm a total of almost USD1.9 million over five years. Schlumberger had also rented vehicles from senior officials at the state-run Petroleum Exploration and Production Authority (PEPA), the body that was overseeing the databank scheme, at hugely inflated prices, and had paid Dhakwan Petroleum, an oil services firm owned by Ali Mohsen al-Ahmar, US$280,000 for processing paperwork. When the company tried to end this deal, it was unable to import equipment, and resumed the agreement, according to the *Journal*.[33] Despite the publicity, no case was brought by COCA or SNACC.

Anti-Corruption Efforts, 'Reform' and SNACC

Despite an effective media blackout and the threat of regime sanctions, allegations of corruption leaked to the Yemeni press while some actors did take a stand against corruption in the early-to-mid 2000's, most notably Parliamentarians Against Corruption, a parliamentary bloc that protested a number of different deals, including the award of an oil exploration block to a company backed by the son of a senior tribal leader; the Yemen LNG deal, which was formally completed in 2005 against the advice of a number of government advisers, and a 2008 compact with Dubai's DP World International for the management of Aden Port.

More importantly, the government came under increasing pressure from the international community from the early 2000s onwards to improve the quality of Yemeni democracy and to crack down on corrupt practices, particularly after Yemen's suspension from the US government's Millennium Challenge Account, a development assistance programme after "backsliding in a number of the... indicators..." particularly "ruling justly."[34] The 2006 USAID corruption report was aimed at least in part at helping donors understand the nature of patronage and corruption in Yemen. The IMF and World Bank both threatened to end cooperation with the government in the early 2000s because of a lack of reform and failure to meet development targets.

In 2006, as part of a wider package of reforms, the government announced the formation of a new anti-corruption body, the Supreme National Authority for Combatting Corruption (SNACC) which was in part formed of members of Parliamentarians against Corruption, and was charged with investigating allegations of corruption and passing them on to the office of the chief prosecutor in Yemen. In December 2005, the minister of development and international cooperation Ahmed Sofan announced a renewed campaign against corruption. In August 2007, the minister of oil Khaled Bahah – who was appointed prime minister in 2014 but resigned the post in January of 2015 - further announced that Yemen was to form a new government body, the "Yemeni Transparency Council" as part of its attempts to join the Extractive Industries Transparency Initiative (EITI). "For a couple of years, we looked like the most forward-facing country in the region when it came to corruption," a former government official says.[35]

Yet interviews with parliamentarians involved with the anti-corruption movement, those working on Yemen's efforts to join the EITI, and SNACC officials describe the 'reforms' of 2005-2007 as largely being a campaign of whitewashing aimed at enhancing Yemen's ranking in the transparency and development indicators needed to encourage donor participation in the country, and to convince foreign diplomats that the regime was genuinely focused on anti-corruption reforms.

SNACC, for example, was not allowed to make details of the cases it was investigating public until they had been successfully prosecuted. Two former SNACC officials complained to the author that the judiciary was "in the pocket" of the regime and that it was impossible to pass cases through the judicial system, making public anti-corruption campaigns largely useless. Bahah was removed from his position as oil minister in 2007, reputedly because of genuine attempts at investigating and bringing a halt to some forms of corruption in the oil industry[36] Yemen acceded to the EITI, but has been twice suspended from the mechanism because of failure to submit its reports on time and failures in complying with the initiative's analytical framework. Those involved in preparing the reports complain of a lack of support from the government and resistance from officials at the oil ministry, state-run and private firms to cooperate in their data-gathering activities.[37] Despite a series of announcements that the government planned to combat the issue of ghost workers, little visible progress was made.[38]

This state of affairs was in keeping with wider trends in governance in Yemen: public and international pressure led to announcements that the government planned on making reforms to improve governance and foster equitable economic growth and development. New government bodies were formed with reformists given key posts to much fanfare. And then, as one official says, it would be death by committee, resistance, and a lack of political will to make anything happen".[39] The state was more interested in creating the perception it was dealing with corruption than actually tackling practices that glued the regime together, using anti-corruption institutions only when there was no other choice or there were political points to be scored.

'Here and Now': Towards New Rules?

Over the course of 2011 Yemen entered into a series of concurrent, overlapping crises. Early in the year, urban protestors, inspired by movements elsewhere in the region, took to the streets initially demanding democratic, economic and anti-corruption reforms and later calling for the ouster of Saleh and the regime. Heavy-handed tactics led to the deaths of dozens of peaceful protestors and precipitated a long-overdue split within the regime. Tribal and Islamist groups, hitherto Yemen's 'loyal opposition', began to denounce Saleh, and were soon joined by military units loyal to Ali Mohsen al-Ahmar. The split in the regime led to violent conflict between pro- and anti-regime military units and militias, and Yemen seemed to be moving down a path towards civil war.

The fighting caused a vacuum in security, power and governance, and badly destabilized an already weak economy, pushing up the cost of living while affecting government revenues so badly that by the end of the year Yemen faced unprecedented humanitarian and fiscal crises. The resultant vacuum was exploited by hitherto marginalized identity groups like the northern Zaydi Shia Huthis, southern separatists, some tribal groups and even AQAP, which seized large swaths of territory in the south.

Fearful that Yemen was on the verge of collapse and that the ensuing vacuum would provide a permanent base for Al Qaeda and cause a major humanitarian crisis, the international community pressured Saleh to step down. In November 2011, he signed a deal brokered by the member states of the Gulf Cooperation Council (GCC) under which he handed power over to Hadi, his deputy of almost 20 years, who was to be made president in a one-man election in February 2012. The deal was not aimed at radically changing the structure of power in Yemen but rather at creating a space in which power could be shared peacefully between the two broad factions from the former regime, with the 'implementing mechanism' of the so-called GCC deal calling for the creation of a coalition government to oversee gradual change and a series of reforms aimed at steadily eroding the Saleh-era nexus of power, along with a six-month national dialogue process aimed at promoting political inclusion, to be followed by national elections.

The deal called for challenges to the status quo, particularly with respect to corruption. The transitional government, the mechanism said, would "pay special attention to the economic and living conditions of Yemeni citizens… *putting an end to administrative and financial corruption*."[40] In 2012, meanwhile, the government, while negotiating much-needed pledges of aid from foreign donors, further agreed to a 'Mutual Accountability Framework', again committed to: "take the necessary steps to allow investigation, prosecution and trial of high officials charged with corruption…Initiate administrative action against civil servants against whom competent courts have issued conviction orders… Ensure autonomy of the Anti-Corruption Commission and establish an anti- corruption court… Observe budget transparency – including revenues from oil and gas and other natural resources… [and] Initiate practical steps towards realizing the autonomy of COCA."[41] Hadi, temporarily appointed president in November 2011 before being formally elected in February 2012, also spoke on a number of occasions about the need to end corruption, as did Muhammad Salem Basindwah, the transitional prime minister appointed in December 2011.

Combatting Corruption?

In 2012 the government took what seemed to be its first steps towards overturning corrupt Saleh-era deals with then-transport minister Wa'ed Bazib announcing that the government planned to investigate the DP World deal for irregularities, arguing that the Dubai firm had not met its investment commitments and that under its control traffic at the port had fallen rather than risen.

The effort was led by members of the Joint Meeting Parties (JMP), an opposition coalition under Saleh that was given half of all cabinet seats in a transitional coalition government in December 2011. "Members of JMP... are investigating ways of overturning deals agreed under outgoing president Ali Abdullah Saleh, in an attempt to build prestige and weaken Saleh's grip on the economy," Gulf States Newsletter (GSN) reported.[42]According to several officials, the government also discussed investigating the YLNG deal but decided not to do so.[43] "The transport minister has decided to go with Aden [port], the new oil minister was told to sort YLNG, but is looking for gains elsewhere," GSN quoted a 'regional businessman' as saying.

In June 2012, SNACC made public its plans to advise the government and parliament to cancel the port deal. In September of that year DP World announced that it was quitting the port, reputedly for a cash settlement of about USD 24million.[44] Members of the transitional government were at pains to represent the decision as a triumph against corruption, but no investigation was made into any wrongdoing around the deal, and no punitive action was taken against those involved in brokering the deal, although port officials involved in the joint venture reported to the author that the JMP treated them with suspicion, on the basis that they had access to crucial evidence that they had refused to provide.[45] The deal was ultimately cancelled because the government agreed to pay a fine to DP World, who later took the lawyers who had brokered the deal for them to court.

From mid-2013, the government turned its attention to the YLNG deal, particularly to the prices being paid for the sale of LNG to Total, GDF Suez and KoGas, the companies that had signed offtake agreements for LNG in 2005. The KoGas deal allowed for a renegotiation of the price five years after the receipt of a first shipment, which had come in 2009, and in February 2014 the government announced that it had achieved a significant increase in the amount the firm paid for its gas. In late 2013, the government also began to pressure Total - whose deal did not have to be renegotiated until 2029 - to renegotiate the price it was paying. The Total contract was particularly troublesome because it was benchmarked against the price of gas in US markets, which had been depressed since 2008, while the company was selling into Asian markets, where prices were double to three times those in the US. In February 2014, Saba, the state news agency announced that chief prosecutor was investigating the Total offtake agreement for corruption.

Yet among insiders this move was, again, seen as a ploy to improve the government's bargaining position with Total and to drum up support for Hadi and the government. In conversation with the author, several officials involved in the YLNG project said that no evidence of malfeasance had been discovered, and that a number of the people tasked with proving the deal was corrupt had in fact been tangentially connected with the original deal.[46]

Since 2012, government officials have pointed to the DP World and YLNG cases as being examples of their commitment to combatting corruption and establishing a new order. Yet further investigation of the deals, and the government's negotiations with its foreign partners do not suggest that their discussions actually focused on questions of corruption, nor that SNACC or any other body was in a position to act on the deals in question. Rather, the government leveraged commercial stipulations within its contracts, and public opinion, to gain concessions from its counterparts. The DP World discussions focused on the ports firm's failure to meet targets agreed at the time of the 2008 agreement and, while the government heralded its renegotiation of gas prices with KoGas, it was not acting aggressively but was acting within the bounds of the existing agreement.

The Total renegotiation, therefore, marks the only attempt the government has made since the beginning of the transition to renegotiate a deal where it does not have the contractual right to do so. Interviews with officials and political observers suggest, however, that discussions with Total do not mark a break from the past but in fact are a continuation of Saleh-era tactics, albeit directed against the commercial interests of the former president himself.

They point to the energy with which Islah held 'anti-corruption' rallies in Sanaa in February 2014, calling for the cancellation of the deal. The same people say that Total, which had historically used regime-approved brokers to negotiate deals on its behalf in the 1980s and 1990s, essentially entered into a direct relationship with Saleh around time the firm won the rights to develop the LNG scheme, both breeding resentment among the president's economic rivals that a potentially lucrative source of revenues had been taken away from them, and leading many regime players to see Total as being the international company most closely associated with Saleh.[47]

"It is no coincidence that at a time when Islah was jockeying for power with the GPC, there was all of this pressure on Total," says a former official. "Hadi was also keen to rein Saleh in and I can understand why he would see this as being a good route; it was something that would be popular, could make some more money for the government, and gave him bargaining power with Saleh, who he clearly sees as a rival. It is not much different from Saleh threatening Ali Mohsen's interests when they were in a similar relationship."[48]

Hadi is said to have used the issue as leverage both against Saleh and in negotiating a more favorable deal with the French company, while members of his administration pushed the idea that they were working to unpick corrupt deals, not least by announcing an investigation into the contracts that underpinned the LNG project.

New Rules?

If the aim of the renegotiation of the LNG contract was to bolster the image of the Hadi administration and the transitional governments he oversaw, it was a failed effort.

Yemenis were well aware that the underlying culture of corruption and patronage remained largely intact. If anything, according to a number of officials including serving ministers, the presence of rival elite groups and a sense of short-termism accelerated the pace at which patronage was being distributed. Current payments – for wages, bills, and overheads – reached successive new record levels in 2012, 2013 and 2014 despite an acknowledged decline in government effectiveness and service provision. According to government officials, Islah and the GPC hired thousands of new employees into the ministries they controlled as a way of disseminating patronage.

Despite a continued decline in private sector output, meanwhile, Yemen Petroleum Corporation, the state fuel distributor, has almost doubled the allocation of fuel to private sector firms since 2011, and the cost of subsidizing fuel was expected to reach a record USD3.5billion in 2014, with at least one minister, Saad al-Din bin Taleb, publicly alleging that half of that amount will be lost to smuggling. The government has also installed temporary power generators that cost an estimated USD 860m to rent before accounting for the cost of the subsidized fuel used to run them in 2013 alone, according to the electricity ministry, creating new opportunities for corruption. News filtered out that aid being given to the country by Gulf donors including Saudi Arabia and Qatar was disappearing, and that at the same time Hadi and presidential family members were suddenly in a position to make large patronage payments and arm their own militias, deepening the sense that Hadi was attempting to reconstitute the Saleh system rather than unravel it.[49]

Yemen's Huthis: Anti-Establishment Outsiders or Quiet Continuation?

Into this context entered the Huthis, once a revivalist movement for the Zaydi form of Islam that is largely unique to north Yemen, today the driving force behind the country's most formidable militia. Between 2004 and 2010, the Huthis, who prefer the name Ansar Allah, or Partisans of God, had been battered by six successive wars in their northern heartland, Saada. The group exploited the security vacuum created by infighting in Sanaa in 2011 to seize control of their home province before expanding their presence beyond its borders over the course of the next two years.

The Huthis backed the popular uprising of 2011, with their leader Abd al-Malik al-Huthi reining in the religious rhetoric of past public speeches over the course of the year to refocus on populist topics including corruption and the government's failure to provide basic services.[50] The group gained widespread support during the early months and years of the transition, presenting themselves as a legitimately antiestablishment force in contrast to Islah, Yemen's main Sunni Islamist party, which had joined the side of the uprising but was widely mistrusted by many protestors because of its historical role as an integral part of the Saleh regime.

In 2014, following successive military victories in the north of the country that had led to Huthi control of Amran, the province that separates Saada from Sanaa, the Huthis began to exploit public anger over a fuel price hike announced in July of that year, calling for widespread protests in and around the capital. As the protests grew in size, with Huthi supporters setting up protest encampments in central Sanaa and around the outskirts of the city, Hadi began to concede to al-Huthi's demands, offering to dissolve Yemen's transitional government, reduce fuel prices and give the rebel group a say in decision-making in the capital.

The Huthis ultimately chose to seize control of the capital by force, arriving on the northwestern edge of Sanaa on 17 September and taking just four days to rout forces loyal to Mohsen and Islah before their supporters set up checkpoints across the city. Over the following month, the group demanded the confiscation of assets belonging to a number of their rivals - Islah members, Mohsen and his family - on the basis that they had been involved in 'corruption'.[51]

Yet after seizing Sanaa, the Huthis did not attack the interests of other players seen as having been similarly mired in corruption. As reports emerged of Huthi coordination with the Saleh family, many in Yemen came to ask why the economic interests of the former president were not being investigated. At the same time, the Huthis froze bank accounts belonging to senior Islah leaders including Ali Mohsen al-Ahmar, and seized property belonging to their rivals, justifying their actions with claims of corrupt activities. The group's moves suggested that, again, the use of rhetoric around corruption had been as much part of a populist approach to garnering support for attacks on their rivals as a strongly-held ideological conviction. A government official interviewed by the author in November 2014 claimed that the Huthis, initially keen to excise ghost workers including those in the military, balked when presented with evidence that many of the biggest beneficiaries of such contracts were among their most important supporters. Similarly, the same official claimed that the Huthis were amenable to removing fuel subsidies once in power, openly admitting that they had played on the issue for political gain.[52] Again, the group has not matched its populist public rhetoric with actual policy, preferring to maintain a status quo now balanced in its favor and following in the footsteps of Saleh and Islah in demanding that its militias be integrated into the police and military, and paid from the public purse.

Conclusion

Where Yemen's political transition offered a chance to renegotiate the 'rules of the game' around patronage and corruption in a manner that might ultimately have led to a more sustainable distribution of rents and improved management of the economy, competition among Yemen's elites has in fact catalyzed the pace at which rents are – unsustainably – extracted.

It seems unlikely, in the current environment, that the situation will improve, further undermining confidence in the government and the legitimacy of the country's historical ruling class. Institutions ostensibly aimed at targeting corruption are still being used as political tools, further undermining their credibility in the long run and making it more difficult to know whether or not actors who claim to be anti-corruption are in fact simply acting as political agents. The lack of action on corruption - and the co-option of ostensible anti-corruption efforts by Yemen's main political players - is emblematic of a wider set of issues posed by the transition itself.

Although president Hadi appears to have had noble aims at the outset of the transition, he did little to control the way the government conducted itself, and often gave in to realpolitik when it came to attempting - often unsuccessfully - to revert to Saleh-era tactics to meet his personal aims, particularly when it comes to competing with his predecessor. The Huthis, meanwhile, having used anti-establishment rhetoric to achieve their political goals, have similarly decided that it is more important to maintain support at the elite level by allowing corrupt practices to continue than to actually attempt to combat corruption.

With the Huthis now in control of Sanaa, meaningful reform of the kind required to prevent Yemen from economic collapse and a political quagmire is just as much of a distant possibility as it was under Hadi and Saleh before him. And as a result the political transition initiated in 2011 is unlikely to yield positive results.

ENDNOTE: The paper draws on the work of April Alley Longley, Sarah Phillips, and Abdulghani al-Iryani along with the author's work with Ginny Hill for Chatham House, along with studies the author has conducted for the UK's Department for International Development, the World Bank and others on political economy and corruption in Yemen.

Notes

1 Rafat Al-Akhali, "The Challenge of Federalism in Yemen" (Atlantic Council Issue Brief, May 2014).
2 Transparency International, Corruption Perceptions Index (2014).
3 Ali Saeed, "Public Funds Prosecutor Says It Is Investigating LNG Sales Contracts," *Yemen Times*, February 8, 2014: http://www.yementimes.com/en/1756/news/3491/Public-Funds-Prosecutor-says-it-is-investigating-LNG-sales-contracts.htm
4 "DP World Quits Aden," World Cargo News, September 20, 2012: http://www.worldcargonews.com/htm/w20120920.361412.htm.
5 OECD, "International Drivers of Corruption: A Tool for Analysis" (2012), http://www.oecd.org/document/8/0,2340,en_2649_34565_37 957768_1_1_1_1,00.html.
6 Phillip Krausse, "Of Institutions and Butterflies: Is Isomorphism in Developing Countries Necessarily a Bad Thing?" (Overseas Development Institute, April 2013).
7 Douglass North, "Limited Access Orders in the Developing World: A New Approach to the Problems of Development" (World Bank, September 2007).
8 Sue Unsworth, "Framework for Strategic Governance And Corruption Analysis: Designing Strategic Responses Towards Good Governance" (Clingendael Institute, October 2007).
9 OECD, "International Drivers of Corruption: A Tool for Analysis": http://www.oecd.org/document/8/0,2340,en_2649_34565_37 957768_1_1_1_1,00.html
10 The OECD draws this definition from the Norwegian Agency for Development Co-operation (NORAD), "Anti-Corruption Approaches: A Literature Review": www.norad.no/en/Tools+and+publications/Publications/Publication+Page?key=119213
11 Transparency International, Corruptions Perception Index, 2013: http://www.transparency.org/country/#YEM
12 World Bank, "Yemen Joint Social Economic Assessment," August 2012: https://openknowledge.worldbank.org/handle/10986/11920
13 Ginny Hill, Peter Salisbury, Leonie Northedge, and Jane Kinninmont, Yemen: Corruption, Capital Flight and Global Drivers of Conflict (London: Chatham House, 2013).
14 April Alley-Longley, "The Rules of the Game: Unpacking Patronage Politics in Yemen," *Middle East Journal*, Summer 2010.
15 Alley-Longley, "The Rules of the Game."
16 Paul Dresch, *A History of Modern Yemen*, (Cambridge: Cambridge University Press, 2000), 204.

17 Daniel Egel, "Tribal Diversity, Political Patronage and the Yemeni Decentralization Experiment" (University of California, Berkeley, January 2010).
18 For a comprehensive discussion of patronage networks, see April Alley-Longley, "Shifting Light in the Qamariyya: The Reinvention of Patronage Networks in Contemporary Yemen" PhD diss., Georgetown University, 2008): https://repository.library.georgetown.edu/bitstream/handle/10822/553065/alleyapril.pdf?sequence=1
19 See Hill et. al., "Corruption, Capital Flight."
20 See Egel, "Tribal Diversity."
21 Sarah Phillips, "Politics in a Vacuum: The Yemeni Opposition's Dilemma," paper presented at "Viewpoints: Discerning Yemen's Political Future," Middle East Institute, June 2009. See also Sarah Phillips, "Evaluating Political Reform in Yemen" (Carnegie Papers Middle East Series, Democracy and Rule of Law Program, No. 80, February 2007).
22 Author interview, April 2014.
23 Author interview, April 2014.
24 See Egel, "Tribal Diversity."
25 Douglass North, "Limited Access Orders in the Developing World: A New Approach to the Problems of Development" (World Bank, September 2007).
26 Hill et al., "Corruption, Capital Flight."
27 USAID, *Yemen Corruption Assessment* (USAID, 2006).
28 Author interview, April 2014.
29 Author interview, April 2014.
30 Jane Novak, "Tawfiq Abdul-Rahim owes 2B?," *Armies of Liberation*: http://armiesofliberation.com/archives/2006/04/20/tawfiq-abdul-rahim-owes-2b/
31 Author interview, April 2014.
32 Latham & Watkins, *International Dispute Resolution* newsletter, September 2008.
33 Dionne Searcey and Margaret Coker, "Oil-Field Giant in Bribery Probe," *Wall Street Journal*, October 8, 2010: http://online.wsj.com/article/SB100014240 52748704631504575532332768800728.html
34 USAID, *Yemen Corruption Assessment*, 1.
35 Author interview, Sanaa, April 2014.
36 Author interview, Sanaa, April 2014.
37 Author interviews, Sanaa, April 2014.
38 *Authorities and Anti-Corruption Agencies – Yemen:* http://www.google.com/url?sa=t&rct=j&q=&esrc=s&source=web&cd=1&ved=0CCoQFjAA&url=http%3A%2F%2Fwww.track.unodc.org%2FLegalLibrary%2FLegalResources%2FYemen%2FAuthorities%2FAuthorities%2520and%2520Anti-Corruption%2520Agencies%2520-%2520Yemen.pdf&ei=3W6KU5aAKMH3O8TQgLgH&usg=AFQjCNE5i6bK5BW32l6anIVNMZ9SarBYcw&sig2=43drnIcsxo3wkloPuCdPRw
39 Author interview, Sanaa, April 2014.
40 "Implementation Mechanism of the GCC Initiative": http://www.lcil.cam.ac.uk/sites/default/files/LCIL/documents/arabspring/yemen/Yemen_21_Implementation_Mechanism_GCC_Initiative_USversion.pdf
41 Government of Yemen, "Mutual Accountability Framework (MAF)," "Economic Transition Priorities," Yemen Donor Conference, Riyadh, September 4, 2012: http://blogs.worldbank.org/files/arabvoices/maf.pdf
42 "Yemen's Interim Ministers Push for Renegotiation of Saleh's Deals," *Gulf States Newsletter* 36, no. 915 (January 12, 2012).
43 Author interview, Sanaa April 2014.
44 Needs to be verified before publication
45 Author interview, ports officials, February–March, 2014.
46 Author interviews, Sanaa, February–March 2014.
47 Multiple interviews, Sanaa, 2011–2014.
48 Author interview, April 2014.

49 See Peter Salisbury, "Yemen's Astonishing Financial Meltdown," *Foreign Policy*, December 11, 2014: http://foreignpolicy.com/2014/12/11/yemens-astonishing-financial-meltdown/
50 Tom Finn, "Abdel-Malek al-Huthi: From Shadow Rebel Leader to Kingmaker," *Middle East Eye*, September 26, 2014: http://www.middleeasteye.net/in-depth/features/abdel-malek-al-Huthi-shadow-rebel-leader-kingmaker-988988591#sthash.ZhhrXrnO.dpuf
51 Author interviews with banking sector sources, October 2014.
52 Author interview, Sanaa, November 2014.

References

Al-Akhali, Rafat. "The Challenge of Federalism in Yemen." Atlantic Council Issue Brief, May 2014.

Alley-Longley, April. "The Rules of the Game: Unpacking Patronage Politics in Yemen." *Middle East Journal*, Summer 2010.

Dresch, Paul. *A History of Modern Yemen*. Cambridge: Cambridge University Press, 2000.

Egel, Daniel. "Tribal Diversity, Political Patronage and the Yemeni Decentralization Experiment." University of California, Berkeley, January 2010.

Government of Yemen. "Mutual Accountability Framework (MAF)." "Economic Transition Priorities," Yemen Donor Conference, Riyadh, September 4, 2012: http://blogs.worldbank.org/files/arabvoices/maf.pdf

Hill, Ginny, Peter Salisbury, Leonie Northedge, and Jane Kinninmont. *Yemen: Corruption, Capital Flight and Global Drivers of Conflict*. London: Chatham House, 2013..

"Implementation Mechanism of the GCC Initiative": http://www.lcil.cam.ac.uk/sites/default/files/LCIL/documents/arabspring/yemen/Yemen_21_Implementation_Mechanism_GCC_Initiative_USversion.pdf

Krausse, Phillip. "Of Institutions and Butterflies: Is Isomorphism in Developing Countries Necessarily a Bad Thing?" Overseas Development Institute, April 2013.

North, Douglass. "Limited Access Orders in the Developing World: A New Approach to the Problems of Development." World Bank, September 2007.

Norwegian Agency for Development Co-operation (NORAD). "Anti-Corruption Approaches: A Literature Review": www.norad.no/en/Tools+and+publications/Publications/Publication+Page?key=119213

OECD. "International Drivers of Corruption: A Tool for Analysis": http://www.oecd.org/document/8/0,2340,en_2649_34565_37 957768_1_1_1_1,00.html

Phillips, Sarah. "Politics in a Vacuum: The Yemeni Opposition's Dilemma." Paper presented at "Viewpoints: Discerning Yemen's Political Future," Middle East Institute, June 2009.

Phillips, Sarah. "Evaluating Political Reform in Yemen." Carnegie Papers Middle East Series, Democracy and Rule of Law Program, No. 80, February 2007.

Transparency International, Anti-Corruption Resource Centre. "U4 Expert Answer: Political Economy Analysis of Anti-corruption Reforms.

Transparency International. Corruptions Perception Index, 2013: http://www.transparency.org/country/#YEM

USAID. *Yemen Corruption Assessment*. USAID, 2006.

World Bank. "Yemen Joint Social Economic Assessment." August 2012: https://openknowledge.worldbank.org/handle/10986/11920

4

Labor, Investment, and Natural Resources in the Yemeni Economy

Charles Schmitz

Introduction

Everyone agrees that the Yemeni economic needs reform, but what people mean by reform varies greatly. The Yemeni state, the Yemeni poor, the IMF, Ansar Allah, and foreign donors all have quite different perspectives on the crisis in the Yemeni economy and its solution. Reform is not a widely agreed upon formula of policies and institutional changes, but a political process of negotiation.

The two factors often mentioned in relation to Yemen's economic crisis are natural resource limitations – principally water and oil – and overpopulation. In a global economy, natural resources are neither the source of growth nor a significant limitation. The fortunes of nations are not tied to resource endowments; natural resource endowments sometimes even hurt prospects for economic growth. Resource endowments are only beneficial if used to enhance the long-term productivity of the economy.

Labor is the source of wealth, and Yemen has plenty of labor. Since the founding of the Yemeni republics, the Yemeni economy has not been based upon the employment of domestic labor. In the coming decades, Yemen's economic fortune will depend upon the wealth created by Yemeni labor inside of Yemen. The issue is how to develop Yemen's domestic labor force.

Current wisdom in economics places the burden of growth on the private sector, but the private sector can be a hindrance to growth as much as a source. Currently, the private sector in Yemen is benefiting tremendously at the expense of long term development of the economy. The key to Yemen's future is inducing Yemenis to invest in their future inside Yemen, which is not the same thing as simply turning the economy over to the private sector.

Reforms require a political foundation. Increasing capacities of state employees does not make them more effective if the social foundations of changing fiscal policy, principally tax collection, state subsidies, and the wage bill are not addressed. Calls of the Friends of

Yemen to implement "effective reforms in government" will fall on deaf ears if the political foundations are lacking.

Crises and Reforms

The Yemeni economy causes a lot of anxiety in many quarters but for quite different reasons. The IMF, for example, is primarily concerned about the effect of fuel subsidies on the fiscal balance of the state because the IMF sees macroeconomic stability as the key to economic success. The Yemeni government is also concerned with the fiscal balance not because of its detrimental effect on the macro economy, but because state expenditure is the political foundation of the government. Declining oil revenues combined with domestic fuel subsidies and paltry tax revenues threaten to dry up the meager assets available to the government. The United States and Saudi Arabia assume a faltering economy threatens political stability and renders the state unable to contain threats to American and Saudi geopolitical interests, as Ansar Allah's ascent demonstrates. For Ansar Allah, reform means rooting out corruption, which it interprets as funding for enemies of Ansar Allah. Others are more concerned with water scarcity and natural resource sustainability because Yemen's resources are limited and its population is still growing fast. NGOs tend to cite food insecurity and malnutrition among children because poverty is a central concern of aid and development workers. For each of these constituencies, the crisis in the Yemeni economy means different things, and each has differing abilities to present its views of the economy; defining the nature of the crisis of the Yemeni economy is itself a political exercise. Economic analysis and policy formulation are not a pure science, but the result of political assumptions, perspectives, and negotiations.

As a result, everybody agrees on the need for reform, deep reform, in the Yemeni economy, but the meaning of reform is always left vague, and the desired outcomes of reform are dependent upon a thick set of assumptions about the ways that economies operate. Is the goal to end hunger, malnutrition, offer employment, or is the goal an honorable living as the documents of the National Dialogue recommend? Is success achieved if GDP per capita rises or is food security a higher priority? If these are the goals, what are the means to achieve the goals? How does reducing the state deficit reduce child malnutrition, precisely? How would an improved investment environment bring an honorable living?

Fiscal Crisis of the State

The state's fiscal crisis is the focus of most calls for reform because the fiscal crisis threatens the state itself and the interests of political leaders most able to articulate their vision of the economic crisis. Over the last two decades, the Yemeni State grew very dependent on oil revenues. Oil revenues filled state coffers while allowing the Yemeni government to avoid the politically and administratively difficult issues of taxation and building the bureaucratic capacity to collect taxes. Now, declining production in Yemeni oil fields is forcing the state to wean itself from oil dependence.

In spite of dramatic declines in production, the state still depends upon hydrocarbons for the vast majority of its revenues (Chart 3). Collecting oil rents is easy for the state; it requires little administrative capacity. The state signs production-sharing agreements with the oil companies that divide Yemen's crude oil between the state and the companies. The government exports a portion of its oil and delivers the rest to domestic refineries for consumption on the local market at subsidized prices. Oil production has been falling steadily over the last ten years (Chart 6) and domestic consumption has been rising. As a result, a growing share of the government's oil goes to the domestic market (Chart 7) where the state receives less than world market prices, and in domestic currency rather than foreign currency.

However, the growing fiscal crisis is forcing the state to make difficult political decisions. On the expenditure side, the state must make cuts because there are no new revenues to replace declining oil revenues. Implementing effective tax collection, the main alternative to oil revenues (see below), is a complicated political issue that will take time to resolve before taxes will generate sufficient income to replace hydrocarbon revenue. Without cuts in expenditures, the state will fall further into debt. Over the last few years, the Yemeni state has been borrowing domestically, rather than from international lenders, and domestic interest payments themselves are becoming a burden on the budget (Chart 1). The current fall in oil prices will aggravate the crisis further.

The Yemeni state's options are limited by its dependence upon foreign states and the international development agencies. For the IMF, the primary economic policy maker among the international actors in Yemen, the key to growth is macroeconomic stability. Hence, the IMF watches closely the fiscal balance of the state because the IMF fears that state indebtedness will lead to printing of money and inflation. While the Yemeni state often fails to implement IMF policies, Yemeni leaders cannot openly oppose IMF recommendations without risking the ire of the United States and Western European allies. Thus, absent new sources of state revenues, the Yemeni State is forced to make cuts. The two most prominent areas that the state is looking to cut are fuel subsidies and the wage bill. Both are deeply entwined in politics.

The IMF and others argue that the fuel subsidies cost the state tremendous revenue (about 25% of expenditure—see charts), while not significantly reducing poverty in Yemen. Most of the fuel subsidies do not go to the poor. The money spent on subsidies could be better spent by targeting the poor for direct transfers, even increasing support for the poor and at the same time saving a significant proportion of state expenditure.

The problem is that the fuel subsidies in Yemen are highly politicized because the subsidies affect a large majority of the population. People feel the immediate impact of any change in fuel costs, and for the majority of Yemenis that are struggling, the lifting of fuel subsidies causes a significant burden. The World Bank estimated that an immediate lifting of subsidies, without effective transfers to the poor, would increase poverty by 8%.[1] Thus, the lifting of fuel subsidies is easy for populist politicians to exploit, as Ansar Allah did in September 2014 when it overran Sanaa. After taking power, Ansar Allah forced the Hadi government to reinstate some (but not all) of the subsidies.

The IMF's claim that subsidies are not an effective means of reducing poverty depends upon effectiveness of the alternative of direct transfers to the poor. Most of the money spent on fuel subsidies in Yemen goes to people who do not need it, but withdrawal of subsidies will increase poverty unless the state gives money directly to the poor in compensation for rising fuel prices. The cost of direct transfers to the poor is far less than subsidizing fuel for all consumers. However, the Yemeni state is notoriously inefficient and the state's ability to translate fuel subsidy reductions to benefits to the poor is doubtful. The poor do not have a real voice in Yemen or at the IMF, and the poor's increased burden will not be immediately felt among the country's political leaders or IMF policy makers. Without a voice for the poor, reduction of fuel subsidies becomes simply a further transfer of the burden of the economic crisis from the state to Yemen's poor.

Similarly, the reduction of subsidies represented a struggle between powerful people that benefit from smuggling oil and those in Hadi's government that opposed them. Smuggling is a major business for some important figures in Yemen [2] and the Yemeni government faces resistance from those that benefit from the smuggling of subsidized fuel. Here again, the policy of subsidizing fuel is a political one whose outcome depends upon balances of political forces. President Hadi gambled upon his international backers and the technocratic elite in the government when he lifted subsidies. Ansar Allah's position to reinstate some subsidies was based upon populist politics, not any love for those from the old Saleh regime that benefit from subsidies, but Ansar Allah may benefit materially from the control of smuggling in the north[3] and therefore stand to gain materially from rolling back fuel subsidies.

A second major focus of expenditure cuts is the wage bill. The wage bill is the largest portion of state expenditures (see charts) and presumably a large proportion of the current wage bill goes to non-existent workers, or ghost workers as they are called. Estimates are that about three percent of government workers do not exist, but that the highest percentage of ghost workers are in the military and security. The Office of the President recently estimated that about seven percent of the military wage bill goes to non-existent soldiers, presumably into the hands of powerful commanders. The Friends of Yemen countries created a framework of mutual accountability to guarantee the effectiveness of donor aid, but the problem of ghost workers referred to specifically in the agreement remains unresolved.[4] Ghost workers are a means for the government to buy loyalty—part of the patronage networks Saleh built—and in order to reform public employment, new political foundations must be built. Ansar Allah upset the political deck of cards in Sanaa. The new Ansar Allah-dominated government has no interest in continuing the patronage networks of the old Sanaani regime with payments to ghost workers and soldiers. The initial demands of Ansar Allah articulated in the Peace and National Partnership Agreement include implementation of a system of ID cards based upon fingerprints for voter registration and for identification of government employees.[5] However, Ansar Allah has since forced the government to employ Ansar Allah fighters in the military and security, effectively reproducing the same system of patronage. Ansar Allah's attack on corruption in state institutions thus far appears guided by the desire to control the state rather than build the state's capacities.

Fiscal Crisis of the State: Revenues

On the revenue side, the Yemeni state faces the challenge of generating income other than oil and gas revenues. Taxation is much more difficult to implement than collecting oil rents because taxation requires bureaucratic and political capacity. Taxation requires competent bureaucracy to develop, implement, and enforce tax collection over the entire population. The Yemeni bureaucracy is notoriously inefficient and lacking in skills. More importantly, taxation requires political legitimacy. Taxation requires particular political foundations in society, something states relying upon patronage tend to lack because the state is paying out patronage rather than collecting taxes. The state must have sufficient support in, or control over, society to broker effective tax policy with domestic constituencies that pay taxes.

In Yemen, domestic taxation has long been a contentious issue. In 2005 the government introduced a tax bill that stalled. The issue was revisited again in 2010. The private sector has strong objections to government taxation because the private sector argues that the taxes it pays do not serve the country. Taxes go to line the pockets of tax collectors instead of improving the country. In response, the government argues that it cannot improve government services without the revenues from taxation. Both are true, but the hard reality is that taxation will have to become the main source of revenue in the future.

Taxation on income, profit, and capital gains constitutes the largest current sources of taxes, followed by sales taxes and then customs revenue, but all of these sources of taxation combined never constitute more than a third of the state revenue (see charts). The lion's share of state revenues is still from oil, but even oil revenues are not covering expenditures. To avoid further indebtedness, the state is trying to increase tax revenues. Hadi urged all tax collecting units to redouble their efforts, but there were no indications that tax collection was any different from the past. Unless there is a major change in tax collection or development of some new source of revenue, the state's fiscal crisis will dominate discussion of the economic crisis.

The Peace and National Partnership Agreement does not address the decline of state revenues. The agreement calls for increasing subsidies, raising salaries, doubling welfare payments, and bolstering the budgets of education and health, but does not address the shortfalls that these measures will cause in the state budget. Because Ansar Allah has been in the opposition, it has not had to grapple with governance and thus the does not address the politically difficult issue of state revenue as of yet. However, in late 2014, Ansar Allah began imposing taxes in some areas. In Ibb, the local government at Ansar Allah's behest imposed a monthly five percent tax on commercial profits.[6]

Investment

Investment is like crisis; interests shape its meaning. Everybody recognizes that investment is good for an economy and that the current crisis, however understood, will be ameliorated by increasing investment. However, investment means different things to different actors. Investment for the state means primarily attracting large-scale foreign investment that will pay taxes. Even in the transition period, the government has worked hard to attract further investment in the oil sector and to expand foreign investment into minerals. The government likes large-scale foreign investment because taxes on these investments are easy to collect.

The Yemeni government has never devoted a significant portion of the state budget to development. In the 2000s, the Saleh regime was awash with oil revenue and still most of state revenues were spent on current operating expenses. The greatest infrastructure achievement of the Saleh regime was the extension of the network of roads. Outside of roads, little was done. In the transitional period, Hadi's government contracted with the Chinese to build gas fired electrical plants that were due to come online in 2014, but little else has been done in recent years to improve infrastructure.

Another meaning of investment is attracting investment from people of Yemeni origin abroad or from Yemenis living in the country that have capital outside the country. Yemeni private capital abroad is attractive because presumably Yemenis know Yemen and they understand how to do business in Yemen. Unfortunately, the causality may be reversed: Yemenis know Yemen and therefore their capital is outside the country. Precisely because Yemeni capital knows that the security of investments in Yemen depends upon political connections, Yemenis do not invest in Yemen, but transfer any accumulated profits and savings outside the country to safer investments. As we will see below, there are Yemenis who profit tremendously from business in Yemen, but these are people with political connections that diminish the risk of business in Yemen. The question of attracting private expatriate Yemeni capital to the country is a political one, but it is not only a question of the state's relationship to the private sector but also the internal politics of the Yemeni private sector itself.

Labor Export

The single most effective measure in the short term for ameliorating Yemen's poverty is allowing Yemeni laborers back into the Gulf. Worker remittances are progressive, they go to rural areas where poverty is concentrated and they go to poorer households. Though remittances do not play the role they played in the economy of the 1970s and 1980s, remittances are still an important part of Yemen's economy. Remittances reached almost US$4 billion in 2013, representing close to 10% of GDP. Yet the return of Yemeni laborers to Gulf labor markets is a politicized issue. The Gulf States are cautious about Yemeni immigrant labor because Yemenis are culturally close to the Gulf and are more likely to build a life in the Gulf rather than simply work and leave. While Saudi Arabia provides by far the largest amount of support and aid to the Yemeni economy, the Saudis expelled tens of thousands of Yemenis working in the Kingdom by strictly enforcing rules governing sponsorship of guest workers.[7] Saudi Arabia would prefer a North America Free Trade Agreement (NAFTA) style solution that keeps Yemenis inside the borders of Yemen.

Foreign Financial Assistance

Foreign aid has played an important role in Yemen's development in the past. During the early years of the YAR, the entire development budget was funded by foreign aid.[8] Even at the height of Yemen's oil economy, foreign donors were working with Yemen. Foreign financial support (donors is a misnomer—most "aid" is not grants, but concessionary loans, with the exception of the large Saudi grants) for the Yemeni economy primarily goes to infrastructure development and humanitarian needs, but some support, particularly from Saudi Arabia, has gone to the state budget or central bank. Foreign assistance provides capital investment to augment the Yemeni state's meager long-term investment funds. Foreign assistance in Yemen pretends to boost infrastructure, both social and physical, to promote growth, but considerations of foreign assistance are never far from politics.

A major donor conference held in London in 2006 promised some six billion dollars in aid, but little of that aid was actually delivered. In 2010, in response to an attack on a US airliner, the GCC states, the permanent members of the UN Security Council, and EU representatives formed an informal organization called the "Friends of Yemen" to coordinate aid efforts.[9] Saudi Arabia and the UK are the main leaders. In the aftermath of the Yemen Arab Spring, the Friends of Yemen promised eight billion dollars in aid, much of which was unspent money from the previous pledge of six billion in 2006. Saudi Arabia pledged the largest portion of the fund, and the Saudis have delivered their pledges and more. The Saudis delivered three million tons of crude oil to the Aden refinery in 2012 when the pipelines from Marib were disabled. The lack of domestic fuel was adding to a volatile political environment that the Saudis wanted to contain. The Saudis also deposited one billion dollars in the Central Bank in 2012 to support the state's budget. In addition, the Saudis have provided subventions to various political clients in Yemen that surely has an impact on the incomes of selected tribesmen.

For Saudi Arabia, foreign assistance intends to keep a weak state from collapsing. The Saudis fear state collapse and the migration of poverty-stricken chaos and violence into Saudi Arabia. The Saudis want the Yemeni state and economy to provide a minimum of security and economic growth in order to contain Yemen's chaos inside its borders.

Assistance from the United States also correlates closely with politics. The United States is principally concerned with threats from AQAP in Yemen. The United States has long trained Yemeni anti-terror forces, but the Obama administration initiated a widespread campaign of targeted assassinations in Yemen using drones in 2009. As criticisms of the program mounted, the United States announced that military aid to Yemen would be matched with economic aid.[10] USAID projects are now geared towards regaining American credibility in Yemen. USAID contracts go to NGO's delivering humanitarian aid in Abyan and in the south, the focus of the American drone campaign. The State Department tried to insist that US assistance be clearly marked with American flags in order to "brand" US humanitarian aid.

The Saudis and Americans are the most political in their aid - the Germans and the Dutch are much less so - and their view of the crisis of the Yemeni economy is tied to security or political concerns. Assistance programs are closely tied to political objectives.

IMF: Stability Without Growth

The IMF and the World Bank do not have interests in Yemen in the way that Saudi Arabia or the United States do. The IMF is the gatekeeper of international development policy and finance, particularly for those countries that do not have access to private international finance, like Yemen. Nevertheless, policy is shaped by politics and the IMF's policies are a reflection of current wisdom among economic elites in Washington, London, and Paris. The IMF oversaw the transition from state-led development models in the mid-twentieth century to the current focus on macroeconomic stability and liberalization. [11] For the IMF, the role of the state in economic development is to provide a stable environment for private sector investment. At first, IMF policy focused on liberalization and privatization, or divestiture of state assets, in order to widen the scope of private sector participation in the economy. Along with liberalization, the IMF focused on macroeconomic stability and containing inflation in particular. When these initial policies, called the "Washington Consensus," failed to deliver economic growth, the common wisdom focused on the capacities of the state, or "governance" issues. Governance is a set of qualities thought to enhance political accountability and hence, state capacity. The focus on governance also conveniently transfers the blame for lack of growth from IMF policy to domestic states: it is not policy that is flawed, but its implementation. Yemen created a special agency to deal directly with donors in order to address accusations that aid was misspent.

For the IMF, then, the economic crisis in Yemen is defined primarily by the fiscal problems of the state, but also by poor state capacity and the structural dependency of the economy on hydrocarbons (though a recent IMF country report surprisingly describes Yemen's economy as "fairly diversified"[12]). The IMF recommends balancing the budget, investing in infrastructure, and strengthening the capacity of the judiciary, tax agencies, and the public bureaucracy in order to provide an environment safe for investment.

Yemen has worked closely with the IMF over the last two decades, liberalizing markets, privatizing state enterprises, and balancing its budget. As in much of the rest of the developing world, liberalization and privatization have had very mixed results in Yemen, and the IMF has slowly come to recognize that a stable macroeconomic environment does not necessarily bring growth. Stability is only a part of the equation. In Yemen's case, the economy did grow under the IMF structural adjustment program; oil exports boosted the Yemeni economy instead of the private sector.

The Private Sector and Growth

Common economic wisdom places primary responsibility for growth on the private sector, but the dynamic growth of the private sector is assumed. The state simply provides a stable playing field and the private sector will compete, invest, and grow. The state educates workers, builds roads and ports, provides energy infrastructure, and builds the institutions of governance that the private sector needs. The state legislates laws to guarantee property and contracts, courts to resolve disputes, and law enforcement to implement the laws and provide security. Once a stable macro environment is established, the private sector will automatically invest and grow the economy.

It is true that the primary challenge for Yemen's future is creating the conditions to harness and focus the energy of its labor. Yemenis are industrious. For centuries, Yemenis have travelled great distances to find work and build countries in Southeast Asia, East Africa, South Asia, and recently in the Arabian Peninsula. The agricultural terraces that line Yemen peaks are testament to the industriousness of Yemeni labor. Yet Yemeni labor today is unemployed and underemployed.

For many, the solution to unemployment is private sector investment. If people are unemployed, it is because there is no investment. For the IMF, state reforms, a stable currency, low inflation, and fiscally conservative policies will attract private sector investment. For the Yemeni government, the solution lies in Yemenis living abroad and wealthy Gulf investors (sometimes the same people), or in Chinese investment. Yemen is attractive to investors from China, Malaysia, and India who are used to dealing with the vagaries of working in unstable political and security environments and the Yemeni government regularly invites delegations from these countries to promote investment.

However, there exists today a private sector in Yemen and the private sector in Yemen is as much the problem as it is the solution. The private sector in Yemen today benefits tremendously from Yemen's current situation. Poverty stricken Yemen is home to some very wealthy people. The powerful commercial elite which holds the contracts for the communication industry, dominates import trade and transportation, and supplies the government and military, thrives on its close relationship with those in power and its control of commercial markets. These people have little interest in changing Yemen's economy; they are doing quite well atop the commanding heights of Yemen's economy.[13]

These wealthy businesses are not stagnant; Yemen's private sector is quite dynamic, and it has adapted quite well to Yemen's economic conditions. Although there are a few import substitution industries and a lot of very unproductive small metal fabrication and simple woodworking shops, most of Yemen's private sector is concentrated in commercial rather than industrial firms. And while agriculture still employs the largest number of Yemenis, about a third of the workforce, it contributes to only about ten percent of GDP, and the qat economy adds only another three percent. Yemen's contemporary economy is based upon consumer imports, transportation, and domestic real estate and construction (see charts). The dynamic sectors of the Yemeni economy import, warehouse, and transport consumer commodities throughout the country and provide supplies to the construction industry in major urban areas. Commercial capital is liquid and it can be moved quickly when threatened. Much more private capital leaves Yemen than enters it, particularly Yemeni capital. When Yemenis accumulate a bit of capital, they invest in safe havens outside of Yemen because the conditions in Yemen are too unpredictable and dependent upon those in power. Only the private sector elite close to the Saleh regime invest in Yemen. Those in the private sector that could not cultivate a workable relationship with the regime left the country.

This private sector is not going to save the Yemeni economy; its interests are in continuing the present state of affairs rather than transforming the economy. The idea that the private sector does only good for the economy, or even that the private sector is by definition more efficient, is simply wrong. Private businesses love a monopoly and will go to great lengths to stymie competition if it serves their interests. Unfortunately, Yemen provides plenty of examples.

Reforming the Yemeni economy means reforming the private sector as well. In order to harness the capabilities of Yemen's labor force, the private sector must invest in labor and not remain complacent in commercial ventures with relatively little risk. Rodrik[14] shows in an analysis of growth patterns over the last half century that the economies in the developing world that nurtured a sustained period of domestic investment significantly enhanced labor productivity and raised incomes. Sustained periods of savings, investment, more savings, and reinvestment at rates of twenty five to thirty percent of GDP over a period of ten years transformed significantly the productive capacity of the economy.

While this may seem obvious, much of contemporary economic policy does not focus on transforming the productive capacity of an economy. On the contrary, the prevailing wisdom is that the most open and stable economies grow the fastest. Stability and liberalization are considered the key ingredients for growth. Foreign capital arriving from beyond is supposed to supply the necessary technological and knowledge spillover effects to jumpstart an economy. The logic is backwards, Rodrik shows in his analysis. While it is true that the fastest growing economies are open, the most open economies are not the fastest growing, or even growing at all. Yemen's economy is very open, at least formally, yet it is not fast growing. Most very open, liberalized economies in the developing world are stagnating. Foreign investment does not create growth, it follows growth, looking for opportunities where growth is already in motion. Liberalization and stabilization are not the keys to growth; domestic investment is the key to transformative growth.

Rodrik's conclusions are important for Yemen. Wealth comes from productive labor, and if Yemen is to create wealth domestically, it must focus on effectively harnessing the growing labor force. Simply allowing the private sector a free hand in the economy is not sufficient or even helpful. Investment must be channeled into those areas of the economy that are most likely to be the basis of future growth and then coordinated with the changing needs of the economy as it progresses. Large-scale transformation of the economy requires long-term coordination of investment by state leaders who provide a vision of economic progress.

Unfortunately for Yemen, Rodrik's conclusions are also dependent upon a number of factors that Yemen lacks. Rodrik saw that social cohesion was a significant factor in economic success. Social cleavages were related negatively with economic performance. Yemen's internal wars are not good indicators of growth potential, according to Rodrik. Rodrik's conclusions also point implicitly to effective political leadership. Transforming the domestic investment environment, refocusing the existing private sector and enabling the growth of new private sector actors, require capable, legitimate leadership. It requires capable and trained bureaucrats who work efficiently and intelligently towards an overall goal of economic growth. Yemen does not have these capabilities.

Natural Resources and Economy

Rodrik rightly refocuses attention on investment and labor productivity as the keys to wealth and growth, but in discussions of Yemen's economy people wonder what Yemeni labor will produce. Soon, exports of Yemen oil will end and Yemen will become an oil importer, scarce water limits agriculture, and there appears to be little else that Yemenis can produce. The LNG exports provide some revenue, but not enough to replace the loss of crude oil exports. The rapidly growing population is underemployed, undernourished, and uneducated. Who is going to employ Yemeni labor and what is Yemeni labor going to produce? Underlying this question is an assumption about the relationship between natural resources and economic growth.

Natural resources—land, water, minerals, fuel—are the basis of an economy, and without natural resources an economy cannot grow, according to this view, which is rooted in the eighteenth century thinking of Ricardo and Malthus, among others. They saw that as population and demand for food increased, farmers brought marginal agricultural land into production. The use of poorer soils caused average yields to fall; hence, the common wisdom at the time was that natural resources limited economic growth. Countries with good natural resources would do better than ones without. Of course, the experience of the past two centuries clearly contradicted Malthus' thinking: Population growth increased exponentially, but so did economic growth. Technological developments in the nineteenth and twentieth century overcame Malthus' supposed limits and allowed for tremendous increases in the productivity of land and labor in farming, and per capita food output has outpaced population growth for most of the last two centuries. On the other hand, some countries famously rich in natural resources are some of the poorest in the world. Sub-Saharan Africa is resource rich, but very poor.

Natural resource wealth can certainly aid economic growth, but only when resources are used productively. The Gulf states know well that natural resources are not the source of wealth; they are trying to use their hydrocarbon rents to educate their populations to become productive workers when oil runs out. In Japan, the situation is reversed; the Japanese have few natural resources, particularly energy resources, but the Japanese are very productive laborers. Wealth is built by human labor, especially in the twenty-first century when transportation costs are so low that producer inputs and consumer commodities are easily transported all over the globe. In the long run, the productivity of human labor determines the level of income in a country. Natural resources are not a source of wealth unless human labor transforms resources into useful commodities, and the wealth of the economy depends upon the ability to apply human labor to transform things.

In fact, if the economy lacks the capacity to productively use natural resources, natural resource rents can cause considerable problems, what we call the resource curse.[15] The resource curse causes problems even in highly productive economies, like the distortions in the Dutch economy during the rise of North Sea oil, from which comes the name Dutch Disease. In an economy at low levels of labor productivity, the influx of resource rents can have even more perverse effects, particularly on the state. Aside from the obvious growth of the temptation of corruption when such large amounts of cash are easily attainable in a poor environment, the biggest perversion is the erosion of the state's capacity to raise revenue outside of resource rents, a problem the Yemeni state is now facing.

Natural Resources and Hunger and Poverty

A corollary assumption is that hunger and poverty are caused by a lack of natural resources. In Yemen people often tie limited agriculture, declining water supplies, and population growth to an increase in hunger and child malnutrition. It is not hard to show that the problems of hunger and malnutrition are related to social access to food rather than the presence or absence of food. The distribution of food rather than absolute scarcity causes hunger and without much relation to the resource base. Outside of Oman there is no real agriculture in the Gulf, yet there is plenty of food. And in spite of the abundance of food, there is still hunger in parts of the Gulf. Similarly, in Yemen, the worst cases of malnutrition and hunger are among those uprooted by conflicts. Forced migration is a major determinant of severe poverty and famine. Those fleeing the conflict in the north, for example, and those fleeing the conflicts with AQAP are the most vulnerable. People with money in Yemen have no problem finding food; it is not a question of the availability of food, but of the social means of gaining access to it. Thus, the relationship between natural resource endowments, economic performance, and human well-being is by no means as straightforward as many seem to believe.

Population Explosion and Natural Resource Limitations

Yemen's transition away from oil dependence is a positive development – diversified economies are far more robust – but making such a transition in the face of widespread poverty, unemployment, and an exploding population appears to be a very daunting task. Yemen's population is growing at one of the fastest rates in the world and young people need health, education, and jobs. The latest figures show Yemen's annual population growth rate at 3.1%, which puts Yemen in rare company. The average population growth rate among the UNDP's low human development countries is 2.3%, and in the Arab Countries, average population growth rate is 2.2%. Saudi Arabia, Qatar, and the UAE have higher growth rates, but other than these outlying rich states, only very poor countries like Afghanistan, Eritrea, Niger, Chad, and Sierra Leone have growth rates as high as Yemen's.[16] The population of Yemen in 1962 is often estimated at six million people, in 1990 twelve million, today twenty five million, and by 2030 Yemen is estimated to reach forty million people. In the lifetime of one person (a slightly longer living Yemeni—average life expectancy today in Yemen is around 65 years), Yemen's population will go from six million to forty million.

However, ironically for observers of Yemen, economists like population increase. More people means more demand and more labor and growth. The population decreases that some European countries are experiencing are a cause for concern because fewer people means less demand, fewer workers, and higher dependency ratios. However, the economist's happy formula for economic growth with population increase depends upon the ability of the economy to train and employ the growing workforce as well as provide the necessary infrastructure for an expansion of the economy. In the developing world, as in Yemen, these conditions do not hold. Yemen is having trouble educating its citizens today (although Yemeni education has achieved much more than is generally acknowledged) and the economy cannot employ the rapidly growing labor force. Rapid population growth can be a great burden for a struggling economy.

Still, there are some positive signs. The Total Fertility Rate, the average number of children per woman, is decreasing. In 1990, the TFR was about eight children whereas today it is about five. In urban areas, it is now less than five. Fertility is falling and Yemeni families are smaller, much smaller than they were two decades ago. Yemenis are becoming more educated, more urbanized, and more women are working. As a result, fertility is falling and will continue to fall.

Nevertheless, the population momentum is so great that Yemen will be forced to accommodate large numbers of new students and workers for decades to come. Yemen's rapid population growth does increase significantly the challenges that the economy faces in the short and medium term, but the challenge is principally harnessing the potential of the young population, not the size of the population in relation to natural resources.

The Decline of Oil and Forced Diversification

Yemen is well past its peak oil, but hydrocarbons will still play an important role in the Yemeni economy in the future. Oil is not depleting as fast as predicted and the recent insecurity in Yemen has slowed both production and investment in the oil sector, ironically allowing for future development. The LNG plant will produce significant revenue for the Yemeni state for the next twenty years. The hydrocarbon sector will remain important to the Yemeni economy, but it will not play as large a role as it has in the past both because oil is declining and the economy is growing.

Nevertheless, the Yemeni economy and government have been so dependent upon oil revenues over the last twenty years that oil's decline presents major challenges, but not because Yemen has limited natural resources. Limited natural resources narrow Yemen's options, but do not prevent economic growth.

Agriculture, for example, is still the largest employer of Yemeni labor, but water scarcity places severe constraints on the development of agriculture. Yemen cannot ease its dependence upon oil by returning to its agrarian past. Yemen's challenge is to diversify its economy by harnessing its great wealth of labor in occupations outside of agriculture.

Conclusion

Yemen's economic crisis and its solutions are politically constructed. At the broadest level, Yemen's economic crisis consists of slow growth, unemployment, low incomes, and increasing poverty. This crisis is born by the weak and the impoverished, but while calls for change are made in the name of the poor, solutions to the crisis rarely address the concerns of the weak. Particular interests reshape this broader description into more focused concerns such as the fiscal crisis of the state, fears of increasing poverty's impact on political stability, or fears about declining water levels in the aquifers and the lack of natural resources. In redirecting the general description of the crisis into particular concerns, political choices are made: some win and some lose. The choice to reduce fuel subsidies passes the burden of the crisis from the state to the poor, given the inability of the Yemeni state to identify the poor and efficiently transfer payments.

Calling for good governance is also a political choice. An independent judiciary and detailed commercial codes do not induce investment any more than elections bring democracy. Installing particular institutional forms such as parliaments and judiciaries, training bureaucrats in skills, and passing new laws mean little if the underlying politics of the state do not support the intentions of these reforms. The IMF and the international development community can call for good governance, but until politics in Yemen support it, governance is a buzzword with little relevance to events in Yemen. The publication of the IMF's country report praising reforms in the midst of the Huthi conquest of Sanaa is indicative.

Likewise, calling for private sector growth without recognizing the politics of the private sector makes little sense. The private sector in Yemen is well adapted to seeking commercial opportunities tied to state power. In fact, the commercial private sector is thriving in Yemen, but such a commercial elite will not transform the Yemeni economy with sustained investment in Yemeni labor. The current private sector is an obstacle rather than the answer to Yemen's problems.

The focus of Yemen's economic future rests in harnessing the productivity of Yemeni labor, not handing the economy to the private sector. The current private sector in Yemen has no incentive to invest in Yemeni labor and Yemenis themselves have no incentive to invest in their futures. Politics in Yemen are too unstable. When leadership emerges that has the capacity to unite the country around long-term economic development, then Yemenis will invest in their future.

Notes

1 Peter Salisbury, *Yemen's Economy: Oil Imports, and Elites,* Middle East and North Africa Programme Paper 2011/02, edited by Chatham House (London: Chatham House, 2011), 9.
2 Sally Healy and Ginny Hill, *Yemen and Somalia: Terrorism, Shadow Networks, and the Limitations of State-Building* (London: Chatham House, 2010).
3 Isa Blumi, *Chaos in Yemen: Societal Collapse and the New Authoritarianism*, Routledge Advances in Middle East and Islamic Studies (London: Routledge, 2011).
4 Saddam al-Kemali, "300 Thousand Ghost Workers Delay Donors' Funds for Yemen," *al-Masdar Online*, September 18, 2014.
5 Peace and National Partnership Agreement, September 21, 2014, Section 3(h) (in Arabic).
6 "The Houthi Group Begins Imposing Five Percent Tax on Merchants," *Yemen Press*, January 4, 2015, http://yemen-press.com/news40554.html.
7 "Government Official: More Than Twelve Thousand Yemeni Expelled from Saudi Arabia Have Arrived since Last January," *al-Masdar Online*, April 5, 2014.
8 Robert D. Burrowes, *The Yemen Arab Republic: The Politics of Development, 1962–1986* (Boulder, CO: Westview Press, 1987).
9 United Kingdom, "Friends of Yemen: Questions and Answers": https://www.gov.uk/government/news/friends-of-yemen-q-a
10 "This year alone, U.S. assistance to Yemen is more than $337 million. Over half this money, $178 million, is for political transition, humanitarian assistance and development. Let me repeat that. More than half of the assistance we provide to Yemen is for political transition, humanitarian assistance and development. In fact, this is the largest amount of civilian assistance the United States has ever provided to Yemen. So any suggestion that our policy toward Yemen is dominated by our security and counterterrorism efforts is simply not true." Transcript of John O. Brennan's remarks at the Council on Foreign Relations, August 8, 2012: http://www.cfr.org/united-states/us-policy-toward-yemen/p28794
11 Tony Killick, *IMF Programmes in Developing Countries: Design and Impact*, Development Policy Studies (London; New York: Routledge, 1995); Tony Killick and Graham R. Bird, *The Quest for Economic Stabilization: The IMF and the Third World* (New York: St. Martin's Press, 1984).
12 International Monetary Fund, "Country Report No. 14/276" (Washington DC: International Monetary Fund, 2014), 11.
13 Salisbury, *Yemen's Economy*.

14 Dani Rodrik, *In Search of Prosperity: Analytic Narratives on Economic Growth* (Princeton, NJ: Princeton University Press, 2003); *The New Global Economy and Developing Countries: Making Openness Work*, Policy Essay (Washington, DC: Overseas Development Council; distributed by Johns Hopkins University Press, 1999).

15 Ian Bannon and Paul Collier, *Natural Resources and Violent Conflict: Options and Actions* (Washington, DC: World Bank, 2003); Paul Collier and Anthony Venables, *Plundered Nations? Successes and Failures in Natural Resource Extraction* (Basingstoke, Hampshire: Palgrave Macmillan, 2011).

16 United Nations Development Programme, "Population Trends": https://data.undp.org/dataset/Table-14-Population-trends/e6xu-b22v

References

al-Arab. "Yemen Is Close to an Agreement to Reduce Subsidies." May 17, 2014.

Bannon, Ian, and Paul Collier. *Natural Resources and Violent Conflict: Options and Actions*. Washington, DC: World Bank, 2003.

Burrowes, Robert D. *The Yemen Arab Republic: The Politics of Development, 1962–1986*. Boulder, CO: Westview Press, 1987.

Carapico, Sheila. *Civil Society in Yemen: The Political Economy of Activism in Modern Arabia*. Cambridge Middle East Studies 9. Cambridge: Cambridge University Press, 1998.

Chaudhry, Kiren Aziz. *The Price of Wealth: Economies and Institutions in the Middle East*. Cornell Studies in Political Economy. Ithaca, NY: Cornell University Press, 1997.

Collier, Paul, and Anthony Venables. *Plundered Nations? Successes and Failures in Natural Resource Extraction*. Basingstoke, Hampshire: Palgrave Macmillan, 2011.

Dresch, Paul. *A History of Modern Yemen*. Cambridge: Cambridge University Press, 2000.

Killick, Tony. *IMF Programmes in Developing Countries: Design and Impact*. Development Policy Studies. London: Routledge, 1995.

Killick, Tony, and Graham R. Bird. *The Quest for Economic Stabilization: The IMF and the Third World*. New York: St. Martin's Press, 1984.

Mundy, Martha. *Domestic Government: Kinship, Community and Polity in North Yemen*. Society and Culture in the Modern Middle East. London: I. B. Tauris, 1996.

Phillips, Sarah, and International Institute for Strategic Studies. *Yemen and the Politics of Permanent Crisis*. Adelphi. New York: Routledge for the International Institute for Strategic Studies, 2011.

Rodrik, Dani. *In Search of Prosperity: Analytic Narratives on Economic Growth*. Princeton, NJ: Princeton University Press, 2003.

Rodrik, Dani. *The New Global Economy and Developing Countries: Making Openness Work*. Policy Essay. Washington, DC: Overseas Development Council; distributed by Johns Hopkins University Press, 1999.

United Kingdom. "Friends of Yemen: Questions and Answers": https://www.gov.uk/government/news/friends-of-yemen-q-a

United Nations Development Programme. "Population Trends": https://data.undp.org/dataset/Table-14-Population-trends/e6xu-b22v

Appendix

Chart 1

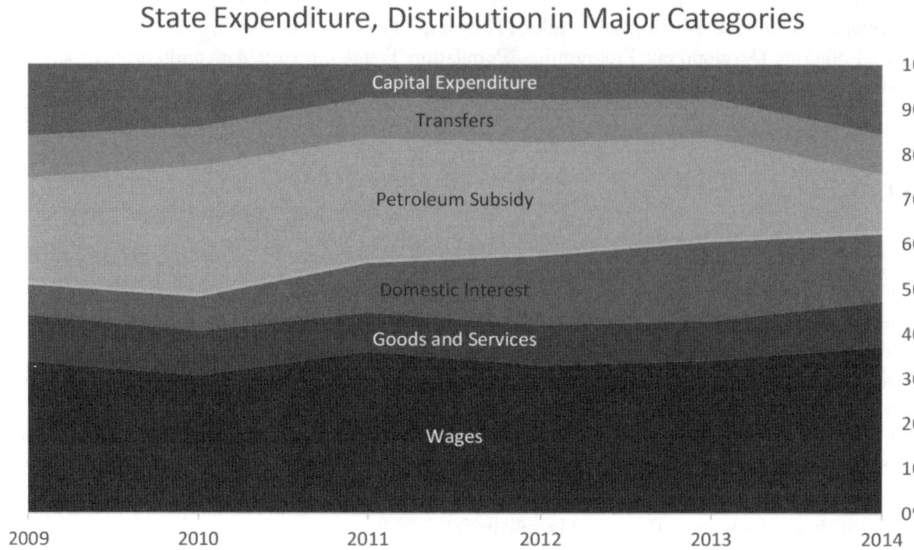

Source: Ministry of Finance, Annual Bulletin 2014, Table 20/1

Chart 2

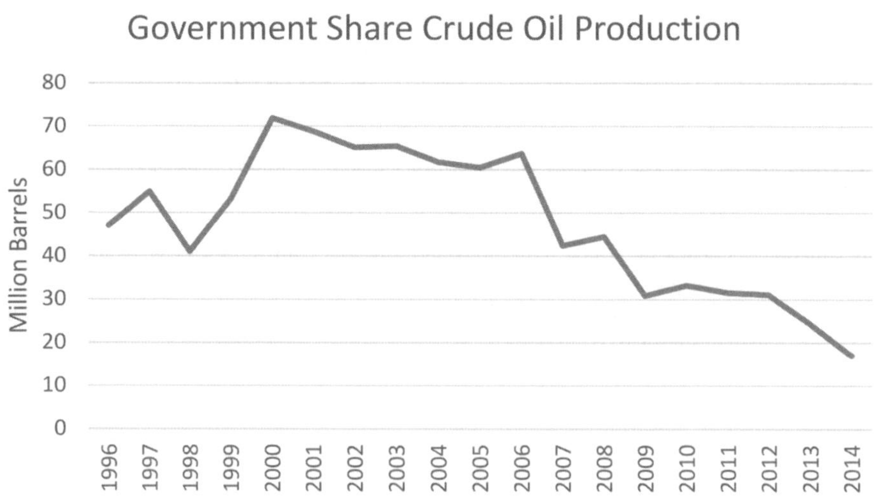

Source: Central Bank, Monthly Closing Newsletter, Jan 2015, Table 26

Chart 3

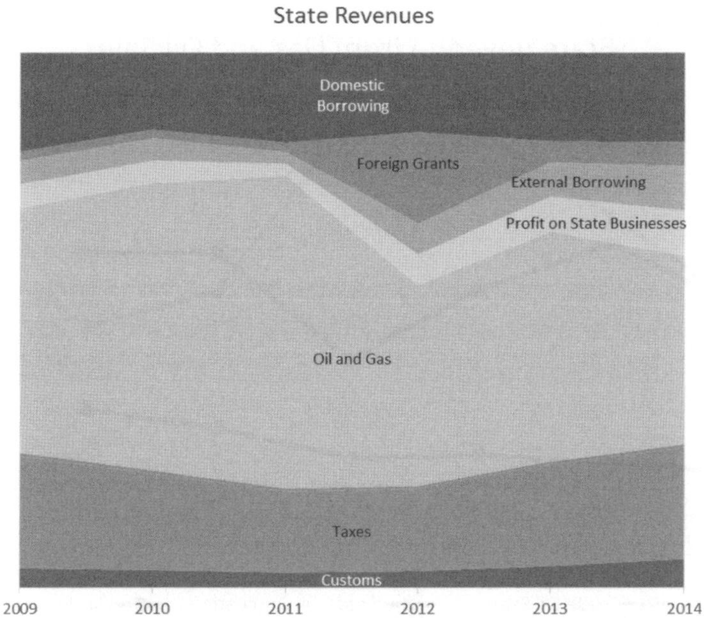

Source: Ministry of Finance, Financial Bulletin 2014, table 11/1

Chart 4

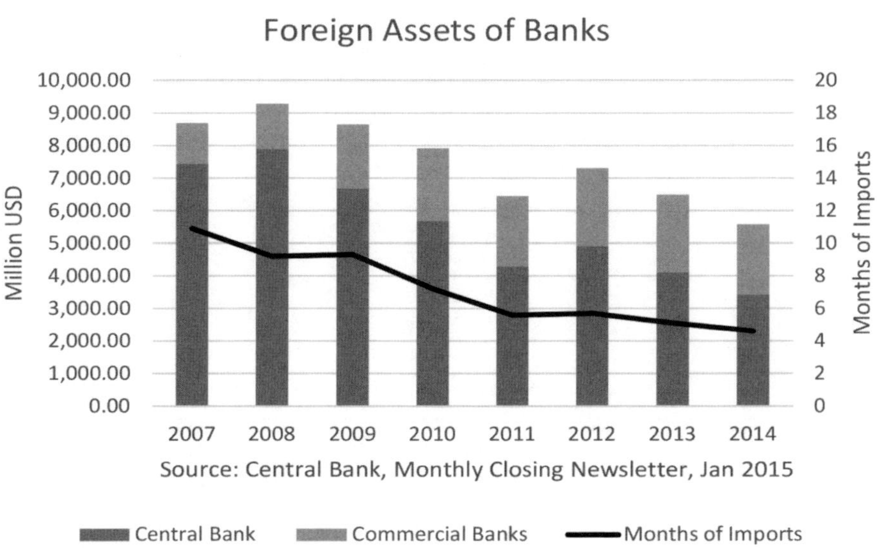

Chart 5

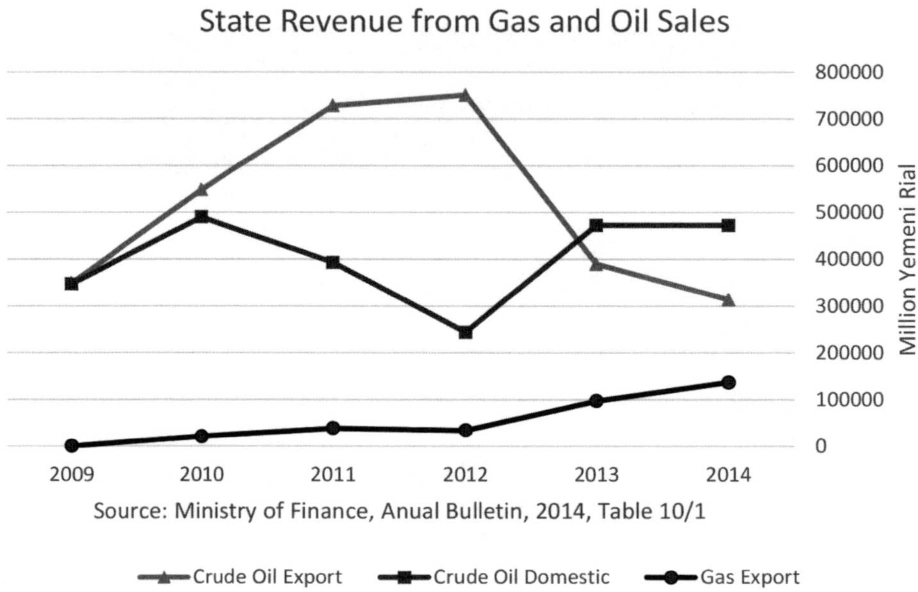

Chart 6

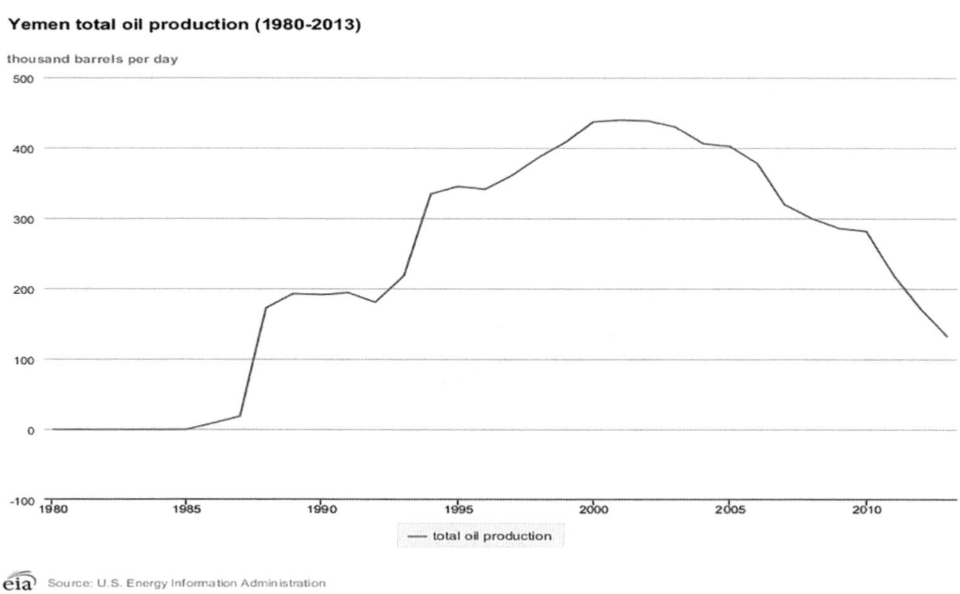

Chart 7

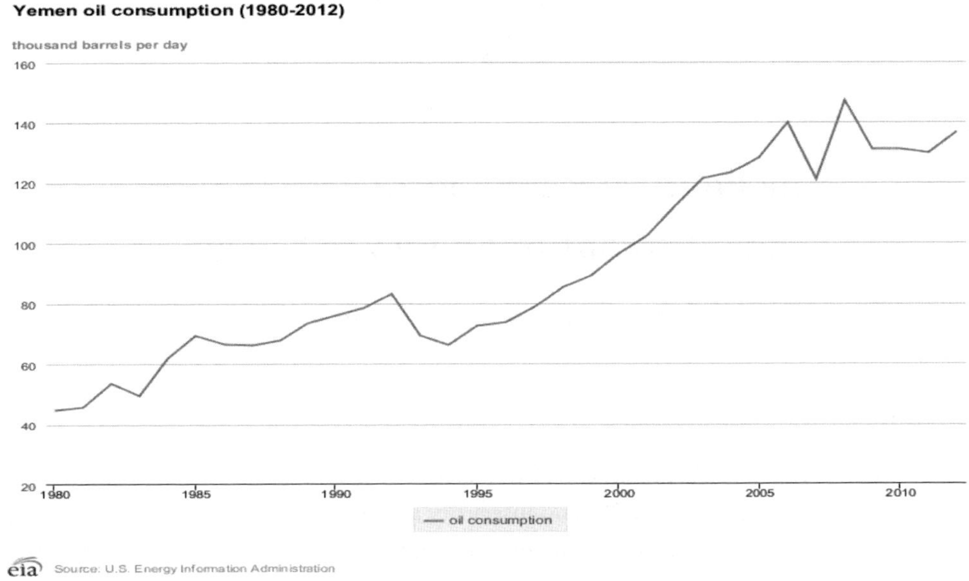

Chart 8

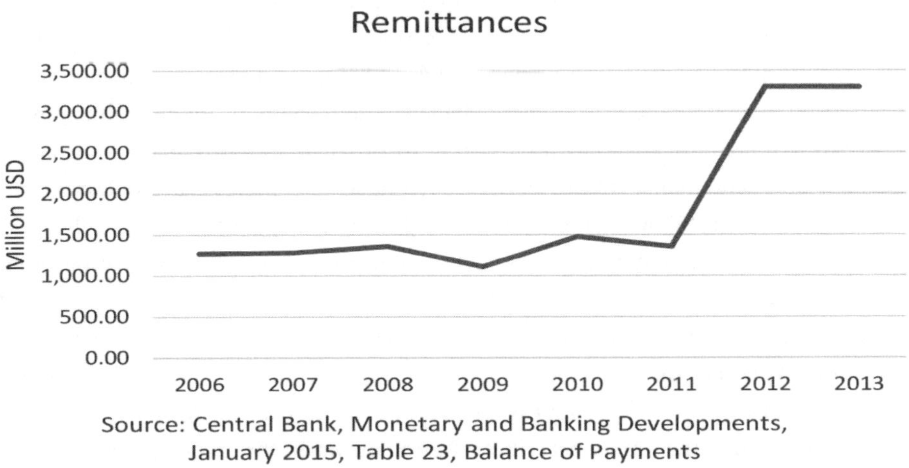

Source: Central Bank, Monetary and Banking Developments, January 2015, Table 23, Balance of Payments

5

The Political Economy of Agriculture and Agricultural Policy in Yemen

Martha Mundy and Frédéric Pelat

Introduction

In 2012 the World Food Programme (WFP) stated that "ten million Yemenis, nearly half of the population, are food insecure."[1] Food insecurity is primarily a rural problem concerning 37% of the rural population.[2] From the end of 2011, Oxfam and the WFP were calling for the supply of emergency food aid to upwards of one quarter of the population.[3] In the wake of the economy's shrinking by 11% in 2011, the overall agricultural sector has been particularly affected by the shutting down of basic supplies and the shortage of inputs – with an estimated drop in output of 16%. Clearly there is no indigenous short-term solution to food insecurity in Yemen in sight: food aid will be required. But it is telling that the food aid will be, in the WFP's packages, 100% wheat grain in a country where sorghum, millet and barley were, until the 1970s, the staple grains, wheat being used for special dishes.

In order to analyze the development challenges and solutions for agriculture and food production in Yemen, we shall begin by setting forth what is known about the changes in agricultural production since Yemen became integrated into the global economy from the 1960s onwards. This is followed by an analysis of the relationship between these changes and the policies and institutional frameworks that accompanied them. An examination of policy since 2011 completes our analysis. The scale of the 2011 protests in Yemen should not be forgotten: Marieke Transfeld has argued that they were in absolute terms the largest in the Arab World.[4] Whether that is true or not, with people marching on foot from Taiz and al-Hodeida to Sanaa the protests sought to unify the city and the countryside symbolically in a manner seen in no other Arab state. From March onwards, the 'international community' engaged in negotiating a settlement to the political challenges, the broad lines of which were drawn up as early as April 2011. This entailed political and legal adjustments but left basic economic policy, and agricultural policy in particular, completely outside the discussion.[5] Hence, in our conclusion, we shall consider the nature of change in policy required to address the structural problems in rural production outlined below and the relation of such economic policy change to the unanswered demands for greater political participation and social justice expressed in the protests of 2011-12 and again in the movement which emerged in 2014.

In this presentation we focus on the rural sector for two reasons: first, Yemen's population remained into the second half of the twentieth century a very rural one: some 85% of the population lived in small villages (or tents) throughout the country as late as the 1970s. Second, as a mountainous country with irregular and at times torrential summer rainfall, the production of people and food over the centuries meant human (and animal) work to make the land that rendered life possible.[6] Yemen's sculpted landscape makes a mockery of the notion of 'the conquest of nature'.[7] And it invites reflection on the absurdity of imposing international 'market value' on Yemeni agriculture in abstraction from this elementary reality. In the rural sector of Yemen the very land of Yemen is at stake.

Concern with Yemen's rural capital thus is not a sign of nostalgia: human knowledge and crafting of physical resources for life have literally built rural Yemen. This physical capital is all the more precious given that the process of the subjection of peasant agriculture to the capitalist economy (in Marxist terms 'primitive accumulation') has in Yemen worked to destroy that capital, not to maintain it for capitalized extraction of profit. Capital accumulation has drawn rather on oil-rent (both that from Yemen's own fields and payments from its richer neighbors), cash remittances from Yemen's migrant male labor force, and the mining of deep fossil aquifers for perishable market crops.

We shall therefore begin by reviewing the character of change in the agrarian sector of Yemen against the background of the country's wider socio-political transformation. In this analysis we present such statistics as are available in graphic form.

The Trajectory of Change in the Structures of Agricultural Production

Today's Republic of Yemen was born from the union in 1990 of the former southern People's Democratic Republic of Yemen (established 1967) and the northern Yemen Arab Republic (established 1962). The south has much smaller areas of rainfed agriculture than the north, but unfortunately a detailed breakdown of land-use between the two former states is not available in the published national statistics analyzed here and on which recent development interventions draw. The quality of statistics remains an issue, there being no systematic land registration throughout most of the country that could reveal holding sizes with reliability, be they the distribution of ownership or the size of tenant farm holdings.[8] Yemen has no decennial agricultural census such as Egypt has had since 1929, a tool vital for charting trends in the rural sector. As we shall discuss in our conclusions, the millions (and soon billions) of dollars expended on rural development projects were decided without systematic statistical knowledge about the structures of farming units and their regional diversity, a necessity for responsible planning and policy debate. Rather such projects presumed that they were in the business of 'knowledge transfer' **to** Yemen so presumably did not need to prioritize Yemen's development of knowledge **of** itself. Indeed today, with the neo-liberal policies governing the state in Yemen, obtaining such rainfall statistics as there are requires payment to the authorities that hold the same.[9] With these caveats, let us here examine what the statistics reveal about overall trends in agricultural production.

Between 1975 and 1990 the rainfed area (see Figure 1) was halved, mostly due to the abandonment or destruction of terraces following a simultaneous increase in the relative cost of production and decrease in the market value of major grain crops (sorghum and barley) in the face of doubly subsidized imported wheat, loss of labor consequent to young male outmigration during the boom years of Saudi Arabia, a very limited transformation of rainfed into irrigated lands and wider expansion of qat cultivation on well watered rainfed land. Male mobility also led to a new division of labor that left to rural women an ever greater part of agricultural labor, although the changes in the division of labor remain unrecorded.

The focus of investment was on irrigated agriculture. The 1970s and 1980s saw the development of unprecedented and unregulated private and public investments in well-drilling (see Figure 1) that served to irrigate flat and mechanizable lands on both coastal lowlands and the dry upper plateaux of the country below terraced escarpments. Investment in groundwater-dependent irrigated agriculture on the plateaux and the coastal plains has resulted in overexploitation and depletion of the aquifers, challenging the very underpinnings of this intensive agricultural economy and even the future of cities such as Sanaa, the capital.[10] The major coastal spate-irrigated wadis saw international development agencies led by the World Bank, offer contracts to international companies for building expensive diversion structures with imported technology in the upper reaches of the flood plain of the wadis.[11] By contrast, the April 2014 newsletter of the 'Spate Irrigation Network' a consortium that spans Yemen, Ethiopia, Pakistan and India, contains a paper on the design of weirs and diversion structures by an Indian engineer for the instruction of Yemeni engineers.[12] The designs concern medium-technology structures, just like those rejected in the late 1970s and early 1980s by the World Bank and its Arab fund partners in favor of permanent high-tech diversion structures built by international contractors, all justified in terms of increasing productivity and production of high-value market-oriented crops for export and Yemeni urban markets. These structures both consolidated inequalities and bequeathed a harsh legacy in terms of their maintenance requirements, which are rarely adequately met today.[13]

The consensus of informed opinion is that over the longer haul, the expansion of cash-cropping has increasingly benefited only a minority of internationally networked wealthy farmers, politicians and businessmen.[14] Irrigation has permitted an increase in the production of fruit and vegetables for export and for the growing city markets as well as of qat for national consumption.[15] It is impossible to document exactly how such changes have impacted the distribution of land tenure given the absence of reliable land tenure data.[16]

To return to the overall pattern of changes in crop production,[17] (see Figure 2) we see a sharp decline in the production of grains between 1970 and 1980 followed by a further gradual

Figure 1: **Agricultural Land Distribution according to Type of Water 1975-2012 (in 1000 ha)**

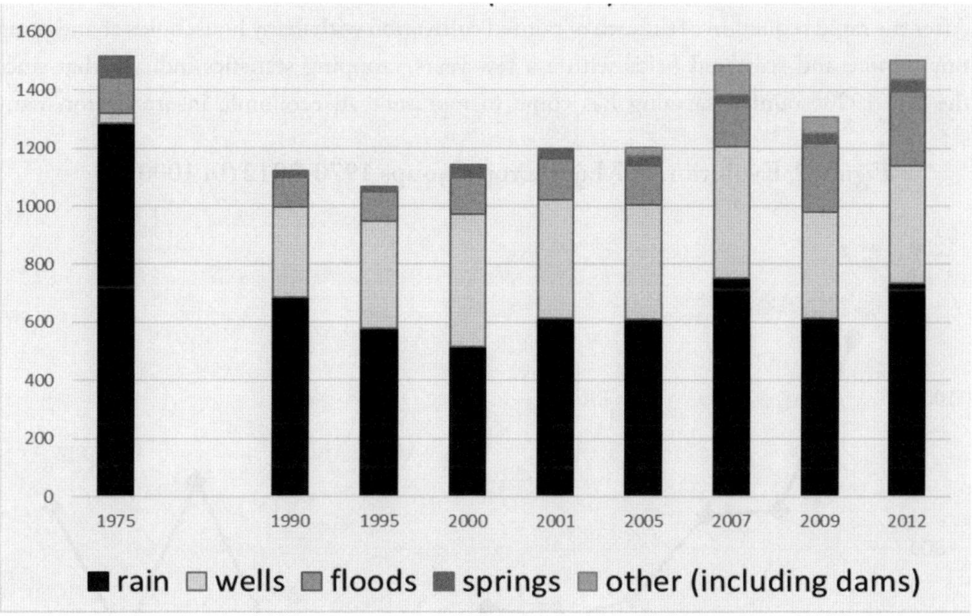

Source: Data compiled from Yemen's Ministry of Agriculture and Irrigation Agricultural Statistics (Year Book) and Republic of Yemen Agricultural Strategy Note, World Bank Report no. 17973-YEM, 1999

decline until 2000. Pulses likewise suffer a relative decline. Qat alone increases notably. Fruit and cash crops do relatively well, although there are changes in the types of fruit crops.[18]

The area planted with grains decreased by 27 percent between 1970 and 1980. Since then, the decline has slowed, but with differences between one cereal and another. According to the World Bank, barley production was halved between 1970 and 1975 alone, from 126,000 tons in 1970 to 64,000 in 1975. Sorghum and millet, taken together, peaked in 1975 to decline until the early 1990s. Alongside the standardization of diets on global models,[19] and in the wake of governmental attempts to introduce high water-demand seeds of "improved" varieties, wheat alone saw an increase in area planted, gaining 56,000 hectares between 1970 and 1990 when, overall, grains lost more than 230,000 ha. Nevertheless, sorghum has remained the first cereal cultivated, as it provides both grain for the family and, given its drought resistance and ability to ratoon, the bulk of indigenous fodder for livestock. Although the areas planted in sorghum were roughly halved, the fact that sorghum continues to be planted today owes as much to its value as fodder as for its value as grain, as well as to the exceptional adaptation of its land races to difficult local conditions (see Figures 3 and 4).[20] As rainfed crops, neither sorghum nor millet has been the object of support from government or international agencies.

Animal production contributes some 28 percent to the total production income for the agricultural sector in Yemen.[21] But beyond such a gross statistic, there is little information to allow an overview of this very important sector.

After the rapid reduction of the area of rainfed cultivation with many households abandoning tiny remote and scattered fields within a few years, cropping statistics indicate that since the late-1990s rainfed farming has come to represent an economic insurance for many

Figure 2: **Evolution of Major Crop Groups 1970-2012 (in 1000 ha)**

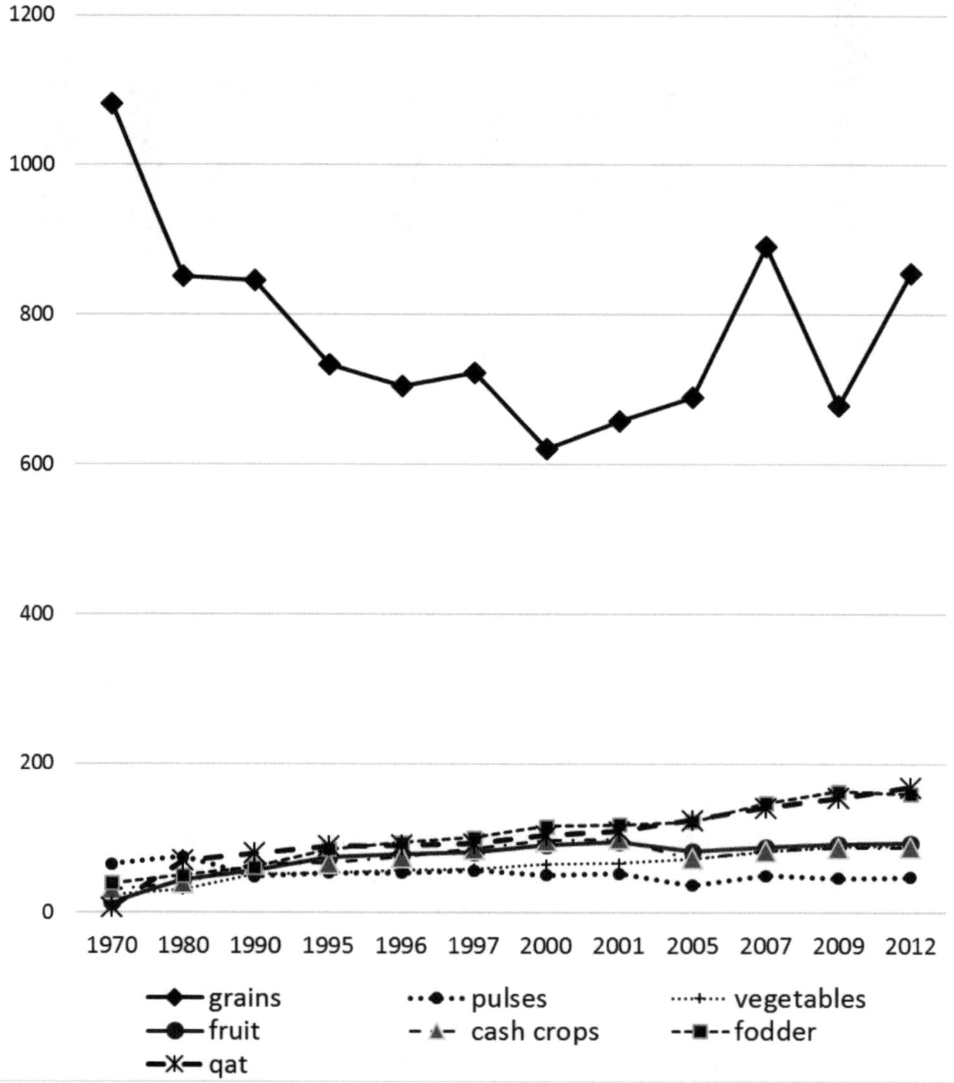

Source: Data compiled from Yemen's Ministry of Agriculture and Irrigation Agricultural Statistics (Year Book) and Republic of Yemen Agricultural Strategy Note, World Bank Report no. 17973-YEM, 1999

Figure 3: **Cereals Area 1970-1996 (in 1000 ha)**

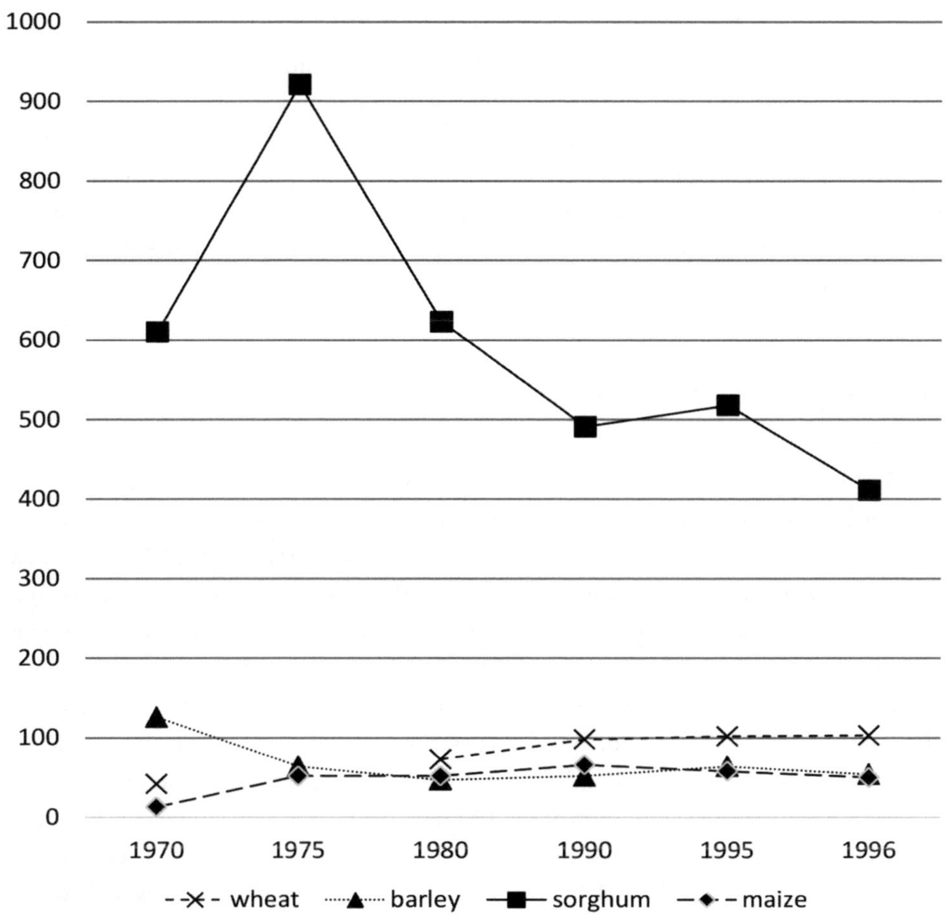

Source: Data compiled from Yemen's Ministry of Agriculture and Irrigation Agricultural Statistics (Year Book) and Republic of Yemen Agricultural Strategy Note, World Bank Report no. 17973-YEM, 1999

families. Families appear to conserve some farmland to be brought back into cultivation when an "urgent crisis" or an "opportunity" takes farmers back to their fields. At this point, the farmers then face the consequences of recent policies: insufficient stocks of local seeds, forgotten knowledge, dislocated community cooperation, and degraded terraces. To what extent such farmers are today women rather than men likewise remains undocumented.

Yemen today imports more than 75 percent of the cereals it consumes whereas in 1970 the figure was 18 percent.[22] In 2009, of the cereals grown in Yemen, 55% by weight, 60% by area sown in cereals, was sorghum; sorghum together with barley and millet formed 69% of cereal production by weight, 80% by area.[23] But in the same year wheat formed 74% of the cereal components of the Yemeni diet.[24] By 2011, 93% of national wheat requirements were imported.[25] This situation was not unpleasing to President Ali Abdullah Saleh whose close relatives controlled the major importing and distributing company, the Yemen Economic Corporation (YECO).[26] The rapid disconnection of social reproduction from local food production, taking place simultaneously with a paucity of public health provision (half of the Yemeni population has no easy access today to health services), the absence of a family planning policy, and an increasingly reactionary approach to women's rights and education, have contributed to rapid population growth. Hence, although wheat production has expanded slightly, its overall contribution to domestic consumption has dropped, roughly from 8 to 4 percent of the estimated needs of the population (see Table 1 in Annex).

Agricultural Policy Since the 1960s

It is not clear that we can speak of an "agricultural policy" in the full sense of the word when the agricultural sector of North Yemen was opened to the world market during the civil war of 1962-71. It was only in the 1970s that governmental and civil institutions concerned with agricultural development were established in both the YAR and the PDRY. The two young states were to pursue very different policies with regard to land tenure, infrastructural investment, crop choice, and marketing. These earlier divergent policies continue to mark the two parts of the country unified since1990.

Although its natural endowment for agriculture was even poorer than that of the north, the PDRY pursued land redistribution, forced cooperative association in agriculture, and dictated control of crop choice and marketing.[27] Notably, the government regulated and restricted the sale of qat.[28] After the 1990 unification of the YAR and the PDRY, agricultural policy, similarly to other policies, was unified on the model of the north. The policies of land redistribution and socialized marketing of the PDRY were cancelled, although farmers in irrigated zones in Hadramawt at the time resisted the wholesale dispossession required legally for the restitution of land to previous owners. Conflict over land is considerable as a result of appropriation of land by government officials from the north, allegedly illegally and sometimes forcibly, in the years after 1994.[29] Such practices – also described for other regions – are invoked today as one of the reasons for renewed calls by southerners for secession from the north.

In the north, with its considerably greater agricultural production, [30] economic and agricultural policy has remained fundamentally unchanged since the 1970s. The only brief departure was during the years of President Ibrahim al-Hamdi (1974-77) who promoted agricultural cooperative association and developmental collective action in rural communities. Aside from this period, the policy, planned or not, basically accepted that the rainfed sector of Yemeni agriculture, exposed to water shortage and with high labor inputs (largely outside the circuit of the market as domestically structured and heavily female), could be left to its own devices. The focus was on zones where delivery of irrigation water could be assured for higher-value, market-oriented production. Until the beginning of the RALP project (Rainfed Agriculture and Livestock Project) in 2008, this basic policy emphasis barely changed, although the water deficit came to be among the most severe in the world.[31] In so far as the issue was addressed, the emphasis was on lessening water loss in irrigated agriculture.[32]

In terms of marketing, Yemen opened its market to imported foodstuffs, subsidized prices of imported grain and other basic foodstuffs on the local market, and refrained from regulating the marketing of produce, especially qat. Labor was encouraged to migrate to the oil-producing states, and it did in large numbers. In short, agricultural policy was effectively based on the premise that the arid and largely mountainous terrain of Yemen was incapable of producing high-quality grain crops, especially wheat, at prices competitive on the international market.[33] Under the guidance of the international development agencies, the focus turned to increasing higher-value agricultural produce from the coastal wadis for the markets of Saudi Arabia and of Yemeni cities more generally. By and large, this policy has been successful. If there has been "failure" in agriculture, this must be ascribed not to any tradition-bound rigidity on the part of farmers who have responded to the policy with myriad changes, but to the policy itself. Thus, further to the statistics with which this paper opened, it is reported that, between 1991 and 2003, areas planted in sorghum and barley declined, whereas those in qat, bananas, mangoes, citrus, and apples increased.[34] A recent UNDP report notes that the land planted in barley and maize halved between 1961 and 2003.[35] Far from stimulating local production of basic foodstuffs, labor remittances fostered consumerism on the Gulf model and supported a rise in food imports. The opening of the domestic market to unrestricted and subsidized food imports, in particular wheat, in order to cover the needs of a rapidly expanding population, inevitably made local production less competitive.

Over the 34 years of President Ali Abdullah Saleh's rule (and with expert international mediation by Dr. Abd al-Karim al-Iryani, the head of the first Yemeni government development agency, the Central Planning Office (CPO), and special advisor to President Abd Rabbuh Mansour Hadi, Saleh's former vice-president who took over as head of state in February 2012), a basic division of labor developed between the expansion of the Yemeni state as a security and military employer and the delegation to international agencies of policy and financing for the rural sector of the country.[36] The GCC agreement and meetings of the 'Friends of Yemen' have confirmed this structural division of labor, the only evident change since the major protests of 2011 being the deepening USA engagement in the military and security organization of the state. Thus, even at the level of what is publicly known about the budget of the Yemeni state, military and security allocations have been further increased in 2014.[37] The Yemeni case thus provides close to a perfect example of the effects of international development policy on an agrarian economy that, in the northern part of the country, was close to self-sufficiency in basic grains until the 1970s.

From the mid-1990s onwards, Yemen was subject to structural adjustment policies supposed to "fight Yemen's impoverishment". The International Monetary Fund demanded the cutting of consumption subsidies and public expenditures with the declared objective to "save public money for the benefit of job-generating and development-oriented investments".[38] Beyond rises in the prices of basic consumption goods and increased competition with local production, those measures led to popular riots – in 1998 and in 2005 – and increased poverty and unemployment. Structural adjustment plans were therefore combined with poverty alleviation programs. This became formalized in the framework of Poverty Reduction Strategy Papers, funded by the World Bank but also by wealthy Arab neighbors, in particular Saudi Arabia.

Today Yemen's agricultural policy is increasingly becoming framed in terms of reduction of food insecurity and poverty alleviation. These categories allow for the agencies to engage with rainfed agriculture and degraded land after decades of neglect but without needing to review the contribution their earlier policies made to present problems. In the name of poverty reduction the Public Works Project and the Social Fund for Development initiated cash/food distribution programmes in 1996 and 1997 respectively. These appear to be generalized in the forthcoming National Agricultural Sector Strategy. These programmes can be directed to support badly needed infrastructural work. But this is done in the name of poverty reduction and targets needy individuals (counted as such, with female 'beneficiaries' counted separately from male) without consideration of the history of degradation of infrastructure, the structure of ownership, and the patterns of access to resources. As we shall see below, alongside this humanitarian poverty-reduction agenda, development aid continues to be cast as 'assistance' to farmers so as to access better markets for products. The next section examines the policy agenda since 2011.

Agricultural Policy After the Uprising

Until the release of the first draft of NASS (National Agricultural Sector Strategy) in 2012 policies and activities in the agricultural sector were more or less framed by overall Ministry of Planning and International Cooperation (MoPIC)-led strategies such as "Yemen's Strategic Vision 2025" (2000) or the more concrete "Poverty Reduction Strategy Paper" (PRSP 2003-2005) and the "Development Plans for Poverty Reduction" (DPPR 2006-2010). Specific agricultural strategies were the responsibility of the Aden Agenda (officialised in 2000), including the interim strategy prepared with FAO support in 2003. All were largely inspired by World Bank strategies and orientations, i.e. the YAR Development of a Traditional Economy report in 1979, followed by the YAR Agricultural Strategy Paper in 1986, and the "Republic of Yemen Agricultural Strategy Note" in 1999. However, since the collapse of extension and research activities in Yemen[39] and the general shrinking of public expenditures on this sector, concrete interventions for agricultural development resulted either from private initiatives mainly in irrigated agriculture or from donor-funded projects as mentioned above. The main funders were above all the World Bank and the International Fund for Agricultural Development (IFAD) sometimes through co-financing, with implementation by Ministries or State agencies;[40] other important funders include the EU, GTZ, USAID, DFID and other European state agencies directly or with NGO implementation.

The drafting of the NASS followed a process similar to other strategies, the "National Food Security Strategy" (NFSS) [41] and in particular the "National Water Sector Strategy and Investment Programme" (NWSSIP) approved in 2005.[42] This programme aimed to coordinate and better to integrate actions in what has become the first sector of investment for development actors since the mid-90s in Yemen: water. NASS is said to be complementary to NWSSIP. Both strategies have institutional, technical and financial mandates. Just as with NWSSIP, the responsibility for NASS implementation lies jointly with the Ministry of Agriculture and Irrigation (MAI) and the Ministry of Water and Environment (MWE), and also in collaboration with other agencies in charge of rural development, rural water supply, health and nutrition. These include the Social Fund for Development (SFD), the Economic Opportunities Fund (EOF), the Public Works Project (PWP), the Pilot Programme for Climate Resilience (PPCR), the Cooperative and Agricultural Credit (CAC) Bank, and Amal Bank, the main micro-finance institution. According to the strategy paper, at the national level, "NASS implementation is coordinated with the Supreme Council for Food Security and with the Food Security Technical Secretariat and Steering Committee within MoPIC".[43] Two specialized programmes of MAI will be directly responsible for NASS implementation: the National Irrigation Programme for all activities and investments in the field of "irrigation and land and water conservation", and the Agricultural Improvement Programme for those in the fields of "crop and livestock development and improvement".[44]

Like NWSSIP for water, NASS plans measures designed to integrate more effectively activities undertaken within the agricultural sector through the strengthening of central authority and at the same time decentralized governance with more responsibility transferred to local stakeholders. The investment programme is "a mix of the ongoing 'projects' which will be progressively consolidated within the NASS and proposed new financing of investments in the NASS". [45] While NWSSIP's budget for 2005-2009 was US$1.5 billion, NASS first investment programme for 2013-2017 should cost US$2.2 billion, of which "US$1.6 billion for agricultural programs under MAI, and US$630 million for broader agriculture, rural development and environmental programmes under other agencies". [46] A priority investment programme has been planned and covers US$1.3 billion out of the $2.2 billion or $668 million out of the $1.6 billion planned under MAI. Those figures are said to reverse "... the pattern of relatively low historical allocations to agriculture under the previous regime, which averaged as little as 2-3% of total government spending 2005-2010".[47] This last figure is hoped to reach 10% annually for the 5-year implementation period, promising a "significant increase in support to the sector" (see in Annex Table 2 summarizing the budget sought for NASS). It should be noted that these projections remain little more than a 'wish list' at present.

In June 2013, MAI's priority agricultural investment program of US$668 million had attracted "firm financing of US$370 million".[48] 300 million were still to be found, maybe as a confirmation of pledges received during the 2012 Friends of Yemen conference. No accurate figure is yet given for the government's direct financing, but it is mentioned that "a number of investments" will be paid "on its own resources" through "the public investment budget and through the Agriculture and Fisheries Production Promotion Fund and the Social Fund for Development (SFD)".[49] It is added that under current crisis conditions (declining fiscal and oil revenues), finding further governmental financing would be a challenge. Private investment and international donor support are therefore required.

In line with this perspective, a first proposal called "Smallholder Agricultural Productivity Enhancement Project"[50] was submitted by the MAI in June 2013 to the Global Agriculture and Food Security Program (GAFSP)[51] for financing, as a "phase one roll out of NASS". This proposal, endorsed by the FAO, World Bank and MoPIC, intends to "implement a time-slice of the NASS in four governorates" (Shabwa, Abyan, Hajja and Sanaa) with what are presented as overall NASS objectives but are seemingly more focused on poverty relief than the general NASS text. The main target population will be food-insecure households and consists of smallholders, tenants and sharecroppers, landless livestock farmers, and households dependent largely on casual labor, but all other farmers are expected to be "secondary target populations" too.[52] Out of 880,000 total projected beneficiaries, the project will target 170,000 women as direct beneficiaries. Representing less than 4% of the overall priority investment program budget, the cost for this first project is US$50 million from which $6,500,000 will be covered by the Government of Yemen and $3,500,000 as a contribution from the beneficiaries themselves. US$40 million is thus submitted for GAFSP financing.

A Critical Reading of the NASS Versions

The 104-page document discussed here is the final National Agriculture Sector Strategy and Investment Plan for the period 2012-2016, known as NASS and approved by the Cabinet on March 13, 2012 (Cabinet decree No 37-2012). Presented by the Ministry of Agriculture and Irrigation, author of the document, with an introduction by Minister Eng. Farid Ahmed Mujawar, NASS was prepared "in cooperation with the United Nations Development Programme"[53] through its Economic Diversification Support Programme (Agriculture Sector). The document tells us that a participatory approach was adopted in the two phases of the strategy development started in 2011: a comprehensive review of policies and strategies and consultative workshops with key participants from the agricultural sector. The resulting draft agriculture sector strategy was then finalized by a "technical committee of multidisciplinary national experts"[54] before being officially approved in 2012. But in 2013 the MAI conducted a "further consultation process" to update the strategy document in order to "reflect a growing emphasis on food security and nutrition, (...) climate change, (...) poverty reduction and natural resource sustainability".[55] A shorter (25 page) MAI-authored document, entitled Summary Interim Update, reflecting "technical and strategic guidance from independent peer reviewers (University of Sanaa and IFPRI) as well as from individual consultants"[56] was temporarily available online. These outcomes were integrated in the final NASS version that, aside from introduction and conclusion, contains five main sections: 1) a short situational analysis, 2) a longer section on the challenges in the agricultural sector, 3) a brief introduction to the agriculture sector strategy, 4) the subsector development strategies, and 5) a description of the sector-wide development strategies in agriculture.[57]

The forthcoming discussion builds on the analysis of both final version and updated summary that were available successively at the same internet link.[58]

The NASS Strategy document was released in May 2013. In the section below we discuss its key points. The justifications given in the NASS document for the action required in agriculture do not clearly identify the origins of the problems but rather address their consequences. The strategy does not question the economic dogmas that have led to the current situation of today's rural populations. In the very short contextual page on "Agriculture and the Yemeni economy", causes and consequences of the problems are blurred and no real categorization is made of the different agro-ecosystems, let alone their respective farming systems. The result is a homogenized and simplified portrait of present problems. The entire agricultural population is categorized as either 'subsistence' or 'commercial' farmers; the first are described as largely poor, with poor productivity on rainfed lands and the latter as dynamic, larger scale, and technologically advancing. The section recognizes that the rapid growth of the latter sector is the result of private and public investments in groundwater-dependant and irrigated agriculture more generally as well as widespread "domestic demand in a market economy".[59] The strategy developed takes these choices for granted without questioning their rationality. Nowhere is it mentioned that the earlier policies, which focused investment on irrigated agriculture both in the coastal plains and in the uplands, benefited a minority of wealthy farmers and business people. Rather the resulting consequences – groundwater overexploitation and depletion, inequity of land and water distribution, small sizes of farms, and resort to qat production to maximize incomes on tiny plots – are cast alongside the risks resulting from climate change as "severe constraints" that have "emerged" to the strategy of increasing agricultural productivity over the last decades.[60]

NASS then identifies low productivity (despite recent improvements in water use efficiency), shrinking public investment (including in services, research and extension), and the weak empowerment of rural women (although they are "providing three quarters of agricultural labor and all the skills in household management, health and nutrition")[61] as major problems. These three factors are said to engender poverty, food insecurity and malnutrition in rural areas as local consequences, and reliance on food imports, and consequent vulnerability to external price and supply shocks, as macro-level consequences. Problems in agriculture are thus presented in such a way as to give the impression that food imports represent simply a response to increasingly insufficient food production. No mention is made of the fact that unrestricted imports of (heavily subsidized) foodstuffs and seeds formed part of the policy adopted since the 1970s by first the North and later by unified Yemen with the blessing of international donors – cheap food imports which rendered completely uncompetitive local unsubsidized production of staple grains and pulses. Instead, the report stresses the difficulties poorer Yemenis now experience to buy food in the wake of higher and fluctuating global food prices since 2008.

In the same way, just as the text does not mention the impact of imported foodstuffs on rainfed farming production and its workforce, it also ignores the impact of the development of irrigated agriculture, producing for urban and export markets, on the rainfed sector. Although for the first time, in the wake of dramatic food insecurity, rainfed agriculture is included as a target of agricultural strategy, it is cast as "poor mountain agricultural areas of the highlands", recognized as "a particular problem, with two thirds of all Yemen's food insecure living in dry highland areas".[62] According to the GAFSP proposal, "NASS' growth strategy in rainfed and smallholder agriculture focuses more on inclusion and adding value to the assets of the poor and on improving their nutritional status", while "growth in commercial largely irrigated agriculture will be stimulated more through support to private sector development, public-private partnerships and strengthening of key public services".[63] Although in the GAFSP document, a paragraph[64] states that cash transfers will be made to the poor for infrastructural repairs (rebuilding terraces, water collection structures, and the like), the thrust in NASS remains purely on increasing incomes through better crop yields and livestock enhancement. In fact the most convincing section of the final NASS document is the long and technical section on the need for veterinary services, research into native animal races, genetic breeding, regulation of the importation of (often diseased) animals, and other support for livestock production, clearly written by the Yemeni specialists who have received negligible funding for many years.[65] But to return to crop production, although the earlier RALP project and the forthcoming final version of the GAFSP may include development of local landraces of rainfed agriculture, their importance, as well as that of local farming knowledge, seems ignored in the final NASS. By contrast, NASS places considerable emphasis on the development of new markets for seeds or inputs; this appears once again in line with the vision of the market as panacea articulated as early as the 1970s by the World Bank. Little in the NASS strategy for agriculture really departs from the judgement in the influential 1979 World Bank report entitled 'Yemen Arab Republic: Development of a Traditional Economy'. This stated that the "new situation required a flexible response from both farmers and Government" and that "instead of clinging rigidly to outdated objectives and traditional farming practices, the agricultural sector should be left free to respond to local market conditions and price/cost relationships just as the economy at large is an open one."[66] In general, given that the chain of actions which led to the present dramatic situation is not recognized, questioned or changed but rather supported by the NASS strategy, does repetition of the market mantra promise any real remedy to the situation wrought in its name over the past four decades?

The absence of recognition of the importance of domestic consumption from the production of rainfed farming makes the real intentions of the NASS strategy for this sector unclear. Nowhere is the objective of increasing rainfed yields linked to diminishing dependence of smallholders on (imported) food grains from the market and/or humanitarian food aid and hence to increasing the degree of self-sufficiency of the smallholders. Rainfed agriculture is targeted by technical solutions dedicated "to increase productivity" but with the objective "to increase incomes", which means, by the standard understanding of the term 'income', increasing production for a market where local rainfed production will never be competitive without strong support and protection measures. In addition, although more research and extension in rainfed agriculture is obviously welcome, in particular on seed multiplication and storage, the strategy does not mention clearly how and towards what this research would be directed. In the NASS strategy, "local knowledge" seems once again to be replaced by "transfer of knowledge", depriving the strategy of an essential resource. Furthermore, what do "improved seeds" really mean? Although for the rainfed sector, it is noted that research would work to improve "land races" (but not necessarily only land races?), the question needs to be asked for vegetables and other crops, when it is known that GAFSP funding combines public and private donors including the Bill Gates Foundation, a supporter of genetically modified seeds, and that the International Food Policy Research Institute, a Consortium of International Agricultural Research Centre (CGIAR) [formerly the Consultative Group] agency, is connected to Western governments and multinational agribusiness. Indeed, what would the proposed privatization and regulation of the seed system in the rainfed sector imply for access and ownership by the farmers accustomed to produce their own seeds?

Land and water management aspects are also addressed by the strategy. Technical measures aimed at improving access to land, rehabilitating terraces and rangeland, limiting degradation and combatting desertification are of great interest, but how will they deal with land ownership and tenure arrangements? A starting point would be to have a review of other projects concerned with land resources, the Groundwater and Soil Conservation Project (GSCP) and Rainfed Agriculture and Livestock Project (RALP) and IFAD projects such as the Dhamar Participatory Rural Development Project and the al-Dhala Community Resource Management Project to see how this question was approached. Concerning water management, the strategy aims to include rainfed farming, although water was until now primarily addressed in relation to irrigated commercial agriculture. Aside from the inclusion of rainfed agriculture, the strategy does not really seem to add anything to policies outlined in NWSSIP or the Water Law. It nevertheless entails the risk of competition between the MAI and the MWE and perhaps other agencies for the implementation of projects (and the related management of funds) in the specific field of agricultural water.

NASS Preparation and Development Rhetoric

Although a new strategy is greatly needed for the agricultural sector, the proposed national strategy reveals no revolutionary solutions. Despite giving the impression of being a grassroots-based creation, it results in reality from an incremental process similar to earlier strategies and builds on past actions. The participatory process may be new by itself as it involved an unprecedented number of stakeholders from various origins and regions, including women, smallholders and other very poor groups, in the wake of the popular movements of the 2011-2012 uprising. However, despite the laudable claims of mass consultation and the inclusion of new dimensions such as climate change or nutrition in the development rhetoric, proposed interventions are '*déjà vu*' and the technical content differs little from other strategies and projects proposed for Yemeni agriculture since the mid-1990s. This can indeed be explained by the fact that NASS is a strategy which links past, ongoing and future projects and is intended to build on "successes" observed from the field. It is unclear to what extent the farmers who participated in the workshops, and in particular the poorest, have been already involved in or influenced by World Bank projects from which the final strategy drew its inspiration. Proposed interventions seem to be directly and solely originating from World Bank projects' components and consequently ignore other local initiatives and NGO-led projects (which World Bank expert teams can easily contact).

Moreover, the process that led to NASS started several years ago. From the mid-1990s to date, interventions in agriculture were first part of general rural development projects, each of them targeting one or a few governorates. Then, as they expanded to more governorates, they began to be more specialized by sector: water and (rainfed) agriculture. On the one hand, national-level World Bank funded projects started in 2001 with the Rural Water Supply and Sanitation Project (RWSSP) for domestic water, and the Irrigation Improvement Project (IIP) for agricultural water. The GSCP followed in 2004. The NWSSIP built on ongoing and past projects in the water sector and planned new interventions in the framework of an investment plan designed for donors and the private sector. It was part of a package of institutional and technical reforms which also included the creation of the MWE and the promulgation of the Water Law. On the other hand, later, in the specific field of agriculture, newly separated from water, the more specific RALP started only in 2008 although IFAD's target population had usually included "poor farmers involved in rainfed agriculture and livestock production". NASS follows the same trajectory as did NWSSIP but is supposed now to address both rainfed and irrigated agriculture thus encroaching on the field of water. The difference, if any, is that NWSSIP was a strategy to frame and to coordinate a well-funded sector with a significant diversity of donors, water being considered as urgent for agricultural and above all non-agricultural purposes, whereas the NASS action plan intends to diversify and to expand a budget in a sector essential for food security but abandoned by donors.

The real novelty of the NASS strategy is the size of funds proposed to be raised for the agricultural sector and the place given to the long neglected and very deserving livestock sector including animal health and production. However, in its general conceptualization the present programme falls in line with the liberalization of the agricultural sector of the 1970s, the structural adjustment policies of the mid-1990s, and after a decade of negotiation,the adhesion of Yemen in December 2013 to the World Trade Organization.

Despite laudable intentions, support to the rainfed sector, the most fragile system of Yemeni agriculture, may need more than technical solutions to be viable and sustainable. This is all the more true given that the proposed solutions are not really new and had already appeared in previous strategies and reports, even though they were not always implemented. Numerous types of "improved seeds" were introduced in the past by extension and research services but never achieved the expected results. And "promising alternative crops to qat" were already identified several decades ago without really being taken seriously. Even though planned actions may now be able to obtain funds for their implementation, rainfed farming remains in direct competition with irrigated agriculture for its workforce and with cheap imports in the market. The economic policy context in which agricultural policy decisions are made may lead it to fail as long as there is no real political support and protection for this weakened sector.

Proposing rural development strategies based on recycled technical solutions may prove not only inefficient but also counter-productive, if framed within neoliberal dogma of the supremacy of a deregulated market. It is time to propose political and economic measures which will protect smallholders, and in particular in rainfed agriculture. Just as with water, coherent legislation should be drawn up to protect (agricultural) land resources, including terraced land, and to acknowledge the multiple dimensions and importance of mountain land in relation to household economies, food production, pasture, ecological integrity, watershed management, and even national heritage. Can there be a Yemen without terraces? Rainfed farming cannot be seen simply as the remains of a 'traditional' agriculture of the past but must be recognized as a vital part of agriculture for the future. Crop production reliant on ground water will prove increasingly problematic, and a growing proportion of today's irrigated land will become rainfed land in coming years. Therefore, farmers' knowledge needs to be valued and safeguarded, especially the knowledge developed over centuries as to how to manage resource scarcity and environmental variability. Indeed, under far more clement skies, governments support and value farming systems, so in Yemen forms of direct aid, incentives or production insurance in support of rainfed production and its physical base should be considered.

Conclusion

NASS and the GAFSP project contain certain positive aspects: a recognition of the existence of rainfed agriculture as central to the livelihoods of the highland rural populations; the recognition, albeit only implicit, of a link between poverty and agrarian infrastructural degradation; a strong technical argument for the need to support livestock production; and an acknowledgement of the interconnection of agro-ecological zones in watershed systems.

Yet, for documents written after the uprising of 2011, there is surprising continuity with the policies promoted in earlier projects. There is no recognition that the neo-liberal policies have led to massive destruction of land, water resources and farmer's knowledge. It is worth reflecting on the issue of knowledge, the central form of capital in the interface between farming and nature. Knowledge has two aspects: that of the farmers in their fields and herders in their pastures and that of a governing order, a state, which develops public policies to enhance the productive capacity of farming and animal husbandry. As we discussed earlier, from the 1970s the international development agencies treated the first as part of the "outdated" "traditional farming practices",[67] rather than as a resource, be it in terms of genetic stock or techniques for water harvesting, soil retention or seed reproduction. And the second was effectively never developed: no on-going census of farming structures, no on-going studies of land-use, no cadastral registration of land ownership, no banks of native genetic material, be it from plants or animals. Lastly, in the strategy documents discussed above, there is no recognition of the responsibility and history of international development interventions in Yemen and the relation of past decisions to the present dramatic crisis. Instead, there is continuity with previous projects with no historical chart of the actual interventions – a silence that itself is but another failure to produce knowledge about the rural world.

It would be easy to conclude that the policy objective has been to create dependence in the classic manner of development 'aid' functioning as a tool in the construction of an internationally articulated ruling class.[68] Certainly the result of 'development' in Yemen has been primarily dependence. The dominant powers (and their tax payers) make substantial payments in 'aid'; yet at the level of the equation of capital flows, it has been shown that for every dollar of 'aid', almost three dollars left the country to 'safe havens'.[69]

Yemeni youth activists opened a brief debate on the role of the aid industry in relieving Yemen's government of responsibilities, in guiding its economic policies, and in patronizing elites ill-placed to challenge fundamental inequality and disfunctionality. By contrast, the international 'solution' entailed increased militarization and direct US and foreign management. In spite of political contestation, small farmers of the countryside, and their concerns, remain without representation in the making of state policy.

What is not said in all strategies is that the very basis of food production needs rebuilding and conservation; that such rebuilding can be done by local groups with government support; that women's rights to land can be built into such initiatives; that women form the backbone of small farming families; that small farming families are the guardians of bio-diversity; that knowledge of cultivation and water-harvesting methods, and of seed and animal types, can be strengthened through both local transmission and the introduction of scientific bio-banks; that a successful family planning programme requires both universal health coverage and less reactionary ideologies in the name of religion; that real estate construction is not productive 'industry'; that it is possible to regulate a market so as to permit qat sales on only certain days as was done in South Yemen; that inequality and the concentration of wealth are not God-given derivatives of the market or property itself but the result of public policy over many years; that such policy can be changed to restructure property rights; that government expenditure on the military and security (as with petrol subsidies) can be redirected to basic production; and that Yemenis need to take back their own government to such ends.

Notes

1 World Food Programme (WFP), "The State of Food Security and Nutrition in Yemen: Comprehensive Food Security Survey," 2012, 18. See also Figures 1 and 2 of the International Food Policy Research Institute (IFPRI) and Ministry of Planning and International Cooperation, Yemen, "Yemen National Food Security Strategy: 1 Overview and Action Plan," 2011. This is a policy paper for estimates of food insecurity in 2009, showing large areas of the country with 40 percent severe food insecurity and 60 percent or more stunting in children, pp. 2-3.

2 Quoted from the GAFSP Project Proposal for Yemen ("Republic of Yemen, Proposal for Yemen: Smallholder Agricultural Productivity Enhancement Program, Phase One Roll Out of National Agriculture Sector Strategy [NASS] for Yemen's Efforts towards Achieving Food Security under Global Agriculture and Food Security Program, Sanaa, June 2013"), 4, in "1.1 Objectives and indicators" section. See for GAFSP: http://www.gafspfund.org/sites/gafspfund.org/files/Documents/4.%20Yemen%20 Proposal.pdf

3 Ashley Jonathan Clements, "Yemen: Fragile Lives in Hungry Times," Oxfam Briefing Paper No. 152, September 2011 and World Food Programme (WFP), *The State of Food Security and Nutrition in Yemen: Comprehensive Food Security Survey*, 2012.

4 "What had begun as small protests in January 2011 developed into a full-fledged, countrywide, popular uprising that lasted for ten months. In absolute terms, of all the countries participating in the Arab Spring, Yemen had the largest protests by far." Marieke Transfeld, "Yemen's GCC Roadmap to Nowhere: Elite Bargaining and Political Infighting Block a Meaningful Transition," German Institute for International and Security Affairs, 2014, 7.

5 Although the degree of outside management of the political change appears exceptional in the case of Yemen, as Georges Corm noted, the political transitions in other Arab states have also not entailed discussion of major change of social and economic policy: 'During the wave of Arab uprisings, Arab and international media limited their focus to the issue of democracy and personal freedoms. Absent from the analysis of revolutionary matters was any indication of the ways and means to reach a renewed developmental style, independent from the neoliberal model popularized by international, regional, Arab and Islamic financial institutions. To our knowledge, no political party, be it Islamic or secular, has been seen to highlight this key issue in its programme and slogans so that the Arab revolutions could reach safe ground.' See Georges Corm, "The political Economy of Democratic Transition in the Arab Situation," *Contemporary Arab Affairs* 8, no. 1 (2015), 22.

6 This is what van der Ploeg terms coproduction of farming and nature in landscape: see Jan Douwe van der Ploeg, *Peasants and the Art of Farming: A Chaanovian Manifesto* (Halifax, Fernwood, 2013), 48–49.

7 Compare Neil Smith, *Uneven Development: Nature, Capital and the Production of Space* (Athens: University of Georgia Press, [1984] 2008).

8 Jens Kanbeck, "Land Disputes in Yemen," in *Why Yemen Matters: A Society in Transition*, ed. Helen Lackner (London, Saqi Books), 200.

9 We are grateful to Helen Lackner for her careful comments on our paper and for noting on this point that 'payment for data is the case for everything'. It would seem that neo-liberal economic policy also entails the commercialisation of the knowledge production of the state.

10 For recent publications on the water crisis and its political causes, see: Milan Karner, "Water Scarcity and Human Security in Yemen, Assessing the Causes and Consequences of Yemen's Water Crisis," 2014: http://mei-nus.com/publications/middle-east-perspectives/water-scarcity-and-human-security-

in-yemen, and Matthew I. Weiss, "A Perfect Storm: The Causes and Consequences of Severe Water Scarcity, Institutional Breakdown and Conflict in Yemen," *Water International*, 2015, accessible at: http://www.tandfonline.com/doi/full/10.1080/02508060.2015.1004898#.VNI4Fy4Rrl4

11 See Martha Mundy, "Tihama II Project: Monitoring and Evaluation Report," Ministry of Agriculture, Yemen Arab Republic, and World Bank/Kuwait Fund, 1980 and "Agricultural Development in the Yemeni Tihama: The Past Ten Years," in *Economy, Society and Culture in Contemporary Yemen*, ed. B. R. Pridham, 22-40 (London: Croom Helm, 1985).

12 April 2014 edition of the Newsletter of the Spate Irrigation Network (www.spate-irrigation.org/spate-irrigation-network/) contained a link to: http://spate-irrigation.org/wp-content/uploads/2014/04/Quick-Start-Design-Manual-for-Spate-Works.pdf

13 See more generally, Frank van Steenbergen, Philip Lawrence, Abraham Mehari Haile, Maher Salman, and Jean-Marc Faurès, "Guidelines on Spate Irrigation," FAO Irrigation and Drainage Paper No. 65 (Rome: FAO, 2010).

14 In the final NASS document to be discussed below, Republic of Yemen, Ministry of Agriculture and Irrigation, *A Promising Sector for Diversified Economy in Yemen: National Agricultural Sector Strategy 2012–2016*, March 2012, 13–14, it is written: "In the highland and coastal plains, the land tends to be owned by large land holders, and small farmers are interspersed among large farms." The source of this information and the problems posed to agricultural planning by the poverty of land tenure data in the absence of land registration and of an agricultural census is not made clear. See also note 28 below.

15 In Martha Mundy, Amin al-Hakimi, and Frédéric Pelat, "Neither Security nor Sovereignty: The Political Economy of Food in Yemen," in *Food Security in the Arab World*, ed. Zahra Babar and Suzi Mirgani, 137–59 (London: Hurst, 2014), we discuss, in some detail, change in the nature of fruit crop production, a secondary but important aspect of the agrarian transformation.

16 World Bank, *Republic of Yemen: Country Social Analysis*, 2006, 15–16 describes trends towards increasing concentration of land ownership in Yemen but once again cannot provide much data.

17 The sources for the statistics given here are Yemen's Ministry of Agriculture and Irrigation (MAI) agricultural statistics for the period 1997-2009 and World Bank, "Republic of Yemen Agricultural Strategy Note," Report No. 17973-YEM, 1999. It should be noted that the data available from the World Bank, "Agricultural Strategy Note," concerns only total tonnage for 1970-1996, not area, for barley, sorghum and maize. Furthermore, the data for 1970-1996 combines sorghum and millet as if a single crop, entered together on Figure 2. Nevertheless, this data has been incorporated here. The agricultural statistics published annually by the Ministry of Agriculture and Irrigation group crops into: grains, pulses, vegetables, fruit, qat, and cash crops (excluding qat, fruit, and vegetables).

18 For a fuller discussion of changes in cropping patterns, see Mundy et al., 'Neither Security nor Sovereignty."

19 See Philip McMichael, *Food Regimes and Agrarian Questions*, Halifax: Fernwood, 2013.

20 A landrace is a domesticated, regional ecotype; a locally adapted, traditional variety of a domesticated species of animal or plant that has developed over time, through adaptation to its natural and cultural environment of agriculture and pastoralism, and due to isolation from other populations of the species. (Wikipedia definition)

21 Yemen Ministry of Agriculture and Irrigation, *Agricultural Statistics Year Book 2007* (Sanaa: General Department of Statistics and Documentation, MAI, 2008).

22 Abdel-Warith Hazza, "Wheat Production Trade and Nutritional Level of Yemeni Population," *Yemeni Journal of Agricultural Research & Studies*, no. 19 (2009): 45–68.

23 These estimates are given in "FAO/WFP Crop and Food Security Assessment Mission to Yemen," FAO, Economic and Social Development Department, December 9, 2009, Table 4: http://www.fao.org/docrep/012/ak342e/ak342e00.htm

24 Ibid., Section 4.2.

25 The sources for agricultural statistics are either the Yemen Ministry of Agriculture and Irrigation year books or the WB's reports. The quality of statistics is poor and should be taken only as rough indicators.

26 YECO is the name for the former Military Economic Corporation (MECO), see Paul Dresch, *A History of Modern Yemen* (Cambridge: Cambridge University Press, 2000), 208. See also Sarah Phillips, "Yemen: Developmental Dysfunction and Division in a Crisis State," Developmental Leadership Program Research Paper 14, 2011, where she writes: "The climate for foreign investment is further undermined by President Saleh's insistence that the shadowy and unaudited Yemen Economic Corporation...be the local partner for prospective investors," p. 27. In note 71, Phillips writes that "YECO was established in the early 1970s and was initially owned by all military servicemen who contributed to its start-up capital, but was usurped and used as a commercial arm of the regime in the mid-1980s. It has business operations in a wide array of industries including basic commodities and foodstuffs, non-lethal military supplies, furniture, textiles, pharmaceuticals, agribusiness, (unlicensed) commercial fishing, and real estate. Many Yemeni observers view the corporation as a vast criminal enterprise." She also notes that "President Saleh used to be the head of YECO,'" but that it is now run by Ali al-Kohlani who "is the brother of Ahmed al-Kohlani (former governor of Aden and now the Minister of Parliamentary Affairs), who is President Saleh's father-in-law," note 71, p. 27.

27 Helen Lackner, *P.D.R. Yemen: Outpost of Socialist Development in Arabia* (London: Ithaca Press, 1985), 171–88.

28 Noel Brehony, *Yemen Divided: The Story of a Failed State in South Arabia* (London: I. B. Tauris, 2011), 71: "Under a law in 1977, qat could only be consumed at weekends and public holidays in Aden. In the qat-chewing area, Lahij and Abyan, it could be chewed at any time. It was banned in Hadramawt and Mahra, where at the time it was not widely consumed." Qat (*Catha edulis*) is a shrub, the leaves of which when chewed have amphetamine with mild hallucinogenic qualities; it is not a narcotic.

29 World Bank, "Republic of Yemen," 15: "2.18 There is a trend towards inequitable distribution of land in Yemen, with ownership increasingly concentrated in the hands of a few influential families. .... 2.20 There is a trend towards increasing private appropriation of communal land." And '2.23 In the southern governorates, in contrast, the holding of large agricultural land owners are expanding at the expense of small farmers. After unification rampant land grabbing occurred, often by influential and powerful figures," p. 16. It should be noted that calls to introduce comprehensive land registration in the unified Republic of the early 1990s were silenced by the 1994 war.

30 According to "A World Bank Country Study- People's Democratic Republic of Yemen, A Review of Economic and Social Development, March 1979," the total cultivated area was 76,985 ha in 1974, 65,678 ha in 1975, 83,344 ha in 1976 and 91,869 ha in 1977. (In the report figures were in acres, here converted into hectares.) By comparison in 1975 the figure for the North was 1,515,000 ha, i.e. according to these figures the cultivated area in the PDRY represented 4% of the total surface YAR+PDRY and North Yemen's cultivated area was 23 times larger than that of South Yemen's one although the total area of South Yemen was larger than that of the North (337,953 km2 according to the same document). In South Yemen, in 1975, there were 25,678 ha of cereals other than wheat, 7,508 ha of wheat, and 11,340 ha of cotton.

31 Yemen Ministry of Planning and International Cooperation, "Yemen's Third Socio-Economic Development Plan," 64 notes "Total annual renewable water resources are estimated at 2.5 billion cubic meters (1.500 billion m^3 of groundwater and 1billion m^3 surface water). However, total annual water consumption stands at 3.4 billion m^3, reflecting a groundwater depletion rate of 0.9 billion m^3 (138%) a year. On average, water tables in most aquifers drop by 6 meters a year, and are thus expected to run dry within 15-50 years...". Less pessimistic is the recent paper by Frank van Steenbergen, Omar Bamaga, and Adel al-Washali, "Groundwater Security in Yemen: Who Is Accountable to Whom?," *Law, Environment and Development Journal* 7, no. 2 (2011): 164, http://www.lead-journal.org/content/11164.pdf, which states some successes at the local level in regulating extraction from the aquifer by pumps and restrictions on the sinking of pumps.

32 See for example the discussion below of the GSCP Groundwater and Soil Conservation Project that began in 2004 and Yemen Ministry of Planning and International Cooperation, "Millennium Development Goals Needs Assessment: Yemen Country Report," 2005.

33 Yemen Arab Republic, "Final Report on the Airphoto Interpretation Project of the Swiss Technical Co-operation Service, Berne Carried out for the Central Planning Organisation, Şanʿāʾ," Zurich, 1978, 13, concerning the region of Turbah south of Taiz notes: "In 1977 some farmers reported that they have stopped the cultivation of wheat because imported wheat is much cheaper than that which is locally produced."

34 Yemen Ministry of Planning and International Cooperation, "Millennium Development Goals Needs Assessment: Yemen Country Report," 2005.

35 UNDP Regional Bureau for Arab States, "Development Challenges for the Arab Region: Food Security and Agriculture," vol. 2 (Cairo, 2009).

36 See Mundy et al., "Neither Security nor Sovereignty."

37 See the useful analysis of the 2014 budget by Muhammad Abduh al-Absi, "Dirasa fi mizaniyyat al-dawla li-amm 2014: http://www.mohamedalabsi.blogspot.com/2014/01/2014_2298.html

38 See Claire Beaugrand, "Une économie en perpétuel sursis," in *Yémen Le Tournant Révolutionnaire*, ed. Laurent Bonnefoy, Franck Mermier, and Marine Poirier, 179–200 (Sanaa and Paris: Cefas-Karthala, 2012).

39 By the late 1990s extension programmes were generally not active, presumably because the whole sector had come to be organized in foreign-funded 'projects'. The history of extension services under the Ministry of Agriculture and Irrigation needs to be documented.

40 Projects are the 1) Tihama Environment Protection Project (TEPP), 2) Southern Governorates Rural Development Project (SGRDP), 3) Raymah Area Development Project (RADP), 4) Al-Mahrah Rural Development Project (AMRDP), 5) Dhamar Participatory Rural Development Project (DPRDP), 6) Al-Dhala Community Resources Management Project (ADCRMP), 7) Pilot Community-Based Rural Infrastructure Project for Highland Areas (RIP), 8) Rainfed Agriculture and Livestock Project (RALP), and 9) Agrobiodiversity and Climate Adaptation Project.

41 http://www.ifpri.org/sites/default/files/publications/yemennote1en.pdf

42 http://www.yemenwater.org/wp-content/uploads/2013/05/1-GEN-Cover-ToC-and-Introduction-December-17th-2008-FINAL.pdf

43 Quoted from the Summary Interim Update of NASS, p. 18, "Implementation structures" section.

44 *Ibid*, pp. 18-19, "Implementation structures" section.

45 *Ibid*, p. 20, "Investment program" section.

46 Quoted from the GAFSP Project Proposal for Yemen, p. 7, in "Investment program for agriculture" section.

47 *Ibid*, p. 12, "1.4 Planned composition and level of spending to implement the components" section.

48 *Ibid*, p. 13, "1.5 Financing sources and gaps" section.

49 *Ibid*, p. 15, "Investment program" section. In fact the SFD is entirely foreign-funded.

50 The proposal discussed in this paragraph is available here (accessed 26 January 2015): http://www.gafspfund.org/sites/gafspfund.org/files/Documents/4.%20Yemen%20Proposal.pdf

51 For more on GASFP in Yemen: http://www.gafspfund.org/content/yemen. GAFSP is a multilateral program assisting in "the implementation of pledges made by the G20 in Pittsburgh in September 2009. The objective is to address the underfunding of country and regional agriculture and food security strategic investment plans already being developed by countries in consultation with donors and other stakeholders at the country-level". It receives contributions from ten donors, from the private and public sectors, including the "Bill and Melinda Gates Foundation".

52 *Ibid*, p. 20, "Target area and population" section.

53 The final version of NASS, p. 2.

54 *Ibid*, p. 4.

55 Idem.

56 *Ibid*, p. 5, "The National Agriculture Sector Strategy (NASS) and the NASS Update 2013" section.

57 NASS also includes two Appendixes: A) National Agriculture Sector Strategy – Implementation Plan (NASS-IP 2102-2016) and B) Preparation of the National Agriculture Sector Strategy.

58 The final NASS is available here: http://www.agriculture.gov.ye/PDF/NASS_Final_March2012_%20 En.pdf

The Summary Interim Update was available at the same link prior to the final one.

59 Quoted from the Summary Interim Update of NASS, p. 4, in "Agriculture and the Yemeni economy" section.

60 *Ibid*, p. 4, "Agriculture and the Yemeni economy" section.

61 *Ibid*, p. 4, "Agriculture and the Yemeni economy" section.

62 Quoted from the GAFSP Project Proposal for Yemen, p. 4, "1.1 Objectives and indicators" section.

63 *Ibid*, p. 10, "1.3 Plan components to achieve the objectives" section.

64 *Ibid*, p. 23, "box 1.1 Land and water management and improvement".

65 Clearly milk production has also been affected by importation of subsidized processed milk products, but we are not discussing it here as we do not have access to relevant data.

66 World Bank, "Yemen Arab Republic: Development of a Traditional Economy," World Bank country study (Washington DC: World Bank, 1979), 32. The report added that "the declared policy of the Government to become self-sufficient in food-grain production no longer seems appropriate in the light of YAR's large foreign exchange earnings which have removed earlier constraints to the importation of basic foodstuffs." Idem.

67 See previous note.

68 See Jason Hickel, "The Donors' Dilemma - Aid in Reverse: How Poor Countries Develop Rich Countries": http://www.globalpolicyjournal.com/blog/12/12/2013/donors%E2%80%99-dilemma-aid-reverse-how-poor-countries-develop-rich-countries

69 "International aid flows to Yemen are dwarfed by outward capital flows, with tax havens facilitating capital flight. For every dollar spent on aid in Yemen between 1990 and 2008, another $2.70 left the country." Ginny Hill, Peter Salisbury, et al., *Yemen: Corruption, Capital Flight and Global Drivers of Conflict* (London: Chatham House, 2013), xi.

References

Beaugrand, Claire. "Une économie en perpétuel sursis." In *Yémen Le Tournant Révolutionnaire*, edited by Laurent Bonnefoy, Franck Mermier, and Marine Poirier, 179–200. Sanaa and Paris: Cefas-Karthala, 2012.

Brehony, Noel. *Yemen Divided: The Story of a Failed State in South Arabia*. London: I. B. Tauris, 2011.

Clements, Ashley Jonathan. "Yemen: Fragile Lives in Hungry Times." Oxfam Briefing Paper no. 152 (September 2011): http://www.oxfam.org/sites/www.oxfam.org/files/bp152-yemen-fragile-lives-hungry-times-190911-summ-en.pdf

Corm, Georges. "The Political Economy of Democratic Transition in the Arab Situation." *Contemporary Arab Affairs* 8, no. 1 (2015): 22–38: http://www.tandfonline.com/doi/pdf/10.1080/17550912.2014.976403

Dresch, Paul. *A History of Modern Yemen*. Cambridge: Cambridge University Press, 2000.

FAO. *Special Report, FAO/WFP Crop and Food Security Assessment Mission to Yemen*. Rome: FAO Economic and Social Development Department, December 2009: http://www.fao.org/docrep/012/ak342e/ak342e00.htm

Hazza, Abdel-Warith. "Wheat Production Trade and Nutritional Level of Yemeni Population." *Yemeni Journal of Agricultural Research & Studies*, no. 19 (2009): 45–68.

IFPRI. *Yemen National Food Security Strategy, Overview and Action Plan*, 2011: http://www.ifpri.org/sites/default/files/publications/yemennote1en.pdf

Kanbeck, Jens. "Land Disputes in Yemen." In *Why Yemen Matters: A Society in Transition*, edited by Helen Lackner, 197–212. London: Saqi Books, 2014.

Karner, Milan. "Water Scarcity and Human Security in Yemen, Assessing the Causes and Consequences of Yemen's Water Crisis." *Middle East Perspectives*, NUS/MEI, 1 (2014): 17–47: https://mei.nus.edu.sg/index.php/web/publications_TMPL/Perspectives-2-Water-Scarcity-and-Human-Security-in-Yemen

Lackner, Helen. *P.D.R. Yemen: Outpost of Socialist Development in Arabia*. London: Ithaca Press, 1985.
McMichael, Philip. *Food Regimes and Agrarian Questions*. Halifax: Fernwood, 2013.
Mundy, Martha. "Tihama II Project: Monitoring and Evaluation Report." Washington. Ministry of Agriculture, Yemen Arab Republic, and World Bank/Kuwait Fund, 1980.
Mundy, Martha. "Agricultural Development in the Yemeni Tihama: The Past Ten Years." In *Economy, Society and Culture in Contemporary Yemen*, edited by B. R. Pridham, 22–40.London: Croom Helm, 1985: http://www.athimar.org/Article-48#sthash.pPV3PfbJ.dpuf
Mundy, Martha, Amin al-Hakimi, and Frédéric Pelat. "Neither Security nor Sovereignty: The Political Economy of Food in Yemen." In *Food Security in the Arab World*, edited by Zahra Babar and Suzi Mirgani, 137–59. London: Hurst, 2014.
Phillips, Sarah. "Yemen: Developmental Dysfunction and Division in a Crisis State." Developmental Leadership Program Research Paper no. 14, 2011: http://publications.dlprog.org/Yemen,%20Developmental%20Dysfunction%20and%20Division%20in%20a%20Crisis%20State.pdf
Republic of Yemen. *NWSSIP, National Water Sector Strategy and Investment Programme Update*, 2008: http://www.yemenwater.org/wp-content/uploads/2013/05/1-GEN-Cover-ToC-and-Introduction-December-17th-2008-FINAL.pdf
Smith, Neil. *Uneven Development: Nature, Capital and the Production of Space*. Athens: University of Georgia Press, (1984) 2008.
Transfeld, Marieke. "Yemen's GCC Roadmap to Nowhere: Elite Bargaining and Political Infighting Block a Meaningful Transition." SWP Comments no. 20. Berlin: German Institute for International and Security Affairs, 2014: http://www.swp-berlin.org/fileadmin/contents/products/comments/2014C20_tfd.pdf
UNDP Regional Bureau for Arab States. *Development Challenges for the Arab Region: Food Security and Agriculture*, vol. 2. Cairo, Egypt, 2009.
van der Ploeg, Jan Douwe. *Peasants and the Art of Farming: A Chayanovian Manifesto*. Halifax: Fernwood, 2013.
van Steenbergen, Frank, Philip Lawrence, Abraham Mehari Haile, Maher Salman, and Jean-Marc Faurès. "Guidelines on Spate Irrigation." FAO Irrigation and Drainage Paper no. 65. Rome: FAO, 2010: http://www.fao.org/docrep/012/i1680e/i1680e.pdf
van Steenbergen, Frank, Omar Bamaga, and Adel al-Washali. "Groundwater Security in Yemen: Who is Accountable to Whom?" *Law, Environment and Development Journal* 7, no. 2 (2011). 164-179: http://www.lead-journal.org/content/11164.pdf
Weiss, Matthew I. "A Perfect Storm: The Causes and Consequences of Severe Water Scarcity, Institutional Breakdown and Conflict in Yemen." *Water International* 40, no. 2 (2015): 251–72: http://www.tandfonline.com/doi/full/10.1080/02508060.2015.1004898#.VNI4Fy4Rrl4
World Bank. *Yemen Arab Republic: Development of a Traditional Economy*. Country Study PUB-2057. Washington, DC: World Bank, 1979: http://www-wds.worldbank.org/external/default/WDSContentServer/WDSP/IB/2001/01/26/000178830_98101903334593/Rendered/PDF/multi_page.pdf
World Bank. *A World Bank Country Study – People's Democratic Republic of Yemen, A Review of Economic and Social Development*. Country Study PUB-2151. Washington, DC: World Bank, 1979: http://www-wds.worldbank.org/servlet/WDSContentServer/IW3P/IB/2001/01/26/000178830_98101903334798/Rendered/PDF/multi_page.pdf
World Bank. *Republic of Yemen Agricultural Strategy Note*. Report no. 17973-YEM. Washington, DC: World Bank, 1999: http://www-wds.worldbank.org/external/default/WDSContentServer/IW3P/IB/1999/09/14/000094946_9906260530330/Rendered/INDEX/multi_page.txt
World Bank. *Republic of Yemen: Country Social Analysis*. Report no. 34008-YE. Washington: World Bank, 2006: http://siteresources.worldbank.org/EXTSOCIALDEV/Resources/3177394-1168615404141/YemenCountrySocialAnalysis.pdf
World Food Programme. *The State of Food Security and Nutrition in Yemen: Comprehensive Food Security Survey*, 2012: http://documents.wfp.org/stellent/groups/public/documents/ena/wfp247832.pdf

Yemen Ministry of Agriculture and Irrigation. *Agricultural Statistics Year Book 2007*. Sanaa: General Department of Statistics and Documentation, MAI, 2008.

Yemen Ministry of Agriculture and Irrigation. *NASS, National Agricultural Sector Strategy: A Promising Sector for Diversified Economy in Yemen: 2012–2016*. Sanaa: MAI, March 2012: http://www.agriculture.gov.ye/PDF/NASS_Final_March2012_%20En.pdf

Yemen Ministry of Agriculture and Irrigation. "GAFSP Proposal -Republic of Yemen, Proposal for Yemen: Smallholder Agricultural Productivity Enhancement Program, Phase One Roll Out of National Agriculture Sector Strategy (NASS) for Yemen's Efforts towards Achieving Food Security under Global Agriculture and Food Security Program." Sanaa: MAI, June 2013: http://www.gafspfund.org/sites/gafspfund.org/files/Documents/4.%20Yemen%20Proposal.pdf

Yemen Ministry of Planning and International Cooperation. *Yemen's Third Socio-Economic Development Plan for Poverty Reduction (2006–2010)*. Sanaa: MoPIC, 2006.

Yemen Ministry of Planning and International Cooperation. *Millennium Development Goals Needs Assessment: Yemen Country Report*. Sanaa: MoPIC, 2005: http://planipolis.iiep.unesco.org/upload/Yemen/Yemen_MDG_2005.pdf

Yemen Arab Republic. "Final Report on the Airphoto Interpretation Project of the Swiss Technical Co-operation Service, Berne Carried out for the Central Planning Organisation, Ṣanʿāʾ." Zurich, 1978.

Appendix

Table 1 Yemen Population and Cereal Needs and Production

Years	Estimated national population	Theoretical national cereal needs	Local cereal contribution	Local wheat contribution
1990	12.2 million	1 952 000 t	39.3%	7.9%
1993	14.5 million	2 320 000 t	35.6%	6.9%
1998	17.1 million	2 736 000 t	30.5%	6.1%
2001	18.7 million	2 992 000 t	23.4%	5.1%
2007	21.6 million	3 456 000 t	27.2%	6.3%
2009	22 million	3 520 000 t	20.1%	4.3%

Source: Data compiled and Calculations made from Yemen's Ministry of Agriculture and Irrigation Agricultural Statistics (Year Book) and FAO *Special Report, FAO/WFP Crop and Food Security Assessment Mission to Yemen,* FAO Economic and Social Development Department, Dec. 2009

Table 2 Table Summarizing NASS Budget Requests (in USD million)

Objectives	Full investment program	Priority investment program
Integrated delivery of community-based investments and services (targeting SO1 and SO2)	(MAI) 325.5	(MAI) 325.5
SO1: increase production, food security and climate resilience	(MAI) 1,071.5	(MAI) 138.5
SO2: fight rural poverty and malnutrition	214.0	204.2
Sub-total MAI program	1,611.6	668.2
Other agriculture and development programmes (not MAI)	(not MAI) 632.5	(not MAI) 632.5
Total MAI and non-MAI programmes	2,244.0	1,300.8

Source: Yemen's Ministry of Agriculture and Irrigation. *NASS, National Agricultural Sector Strategy: A Promising Sector for Diversified Economy in Yemen: 2012-2016* and Yemen's Ministry of Agriculture and Irrigation. *GAFSP Proposal-Republic of Yemen, Proposal for Yemen: Smallholder Agricultural Productivity Enhancement Program, Phase One Roll Out of National Agriculture Sector Strategy (NASS)* (Links available in References)

6

Yemen Urban Water: Extreme Challenges, Practical Solutions, and Lessons for the Future from the Case of Taiz

James Firebrace

Scene Setting: Taiz in the Wider Context of Yemeni Groundwater Depletion

This paper is largely based on substantial in-country research conducted by James Firebrace Associates[1] and funded by the British Conflict Prevention Pool. The study was the first to look comprehensively into the wider social, economic and organisational aspects of urban water scarcity. Research took place from late 2010 to early 2014, a period of great turmoil in Yemen. When relative peace returned in 2012 after Yemen's 'Arab Spring' uprising, the extreme water predicament of Taiz was soon back at the top of the national agenda. However at time of writing in early 2015, security issues and the stability and legitimacy of national government were once again dominant concerns.

The city of Taiz is now facing a water scarcity challenge of such magnitude that it not only imposes great hardship on the majority of its citizens but also threatens the local economy and this great city's ultimate viability. Taiz has the unenviable distinction of being the most water challenged city in the world. It has long attracted the attention of international water experts, and is considered by many to be the ultimate 'iconic' challenge[2]. Even within the Yemen context, Taiz faces extreme water scarcity - an increasingly saline and undrinkable resource at high altitude in a poor country facing a raft of political and economic problems and a history of conflict over water often resolved through violence. This has led some commentators to put forward the most drastic of solutions, including the enforced relocation of the city's population to the coast or the military occupation and control of surrounding hinterland where groundwater can still be found. This paper argues that such solutions are neither realistic nor necessary.

The origins of Yemen's urban water crises lie in aquifer depletion combined with population growth caused by high birth rates and migration to the cities. Yemeni cities have found individual and often highly entrepreneurial and inventive solutions. By mapping the progressive deterioration of the Taiz water supply over time we show that there is now little further potential for demand management as the quantities used by households and industry are already so heavily constrained. While some supply wells are within Yemeni city limits, most are outside in rural areas. The cities taking water from the hinterland puts them in conflict with local farmers. These conflicts flare up easily, leading to cessation of pumping and thus even greater shortages in the city. Taiz again has seen the worst of these conflicts.

While there are a range of options for improving Taiz's water supply, our research has indicated that the only sustainable way forward in practice is to bring desalinated water to the city from the coast. Other supply options can contribute to the overall solution under an Integrated Water Resource Management approach.

The economic impact of extreme water scarcity particularly affects Taiz's large and well-developed industrial sector. The uncertainty of supply and negotiation needed to secure water have deterred investment and led to a fear for the very future of Taiz. The city's population will inevitably continue to grow rapidly, adding to its vulnerability. Conversely the provision of new water will have a major impact on businesses, investment and jobs, and hence support Yemen's political and economic stability.

The possibility is often raised that Yemen's highland urban centers, including Sanaa the capital itself, will in time no longer be viable and that a population shift to the coast will be inevitable. There are numerous examples from history where lack of water has led to the collapse of a city or indeed of an entire civilization[3]. However significant population shifts are unlikely in the short to medium term – there are many constraints on the major investment that would be required in businesses, plant and essential infrastructure to create the jobs to make such a population relocation viable.

Solutions bringing desalinated water from the coast to the highland cities have been too readily dismissed as 'unaffordable'[4] without a serious analysis of actual costs and the reality of concerns about the potential vulnerability of pipelines to future political conflict. In the case of Taiz such anxieties are overblown and misplaced. Affordability of desalinated water is indeed a key issue, but with good planning and adhering to a number of key conditions, this water will be both 'affordable' to Taiz households and financially sustainable; poorer households will benefit more than the better off.

Taiz's lower altitude, at around 1,000 metres, and location in an area of relative stability give it cost and security advantages over highland cities at greater altitudes. Furthermore in Taiz most groundwater is now undrinkable because of high salinity (unlike many other cities), and a desalinated supply overcomes this key problem. The situation of each city and town in Yemen will be different, and each will in time need to find its own solution to groundwater depletion, tuned to local circumstances.

Taiz's extreme water challenge can indeed be solved, and that this is achievable (albeit once Yemen moves on from current political uncertainties), even in the current context of an under-performing local utility demoralized by the dwindling and polluted resource it is tasked to manage.

Conflict Issues around Taiz Water

City – Hinterland Conflicts over Water

The key conflict over water for Taiz City is between the local utility and the rural areas from which it seeks to draw its water[5]. One area in particular, Haima to the north-east of Taiz (see *Figure 4* towards end of this article), has been a constant source of tension, erupting occasionally into armed confrontation.

The Haima story has been pivotal in the development of Taiz water. While the drilling in the Haima / Habir area in the mid-1990s 'rescued' Taiz from its first major water crisis, it sowed the seeds of mistrust and unrest that have characterised the situation ever since. The situation remains unresolved – tense, unstable and clearly unsustainable. It resurfaced in early 2013 when local communities forced an extended closure of the utility's Haima well fields. Utility water supplies were massively reduced and there were serious implications for water quality as the utility compensated by using water from the highly saline aquifers of Hawban and Hawgala.

Another nearby area, Wadi Warazan to the south, became the scene of a major standoff in the late 1990s between armed tribesmen and the crew of a drilling rig hired by the local utility, leading to the hurried intervention of the governor and the withdrawal of the rig[6]. Following the Haima experience the people of other hinterland areas were not going to allow 'their' water to be taken for city supplies without a major showdown. Since then the Taiz Water and Sanitation Local Corporation (TWSLC) has been unable to extend its drilling to new areas.

With mobile phones now ubiquitous, it is even easier to mount an effective opposition by summoning armed tribesmen to 'defend' local community water rights. The 'Three Wadis Drilling Project' which a decade ago showed some promise, no longer has the substantial volumes required for viability and, given the potential for conflict with those dependent for livelihoods on existing groundwater, is most unlikely to be undertaken.

The reality is that the local water table in the Taiz hinterland is in relentless decline, limiting the groundwater quantities available in all existing extraction areas and raising the prospects of increasingly severe conflict over access to water. In many areas the annual extraction is limited to pumping up the year's infiltrated rainfall. Two successive years of poor rainfall, which is more likely with the increased variability brought by climate change, could lead to even more serious conflict than that witnessed to date.

Climate Change, Tipping Points and Food Vulnerability

The most authoritative recent study on climate change in Yemen[7] reports "that temperatures will steadily rise and that there is likely to be an increase in variability and intensity of rainfall". Rising temperatures mean higher water requirements for household drinking and washing. Higher evaporation rates lead to reduced groundwater recharge. Climatic variability and unpredictability will produce more extreme events. Intense rainfall results in lower groundwater recharge for the same volume of rain. Flooding and fast flowing water through the wadis lead to greater losses of water (and of soil) from the catchment area.

Pumping of groundwater has been a feature of rural Yemen since the 1980s and has proved difficult to control despite numerous attempts to regulate and license drilling. A growing consensus is that Yemen's groundwater reserves are likely to be depleted in the next two or three decades[8], and the effect of this on the Yemeni economy - a potential reduction in agricultural incomes by as much as 40% - is likely to dwarf climate change impacts. With groundwater depletion furthest advanced in the Taiz governorate, the region can be seen as a bellwether for the country as a whole and an example of the need for radical measures to be taken.

Yemen's rural population is already highly dependent on cash sales of produce, both food and non-food, and on remittances home from family members in the cities[9] or working overseas. The Taiz governorate has traditionally been an area of high emigration. Yemen is experiencing very high rates of food vulnerability particularly outside the cities, with 27% of rural populations judged 'severely food insecure' as opposed to 9% for the urban population[10]. Within the rural population, agricultural wage labor is the sector most vulnerable with 37% food insecure. Food vulnerability has been driven by water scarcity but also by escalating international food prices. Looking forward, the greatest impact of climate change on Yemen may prove to be from the expected rise in global food prices rather than direct impacts on domestic agriculture[11].

Conflict Mitigation Looking Ahead

Ensuring Significant Benefits for the City Population from Desalinated Water

Our assessments for Taiz indicate that the delivery of desalinated water will benefit the population very substantially. It will end uncertainty over supply and lead to radically better quality water, removing the need for a dual supply between drinking quality and undrinkable water. Most importantly given low incomes, household expenditure on water will be reduced by the use of less expensive water from new tankers, lower costs for water provided by private networks, and the removal of the need for expensive drinking water from local desalination units. Additional benefits will include the opportunity for industrial revitalization, improvement of health by the supply of clean unpolluted water, and freeing children and women from fetching and carrying water.

The key issue for the transition will be keeping the consumer price of new water as low as possible. The most important drivers of price are the scale of future demand, the cost of energy, the extent to which capital grants or soft loans are obtained for investment in infrastructure and the size of the potential cross subsidy from industry and other high-volume consumers. Poorer households will benefit more than the better off, as they currently have to spend a higher proportion of household expenditure on expensive drinkable water from local desalination units (*kawthers*) dispersed throughout the city.

Winners and Losers Within the Water Sector

Based on future broad estimates of employment in the water sector, there will be far-reaching change. The key issues will be:

- the need to address the over-staffing of the utility (the para-governmental supplier distributing through a piped network) where major reforms will be necessary
- initially at least there will be a major shift from tankers collecting water from wells to tankers distributing from the new tanker filling points for the desalinated water.
- private or community networks that will be major beneficiaries from the arrival of new water
- The local *kawther* water purifiers will experience the most major change as they will be unable to compete with cheaper and better quality water.

Pipeline Communities and Pipeline Security

This has been a major concern for the international community, alarmed at the sabotage of oil pipelines and electricity lines from Marib in the east of Yemen. However the situation is different for a Taiz pipeline supplied from Mokha on the Red Sea coast, as it will run through areas where the local people have a very different history of settling tribal grievances, have a different relationship to regional and central authority, and often have close relatives living in the city.

The dedicated study we made on this issue showed that the villages along the pipeline route often have poorly functioning water projects, and in a few cases, no water supply apart from tankers. Generally, the water quality was found to be good, although this may well change as villages and small towns grow and groundwater over-extraction becomes a problem. The best conflict avoidance measure is to provide these communities with support to their current water projects, where necessary upgrading existing infrastructure and allowing access to the new desalinated water at low cost. This would also provide compensation for any disruption from building works during construction, including the relocation of a market. These measures should be implemented well before the arrival of desalinated water to Taiz. Such small and relatively inexpensive projects should be branded as part of the Taiz desalination scheme so that the link is clear to beneficiaries. They could be financed separately by a donor with rural water as a funding priority.

Extraction Zone Communities

Extraction from the best of existing wells should continue after the arrival of new desalinated water and will play an important role in keeping down the price for utility-connected households. Future treated waste water could be piped to areas like Haima and Wadi Dhabab to support agriculture there as compensation for continued extraction.

The Need for New Water: A City Adapts to Extreme Water Scarcity

Taiz Coping Strategies in the Face of Extreme Water Scarcity

Far-reaching measures are now taken by Taiz households to adapt to a situation of extreme scarcity. Over the years a thriving water economy has developed in parallel to the local utility (TWSLC) to ensure households across the city get enough water for general use, and enough of drinkable quality.

With only half the city covered by utility supply and with infrequent and irregular delivery, households must use expensive tankered water. Both utility and most tankered water is of very poor quality (well below the WHO standard[12]), so households must buy drinking-quality water from *kawthers*. In 2013 these accounted for some 40 to 60% of household expenditure on water. The poor paid a higher percentage within the household budget: whilst they could economize by cutting water for washing they still needed to buy water for drinking. In practice the extent of this expenditure is less visible within household expenditure as *dabba*s (small 5 to 20 litre plastic containers) of *kawther* water are now bought regularly from local retail outlets as part of the household shopping.

Rainwater collection is extensive, but limited to those that can afford the roof tanks and pipework or who have access to the external space needed for rainwater collection and storage. Some households, particularly in the vicinity of Jebel Sabir to the south, have access to free spring water. The poorest households rely on free water from mosques, wellheads or from the houses of the rich.

Best Estimates for Quantity and Quality of Water Consumed in Taiz

The surveys conducted in 2010 produced for the first time broad estimates of the extent of water use and of consumer prices in Taiz. Much had changed when in 2013 we compared the current situation with our earlier results, but also extended the analysis to 'Greater Taiz', including the extensive new housing areas beyond the traditional city. This wider city now has a total estimated population of close to 840,000 and an estimated annual growth rate of around 3.5% in central areas and 7% in the outlying areas where most new building is taking place.

We also reviewed in more detail the crucial 'affordability' question. Asking direct questions in the 2010 household interviews on incomes and 'willingness to pay' had proved unsatisfactory in spite of using best practice methodologies. In 2013 a new range of questions was therefore included to assess household income and thence the percentage of this spent on water. With water competing with other items of the household budget, particularly food, rent and electricity, this percentage spend was judged to be the prime determinant of 'affordability'. In both surveys the challenge was how to best interpret the answers given by households during interviews on their doorsteps, as against the responses of the various water suppliers, as perceptions were often widely different. Further in-depth interviews, with the time to really assess what was going on, allowed better judgements on the likely reality.

Household Water Usage

Household usage from the survey totalled 19,600m3/d across Greater Taiz, comprising

- Local utility (TWSLC) 8,000m3/d (41%) but delivered once every 4 to 12 weeks with longer intervals for homes at higher elevations requiring greater pressure
- Private tankers 7,500m3/d (38%)
- *Kawther* local purification units, 1,500m3/d (8%)
- Other, private networks, free water, bottled water and rooftop collection 2,500m3/d (13%).

Per capita consumption averaged only 23 litres per person per day (l/c/d[13]) overall for Greater Taiz, with higher consumption for those households with TWSLC connections and therefore access to cheap water, and less than this for those located outside the area served by the utility. The World Health Organization (WHO) recommended minimum is 50 l/c/d.

Quality of water is a major issue in Taiz and obtaining drinking quality water through the kawther suppliers is a major expense. TWSLC water salinity and contamination was measured at 5,600 µS/cm, which is almost four times over the WHO minimum quality standard of 1,500 µS/cm. Tanker water was little better, although some wells used by tankers, such as in Wadi Dhabab, were relatively non-saline (and consumers were prepared to pay more).

Industry and Business Water Usage

The survey included an assessment of water used by hotels, restaurants, hospitals, mosques and government. Total consumption over the city was estimated at 5,700m^3/d, supplied by

- Hayel Saeed mini-desalination plant at Mokha 3,200m^3/d (56%)
- Tankers drawing from local wells 1,500m^3/d (26%)
- TWSLC supply 1,000m^3/d (17%).

Table 1 Trends in Taiz Water Use 1996-2013 (best estimates)

Taiz Data	1996	2004	2010	2013
Population Greater Taiz '000	320,000	570,000	750,000	840,000
TWSLC (piped water)				
TWSLC Water Sold Mm^3/yr	2.4	4.1	4.5	2.9
No of water connections	30,000	41,465	47,357	50,276
No of sewerage connections	20,000	26,000	36,000	40,000
% Population of Greater Taiz served	72%	56%	49%	46%
TWSLC total water supplied in Taiz m^3/day	4,406	11,400	12,900	8,000
TWSLC Water Quality EC μS/cm	2,000	3,500	4,000	5,600
TWSLC Water Delivery Interval (weeks)	2-3	2-3	4	4 - 12
Tankers				
Tanker users (% households)	28%	48%	58%	80%
Tanker price riyals / $3m^3$ (average over year)	650	1000	2150	2900
Tanker deliveries to Taiz households m^3/d	960	2,850	6000	7500
Number of tankers operating in Greater Taiz (all)	70	200	480	740
Kawther water				
Dabba users (% households)	5%	75%	85%	84%
Dabba Water price riyals / 10litres	15	20	40	50
Dabba water total m^3/d	500	900	1,300	1,600
Other water (private networks, free water, springs, rooftop harvesting, bottled)				
Other water total supplied m^3/d	1,200	1,800	2,200	2,500
Totals (LC + Tanker + Kawther + Other)				
Total supply to Greater Taiz m^3/d	7,066	16,950	22,400	19,600
l/c/d over whole population	22.1	29.7	29.9	23.3

Source: JFA Research Report "Reducing Conflict through the Provision of Affordable Water and Increased Employment in Taiz, Final report April 2014" (funded by the UK's Conflict Prevention Pool)

Escalating Prices: Water Payments a Heavy Burden on Household Budgets

The price of water to consumers varies considerably depending on the source and quality. TWSLC charges \$0.9/m^3 average (over all tariff bands) for water of poor to very poor quality, none drinkable. Tankers charge USD 4.5/m^3 average, but this varies with season, size of tanker, distance from source, and quality (some drinkable quality from wells in Wadi Dhabab, the rest undrinkable). *Kawther* water costs \$USD 23/m^3 average, with again some variation depending on season and size of container.

Household expenditure on water is estimated in the 5% to 15% range for 80% of the population of Greater Taiz with some households at the poorer end spending as much as 20%. Households at the time of the 2013 survey were spending in the range 3,500 to 7,500 Yemeni riyals monthly on water depending on household income, with the average at 4,500 per month.[14]

Taiz Water – From Bad to Worse, a Humanitarian Emergency in Waiting

Our surveys of 2010 and 2013 and the extensive data collected by team member Dr Chris Handley during the late 1990s to early 2000s[15] provided the opportunity to assess longer term trends as well as recent developments. Reality checks were carried out by interviewing local professionals with a close experience of the water sector throughout this period.

As Table 1 above shows, the situation degraded very considerably over this last decade. In particular there has been an accelerated deterioration since from January 2011 as a result of the instability and strife of the political transition, exacerbated by higher fuel prices and continued conflict with the rural water-supplying areas. Many consider that the Taiz water situation has already reached the point where it should be declared a humanitarian emergency.

Utility Household Supply

The TWSLC has had some success in increasing the number of piped connections (to over 50,000 households), but with the population of Greater Taiz growing fast, the percentage connected had dropped to 46% from a high of around 70% in the late 1990s. The utility's supply faced many problems in 2013 (the last year in the above table), in particular the resumed conflict with Haima, which led to a steep drop in total water supplies to around 8,000m^3/d and increased extraction from the highly saline and polluted Hawgala aquifer. Water quality has continued to deteriorate, and there has been a dramatic fall in the interval between deliveries - which has quadrupled in the last decade from some two weeks to around two months. This interval can reach three months or more for those living at higher altitudes within their supply zone.

Cartoon in *al-Jumhuriyya*, Nov 2013, showing Taiz's current dependence on tankered water, while piped connections deliver only once every two months.

Tankers

With the decline in utility supply there has been a massive increase in the number of tankers supplying households with well water, probably now to over 500. Tanker prices continue to rise (driven by scarcity and rising fuel costs) and have reached around 4,000 Yemeni riyals for a $3m^3$ tanker (this varies according to season and the distance to the house), a rise of 35% in three years. It is now three times the price it was a decade ago.

Kawther Water

This locally desalinated / purified drinking water is now used by 85% of households (all but the very poor), and has been a feature of Taiz life ever since the first serious deterioration in the quality of water over a decade ago. Prices have now reached 50 riyals for a 10 litre dabba, an increase of 20% over the last three years and now are 2.5 times the price a decade ago.

Overall

Taiz households have reacted to the escalating prices by trying to get by with progressively less water (average now 23 l/c/d, down from a high of around 30 l/c/d in the 2005-2010 period.) This highlights the very limited amounts of water now being used by the Taiz population, with the average amount being less than half the WHO recommended minimum. It also underlines the fact that there is very limited potential for further water conservation at household level; most households are already operating well below what is desirable.

Alternative Sources of Water, Limited Conventional Options

In 2010 our research trawled all available water supply studies and, with the local office of the National Water Resource Agency (NWRA), we estimated the contribution each source of supply could make in the future and the likely issues each faced. None could provide a sustainable long-term solution for Taiz. This left coastal desalination as the only viable long-term option, but combined as far as possible with other cheaper (but limited) supply options to bring unit prices down.

In 2013 we reviewed our earlier 2010 work, and concluded that the options had narrowed yet further. The various supply options, along with the issues faced by each, are:

Mokha – Taiz Desalination

We have analyzed this desalination option in considerable detail. It will provide abundant supplies of good quality water. Capital support will be necessary to deliver affordable water and the distribution of water in Taiz will require careful planning. Support for the water supply projects in the pipeline communities should be integrated within the desalination project. In the long term such a project will contribute to rising salinity in the Red Sea, but Yemen's contribution to this (compared with the much larger schemes in Saudi Arabia) will be tiny.

New Dams in the Wadi Rasyan Catchment

Dams could make a contribution, but volumes are limited and only available seasonally. There is a dam at al-Amira, the only suitable location, which operates in the wet season only and is already badly silted up. There is a poor history of success for dams and their viability would need to be carefully demonstrated. Potential problems with dams generally include silting, leakages and water evaporation. There are also potential major conflict problems with downstream users in the catchment.

Hawban / Hawgala Desalination of Brackish Groundwater

This area is already extensively used by the city (both TWSLC and tankers) and by local villages for irrigation. It is now highly stressed and polluted. There is a major environmental challenge in managing the city's waste water, which ultimately consists of polluted saline residues, now flowing through this area. Volumes of waste water will increase once a new desalinated water supply is operational which would mean that such a project would then become more economically attractive. However the aquifer is unlikely to be replenished as all potential recharge water is increasingly put to use in urban areas. This project would face severe conflict management issues with agricultural users.

Burayhi Sewage Treatment

Currently waste water no longer reaches Burayhi, although this could change when greater volumes are used in the city following a desalination scheme. The output from a treatment plant would only be acceptable for agriculture, but would support groundwater recharge. It would require satisfactory sewerage infrastructure in Greater Taiz. Importantly such a scheme does offer the potential for compensating communities where water is extracted, such as Haima.

New TWSLC Drilling in the Three Wadis Earlier Identified

This is not viable in practice and would generate considerable conflict. Recent assessments indicate that only small quantities would be available and would need to be pumped uphill from distances of 45 to 60 kilometres from Taiz. Even less water would be available if local communities were also supplied as occurs in existing rural-urban transfers. TWSLC's earlier plans have now been abandoned and the NWRA no longer see this as an option.

Run-Off Management, Especially of Flood Waters

This has some limited potential. The run-off water from rainfall presently ends up in the Hawban-Hawgala-Amira area where it is already captured. Whilst roads could be surfaced with material allowing water penetration this would be extremely expensive. Household recharge pits could be encouraged, but these are expensive, silt up, fill up with garbage and promote malaria. Rainwater catchment is preferred by households if they can afford the cost.

Roof-Top Rainwater Harvesting

This is already in place in most of the houses that have the space for rainwater harvesting and can afford the high costs of storage tanks (so this is limited to the better off). Overall it is cheaper to collect water downstream in the areas in the Hawban-Hawgala-Amira catchment, but this suffers from greater pollution than freshly collected water.

Fixing Leaks in TWSLC Supply

The utility has already invested within the last decade to reduce leaks from 40% to 25%. Further investment is possible but is expensive and will only achieve a limited increase in supply. However fixing leaks and TWSLC reform will be key if desalinated water is supplied through the network. The history of Taiz water indicates that leak development has exceeded leak fixing, except at times of major infrastructure overhaul.

In summary, coastal desalination is the only long-term means of ensuring sufficient sustainable resource although these other measures can enhance supply and quality. Desalination will comprise the major part of the future Integrated Water Resource Management (IWRM) for Taiz city, while not being the only resource. Most importantly it can be done without generating the conflict that other – only partial solutions – will provoke.

The Taiz Economy: Vulnerability to Water Scarcity and Extent of the Water Dividend[16]

Impact of Water Scarcity on the Taiz Economy

Taiz is the main center of industry in Yemen, directly employing over 25,000 people and indirectly contributing to the livelihood of many times more. The business sector represents around one quarter of Taiz's total water usage, and this proportion will rise if water availability stimulates a healthy rate of industrial expansion that outstrips the rate of population growth. Taiz's factories include many large water consuming industries and some of these industries, particularly in food and drink production, require high quality pure water.

Taiz business leaders point to reduced competitiveness and the diminishing attractiveness of Taiz as a business location, with the rising cost of living – exacerbated by increased water prices - and a more difficult living environment as a result of poor quality water and its impact on health.

One major commercial grouping in Taiz has explored the implications of relocating some industries. Relocation has always been rejected given the high cost of relocating a workforce and providing accommodation, infrastructure and services, although some expansion is now occurring in al-Hodeida (on the coast) if there are already existing factories there.

Assessing the Impact of Affordable Clean Water – Important Multiplier Effects

Our study conducted surveys of industry focusing on the food sector, soap and detergents, cement, as well as hospitals and hotels. The results showed that cost savings due to cheaper water were not as significant an issue as expected. The key costs within production tend to be labour and energy, with water often representing only 1% of the cost base. In practice other factors relating to water scarcity prove much more important than potential cost savings.

Taiz has become an important and growing health service centre. There are strong cross-sectoral linkages here, with a significant proportion of the hotel trade coming from people visiting Taiz for health care. There are also important productivity benefits; cleaner, more plentiful water leads to a healthier and more productive working population.

The diagram below shows the three key economic pathways directly driving industrial growth – reduced production costs (to the right), health productivity (in the centre) and increased employment (to the left).

Our study also examined the various 'multiplier' effects of greater economic activity in addition to the *direct impact* of increased employment and productive work generated. This is shown in the diagram below. The *indirect effects* on stimulating supply and distribution chains and generating further employment and incomes were found to be strong on the distribution side (because the products are largely distributed in Yemen), but weaker on the supply side (as much of the raw materials is imported). The *induced effects* of spending wages in the local economy and the stimulation of other enterprises were assessed as important factors. We estimated the most significant of all were the *dynamic secondary effects* on the

Figure 1 **Pathways to Wealth and Employment Generation**

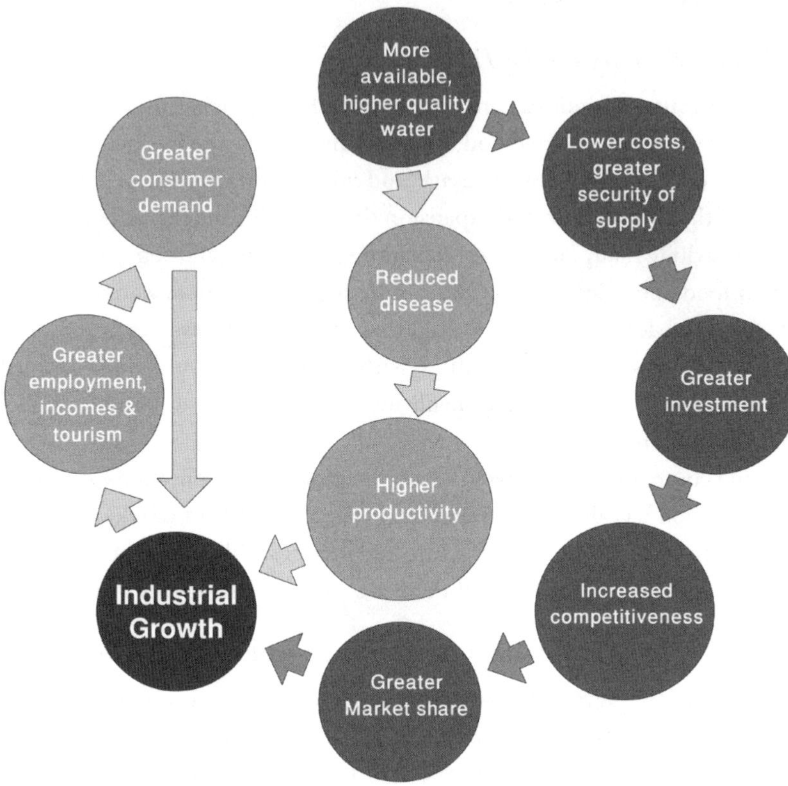

Source: JFA Research Report "Reducing Conflict through the Provision of Affordable Water and Increased Employment in Taiz, Final report April 2014"

economy through improved infrastructure, skills, human and resources and innovation, as Taiz takes up the opportunity to re-emerge as a vibrant economic centre.

Creating a 'Stabilizing' Urbanization

The effects of future water supply certainty point to a scenario where Taiz experiences a beneficial 'stabilising' urbanisation driven by economic revitalisation, as opposed to a 'destabilising' urbanisation from forced immigration from an impoverished countryside. With the increasing difficulties of earning a viable living in the villages, much of Taiz's recent growth has come from an influx of neighbouring rural populations (whole families or individuals sending remittances home) usually driven by the scarcity of water – exacerbated by the city's own extraction. In the absence of sufficient urban jobs this acts as a 'destabilising' urbanisation, associated with increased unemployment particularly among the young and a greater strain on city services.

For Taiz, population growth has been moderated somewhat by emigration of its people both to Sanaa, where there are substantial areas of the city populated by Taizi migrants[17], and beyond to Saudi Arabia and the Gulf where job prospects are better, though prone to sudden reversal[18].

Another relevant issue in terms of economic revival is the relative impact on jobs and the economy of water used by industry and services over water used in agriculture[19].

Figure 2 **The Linkages Between Cheaper, Higher Quality Water and Industrial Growth**

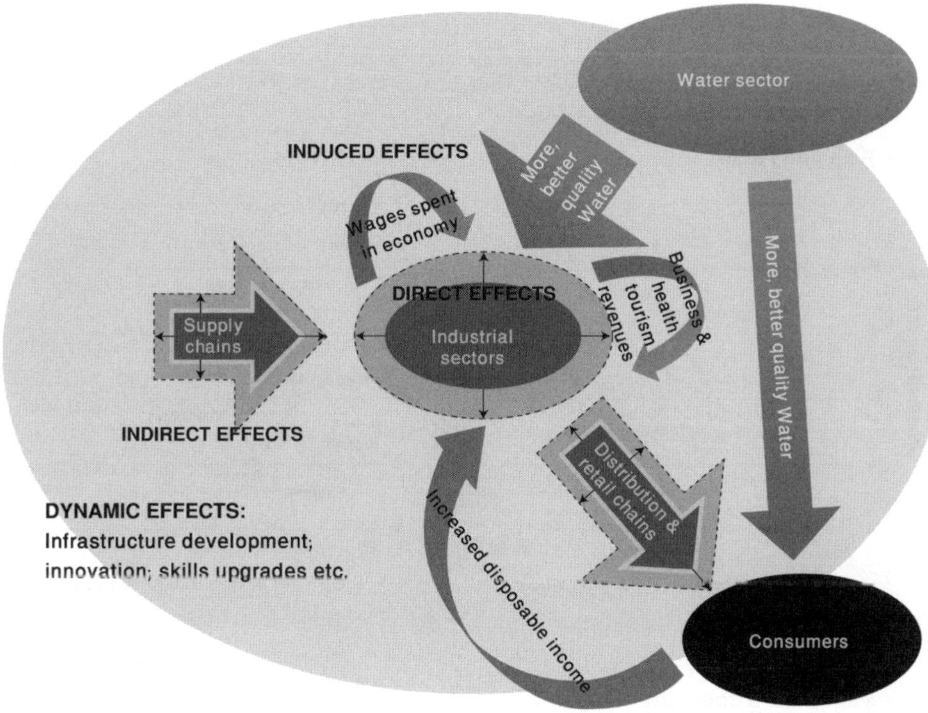

Source: JFA Research Report "Reducing Conflict through the Provision of Affordable Water and Increased Employment in Taiz, Final report April 2014"

Dr Handley's earlier seminal work[20] on Taiz estimated 21 times the number of jobs were created by industry per unit of water over agriculture per unit of water, and the ratio of wealth creation at 275. Ratios of these orders of magnitude still apply a decade later.

These reflections raise fundamental issues for the strategic choices facing a developing water-scarce country. The chart below[21] starkly illustrates this choice – between an urban economic revitalisation that attracts a needed and employable workforce, or a rural economic collapse that throws out the population it can no longer support into urban slums, poor housing and high unemployment.

Coastal Relocation Reassessed

A fundamental issue in discussions about water scarcity in Taiz, and indeed Sanaa, is whether the best solution would be to 'relocate the city' to the coast. We reviewed the earlier costs of relocation produced by McKinsey[22] and concluded that, quite apart from the social and security viability of such a scheme in a country with so many political challenges, these costs were several orders of magnitude greater than the alternative of importing water from the coast.

Figure 3 **Urbanization and Prosperity: Lessons From East Asia and Sub-Saharan Africa**

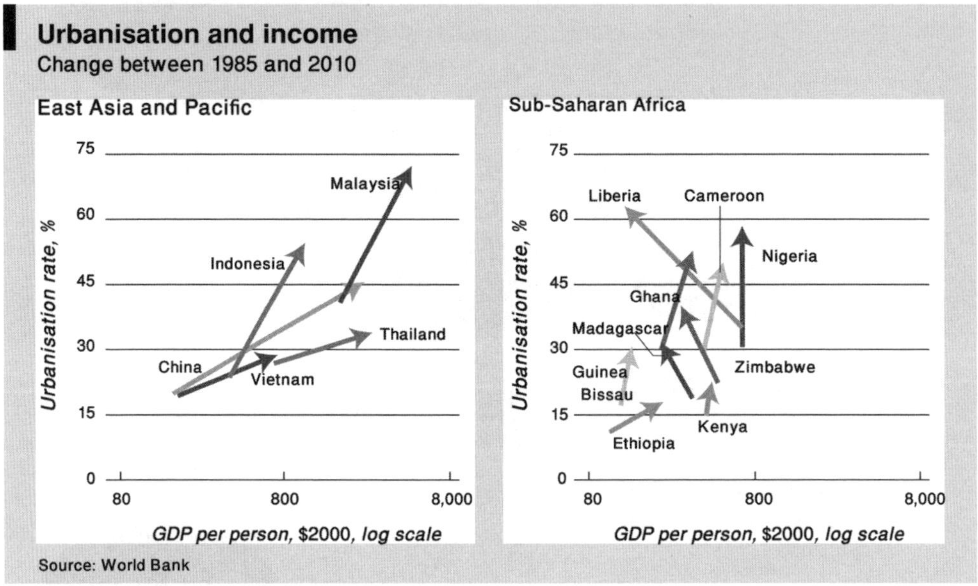

People will move if there are jobs, so the issue is whether industry will invest in new or expanded coastal operations. Stimulated by the worsening water situation in Taiz, relocation of industrial plants has been discussed by Yemen's largest major industrial group. It and others concluded that the costs of relocation (closing current locations and re-establishing elsewhere), re-training, providing new facilities and managing the disruption were not economically viable. On the other hand, the expansion of existing operations to the coast was found to be viable and to a limited extent this is now taking place. Some companies have set up operations in al-Hodeida to secure a more reliable and better quality of water supply as well as to take advantage of the port facilities.

We looked into the economic issues associated with relocation from a household perspective. Although significantly more water and electricity would be used on the coast, as more water is needed for washing and more electricity for air conditioning, it is at present on balance cheaper, but not significantly so, to live on the coast. However this balance will shift as water becomes less available and more expensive from coastal wells, already threatened by saline intrusion as a result of over-extraction, while new water will reduce the overall water bills for households in Taiz.

Locating industry near a coastal desalination plant would save on the considerable energy required for pumping it to the highlands. However in the short-term there is insufficient essential social infrastructure, such as housing and schools on the coast. The carbon footprint of supply and distribution networks is another factor. Shipping in raw materials to a coastal location would involve less energy expenditure but needs to be balanced against greater energy used in freighting goods to major population centres in the highlands including Taiz itself.

Thus while there are longer-term advantages in a shift of population to the coast more work needs to be done to evaluate this systematically. In any event the implied timescale is well beyond the short-term issues of the water crisis in Taiz, and the argument cannot be used to detract from addressing the urgent needs of the city.

Transition Planning for Greater Taiz

Groundwater used to supply the TWSLC, the fleet of tankers, the network of kawthers as well as local irrigated farming, is rapidly diminishing. Well yields are falling - more than half of former productive wells have already run dry, and new drilling or deepening of existing wells is often unsuccessful. The apparently straightforward 'technical solution' of desalinated water does carry financial and organisational risks. These can be managed, but it is essential that this begins with the detailed transition planning, within a longer term vision for Greater Taiz.

Key elements of such a transition plan include:

- The continuing need for integrated water management using traditional sources as well as new water to keep unit costs down
- Ensuring the financial viability of the new scheme by differentiating between secure payers (industry, new tanker filling points, private networks) and the utility which may still be facing management challenges and poor operational efficiency
- In the case of utility water, ensuring the final product is of drinkable quality, by blending with the best of existing groundwater
- Ensuring the water transmission line reaches a main reservoir in eastern Taiz, the foremost industrial area and site of much new housing and services
- Establishing of waste water treatment once volumes have built up - potentially delivered to continuing extraction areas as agricultural water to address degradation issues
- Careful siting of new water tanker filling stations to minimise numbers of tanker trips per day and address congestion;
- Establishing target groupings suitable for private networks in developing areas of Greater Taiz

- Developing/negotiating of Groundwater Protection Areas to increase the viability of the hinterland for agriculture and ensure public health by protecting consumers from shallow abstraction.

Figure 4 below illustrates potential early steps in the transition, with city distribution building on successful existing Yemeni enterprise models of private tanker delivery and private networks, alongside institutions in need of reform (the utility is marked LC on the map). The plan will need to be placed in the context of a renewed Taiz City Development Plan, building on consultation with local communities and other stakeholders, so that new water infrastructure can link with housing, roads, industrial development, health and education infrastructure, areas of cultural or environmental importance and land purchasing.

Figure 4

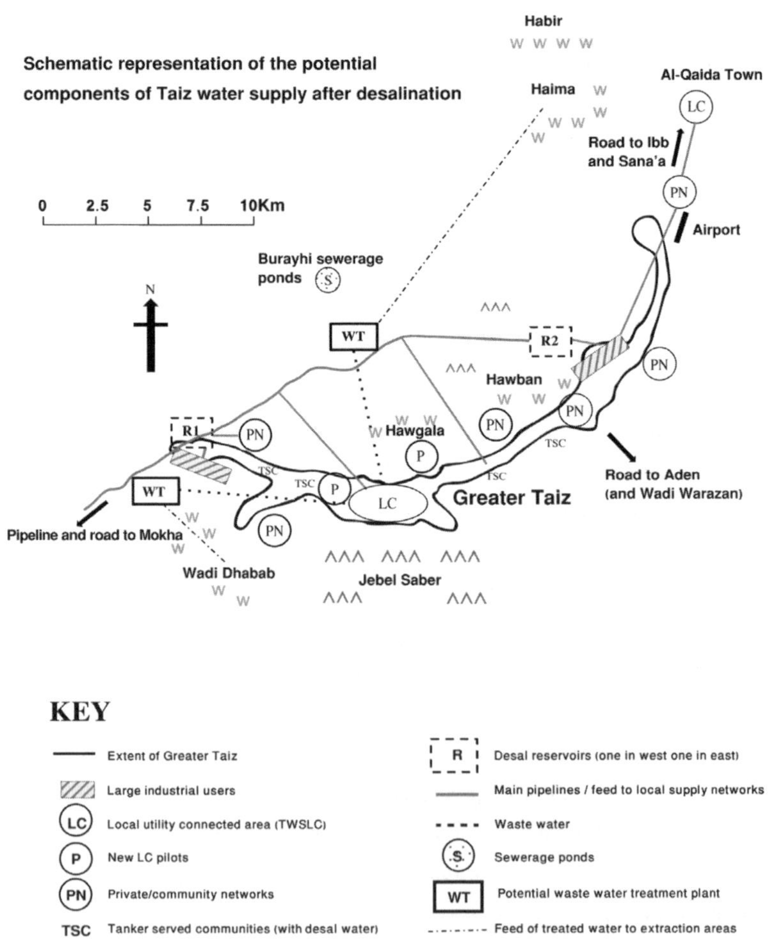

Source: JFA Research Report "Reducing Conflict through the Provision of Affordable Water and Increased Employment in Taiz, Final report April 2014"

Utility Reform

To ensure long-term institutional sustainability, planning for the much-needed reform of TWSLC needs to take place as soon as possible after the trigger of the first major grant for the desalination scheme is in place. We recognise that in the context of diminishing supply, the realistic prospect of new water will be needed as an incentive for reform.

Our study discussed two potential approaches best described by using the analogy of the medical options available to a patient with a severe heart condition. A *'Heart Transplant'* would involve a comprehensive drive at far reaching reform with the temporary 'transplant' of a new management team with the necessary experience and confidence. This will cost more in the short term, but would address the risk of yet another failed attempt at reform. Previous attempts have taken place without the reform imperative that a desalination project brings and without a revitalised Taiz leadership committed to change. A *'Heart Pacemaker'* would deliver progressive reforms over time. These may in the end cost as much as the radical approach but the benefits obtained would take longer to realise, at a time when the utility needs to be in good shape managing revenues and leaks in preparation for the arrival of desalinated water in Taiz.

Analysis of Forward Demand

We made a detailed analysis of future demand for desalinated water, based on the results of the full range of our surveys covering both suppliers and customers. Forward assessments clearly involve a whole range of assumptions about how customers (households, industry and business, and communities outside Taiz) will behave when faced with the option of new water. Our surveys provide for the first time reasonable estimates of demand. Past reports have included some highly exaggerated claims for both current water usage in Taiz and demand projections. A realistic sizing of the desalination project is now possible. The desalination plant itself can be extended progressively by building one module at a time, but it would be best if the pipeline allowed for much higher future demand in Taiz and other communities served, while also allowing for potential extension, to Ibb for example.

Given the extent of uncertainty over both final design issues and consumer behavior, an initial demand (after a settling-in period) in the 25 to 30 mld range is foreseen, but rising rapidly, driven by population growth and economic revitalization, to over 50 mld in the first decade.

Expected Consumer Prices

Water pricing strategies will be very dependent upon final 'as-constructed' costs, in particular on the levels of donor capital support achieved, on ongoing energy unit costs (which will vary according to fuel used), on initial volumes sold and the rate of water demand development relative to each supplier.

Our study developed a cost and revenue model to investigate these different scenarios. With a best assessment of an initial demand of 28mld (two years from first water) we estimate a desalinated water cost at Mokha of USD 1.66/m^3 and a wholesale price at the delivery point (the new reservoirs / tanks) in Taiz of USD 2.75/m^3. This is based on the additional assumptions of energy at 12¢/kWh (which may need to be revised if fuel subsidies are reduced), and the construction of a grant-supported pipeline from Mokha to Taiz. For energy at 16¢/kWh, the wholesale price in Taiz rises to USD 3.18/m^3, demonstrating the need to secure as cheap an energy source as possible[23].

Table 2 **Taiz Water Demand Analysis Following Arrival of New Water (2018–2026)**

All figures in mld (or 000m^3/day)	2013 Current Situation	Scenario 2018 (after 2 years 'settling' from desal water first arriving 2016)			Scenario 2026 (10 years after arrival of desalinated first water)		
		Non desal	Desal	All water	Non-desal	Desal	All water
1. Greater Taiz (households)							
Total	19.6	11.5	17.4	28.9	10.2	40.0	50.2
l/c/d	23.3			28.3			35.1
2. Greater Taiz (industry, business, government, services)							
Total	5.7	1.0	5.1	6.1	1.0	8.5	9.5
3. Outside Greater Taiz (Mokha, Barah, Pipeline villages, al-Qeida)							
Total	4.5	2.0	5.5	7.5	2.0	7.5	9.5
Grand Totals for all areas to be supplied with desalinated water							
Grand Total	29.8	14.5	28.0	42.5	13.2	56.0	69.2

Source: JFA Research Report "Reducing Conflict through the Provision of Affordable Water and Increased Employment in Taiz, Final report April 2014"

Attractiveness and 'Affordability' of New Water for the Main Urban Delivery Options

The key changes that come with the provision of desalinated water are:

Availability

A major improvement for utility customers can be expected. They are currently experiencing one to two months' delay for water delivery and have to rely on tankers to fill the gaps. Following the arrival of desalinated water, the utility may not initially be delivering continuously (this depends on the extent of management reforms), but it is expected that delivery can quickly be reduced to every week as a step towards the target of continuous availability.

New water tankers will also be able to deliver faster (much reduced time from order to delivery) once water delivery points are available at locations throughout the city. Currently tankers have to drive across town in dense traffic and may face long waits when filling at the well particularly in the dry season.

Quality

Households will no longer have to buy expensive locally desalinated *kawther* water, as water supplied by the utility, new tankers and private networks will all be of drinkable quality.

Cost / Affordability

This was analysed in detail by reviewing overall household expenditure. As at present, new water will be available by the three routes of utility, tankers and private networks. New (clean) tankered water will be cheaper than existing tankered water providing fill-up points ensure that new tankers will make more and shorter trips per day. Utility and private network water will cost more but will be available more frequently (in time continuously) and of drinkable quality. Expensive *kawther* water will no longer be needed, thus reducing household costs. As discussed earlier, all households benefit from no longer having to buy the most expensive *kawther* water, but poorer households benefit more. Table 3 below summarises the overall changes expected.

Conclusions and Recommendations

The following are crucial for addressing Taiz's water scarcity and water conflicts, for the successful introduction of desalinated water and for the smooth management of a major transition.

Donors and the International Community

Urgent consideration needs to be given to supporting the overall Taiz programme (desalination, energy supply, transmission, city distribution). The first major infrastructure grant will act as the trigger for other needed areas of support. Initial steps can be low risk and need not involve large financial outlay. Concerns about the management of such a project in the current context of political uncertainty can be mitigated by a clear transition roadmap, with realistic timescales recognizing that major transitions take time, and with key risks identified.

There are different options for structuring the package for new water between the desalination plant, power plant, pipeline and Taiz water suppliers[24]. The key issue is to ensure a clear cut route for sustainable revenues to be passed back to the desalinator, while taking every economic measure that reduces consumer price, which in turn is critical to the speed and stability of the transition.

Table 3 **Prices, Quality and Availability Summary (before desalinated water and after)**

Situation now	**Cost USD/m³**	**Quality**	**Availability**
LC connected	0.5-1.5 inc sewerage	Very poor	1-3 months
Tankers (wells)	4.0- 4.8	Variable quality, some drinkable	May need to wait a day
Kawther	23	Drinkable on the whole	On demand
Private networks	1.2 – 1.6	Poor, undrinkable	On demand
Situation after desal	**USD/m³**	**Quality**	**Availability**
Utility connected (50:50 desal + better groundwater)	c. 3.0 inc sewerage	Reasonably good, Drinkable	Initially perhaps every two weeks depending on LC reforms, then continuous
Tankers (desal)	c.4.0	Good, Drinkable	On demand
Kawther (now retailers of small quantities)	c.5 say	Good, Drinkable	On demand
Private networks	c.3.4	Good, Drinkable	On demand

Source: JFA Research Report "Reducing Conflict through the Provision of Affordable Water and Increased Employment in Taiz, Final report April 2014" (funded by the UK's Conflict Prevention)

Transition Planning

The development of Taiz water infrastructure – mains pipelines and reservoirs, utility pilots, new water tanker filling points, tanks for private networks, sewerage outfall, future water treatment, and ground protection zones – needs to be placed within the context of an updated Taiz City Development Plan, building on consultation with local communities and other stakeholders. Water developments can then link with housing, roads, industrial development, health and education infrastructure, areas of cultural or environmental importance and land purchasing.

Utility Reform

The utility currently faces many difficulties, and far reaching reform will be necessary between the project trigger of first grant and first new water availability in Taiz (minimum of three years estimated). There is a choice between a more radical transformational approach and piecemeal reform over a longer time scale. The former is preferable as it will mean less delay in arriving at a well-functioning system, but this choice will be driven in large part by the extent of available finance.

Utility reform will need to be supported by both 'soft' measures focused on management and systems, and 'hard' support through essential equipment and potentially smart technology. The reform programme should concentrate initially on areas that are easiest to address and thereby create early benefits.

Price Target for New Water

A well-planned and implemented project can bring important financial benefits to households across the income range. A key target in ensuring this to minimize the 'wholesale' price of desalinated water at the first Taiz reservoir. USD 2.75/m^3 makes a suitable target, and attention to energy costs will be key to achieving this.

New Water Distribution in Greater Taiz: Tanker Filling Points, Community Networks

Given the multiple challenges faced by the local utility, and the fact that private tankers and private networks function well in the Yemen context with a track record of low levels of leakage and income loss, a simple enabling environment needs to be developed for new water tanker filling points and community networks. This should include simple regulation to ensure quality and clear differentiation between clean new water and old water - such as a color-coding system for all tankers - and access of small businesses to financial loans. The emphasis should be on realism and simplicity.

New water tanker filling points need to be located close to the communities they will serve - to bring down the consumer price while reducing carbon emissions and city congestion. In time it is expected that the new water tanker filling points will transform into franchised private or community networks, which can deliver water more cheaply and without the need for household storage. These in turn may be subsumed within a wider utility, if and when reforms are successful. Private community networks should be kept to less than 1,500 household connections - beyond this they are likely to lose their close relationship to the people they serve.

Pipeline Communities

Support needs to be given to the communities along the pipeline route to ensure their own water projects are upgraded and are operating before the arrival of 'first new water' in Taiz. Local water along the pipeline route is generally still relatively plentiful and of good quality, but if necessary these village projects (and Mokha itself) should receive desalinated water from the pipeline at close to cost.

Mitigating City – Hinterland Conflicts

The arrival of new water will relieve the tensions and conflicts between the city and its hinterland. Future treated waste water from the city should be directed to areas which will continue to be used for city water extraction such as Haima and Wadi Dhabab. This treated water would support and potentially revive local agriculture while acting as fair compensation for continued groundwater withdrawals.

Reviving Taiz's Economy

New water will play a critical role in the stabilization and revitalization of Taiz's industrial economy. The arrival of new water will provide the opportunity to launch a Taiz investment campaign, highlighting the benefits of a new stable quality water supply for the attractiveness of the city, while reinforcing Taiz's current educational and health advantages. The city will need to be prepared to expand and enhance its technical training, much of which already operates to a high standard, and to ensure it remains in tune with the needs of employers in industry, small businesses and the service sector.

Implications for the Future of Yemen

Providing a reliable, clean and sustainable source of water for Taiz will act as a major incentive for new investment in the city and its industries, generating jobs and improving health and school attendance (particularly for girls). New water for Taiz presents major opportunities for Yemeni enterprise in the water sector itself – from efficient new tanker delivery to private networks in more peripheral locations and nearby communities.

The creation of urban jobs is becoming increasingly important as both town and rural populations expand; urban water stability will be a pre-condition for investment. Rural livelihoods will change radically in the next two decades with the widespread depletion of rural ground water and much higher cost of irrigation water, which is likely to be increasingly used only as a supplement to rain-fed supply. This will put yet more pressure on Yemen's urban centers.

A successful new water scheme in Taiz will provide both a model and many lessons for coping with the urban water crises now escalating in other Yemeni cities including Sanaa - while recognizing each case has distinctive characteristics and supply options. Common themes will be the need for sound socio-economic analysis, a conflict prevention perspective and sound transition planning.

The transformation and reform of the Taiz water utility in particular will create important lessons for other malfunctioning Yemeni governmental or quasi-governmental institutions. The Mokha – Taiz desalination scheme raises important issues around the price and reliability of energy in Yemen as well as the challenging issue of subsidies. Longer-term options are available (energy imports, renewables) to help address this.

The study has raised issues around the role of legislation and regulation in Yemen, as well as its enforceability in practice. Many of these issues reflect 'tragedy of the commons' situations where the wider common good needs protection against narrower interests. There is clearly a popular mandate for such issues and tapping this will be essential to Yemen's future, whatever the future constitutional arrangements adopted.

Notes

1 The key members of the JFA team were Abdullah Saleh Saif (Taiz coordinator and survey management), Shoqi Maktari (conflict assessment), Dr Richard Franceys (urban water distribution issues), Dr

Christopher Handley (survey design and supply alternatives) and Dr Christopher Coles (economic impacts).

2 Phrase used by Prof Tony Allan, winner of the Stockholm Water Prize for his pioneering work on virtual water

3 The abandonment of the Moghul city of Fatehpur Sikri in 1585 appears to have been largely due to lack of water. J. Diamond writing on the causes of societal collapse, gives a number of historical examples of societies failing to manage the loss of natural resources, including both the Maya and Anasazi in Central America where water was the major issue; see *Collapse: How Societies Choose to Fail or Survive* (London: Penguin Books, 2005).

4 Many researchers simply repeat earlier scepticism on the costs of bringing desalinated water to highland locations. See for example M. Weiss, "A Perfect Storm: The Causes and Consequences of Severe Water Scarcity, Institutional Breakdown and Conflict in Yemen," Water International, International Water Resources Association, 2015.

5 Other water conflicts affect primarily rural areas – between upstream and downstream users, between farmers over groundwater use, and between well owners and the rest of the community over prioritization for domestic use. See C. Ward, *The Water Crisis in Yemen: Managing Extreme Water Scarcity in the Middle East* (London: I. B. Tauris, 2014).

6 See C. Handley, *Water Stress: Some Symptoms and Causes; A Case Study of Ta'iz, Yemen* (London: Ashgate, 2000) for a fuller description on the Wadi Warazan incident.

7 Assessment by H. R. Wallingford, outlined in World Bank, "Yemen: Assessing the Impacts of Climate Change and Variability on the Water and Agriculture Sectors and the Policy Implications," Report No. 54196-YE (Washington, DC: World Bank, 2010).

8 See World Bank, "Assessing the Impacts of Climate Change," Key Messages.

9 See Introduction section of H. Lackner, ed., *Why Yemen Matters: A Society in Transition* (London: Saqi Books, 2014).

10 WFP, *The State of Food Security and Nutrition in Yemen 2012, Comprehensive Food Security Survey* (World Food Programme, 2012).

11 See for example the analysis of C. Breisinger et al., "Climate Change, Agricultural Production and Food Security: Evidence from the Yemen" (Kiel Working Paper No 1747, Kiel Institute for World Economy, Kiel, Germany, 2011).

12 The WHO standard for drinking water is an electrical conductivity of 1,500μS/cm. Most Taiz well water measures over 5,500.

13 l/c/d (litres per capita per day) is the unit used for consumption levels

14 At time of usage there were 215 Yemeni riyals to one US dollar

15 While researching his book on the Taiz water crisis, Handley, *Water Stress*.

16 This section and Figures 2 and 3 are based largely on the work of Dr Chris Coles, JFA team member (see J. Firebrace et al., "Reducing Conflict through the Provision of Affordable Water and Increased Employment in Taiz" [CPP Report, London and Sanaa, 2014], Chapter 6).

17 The extensive al-Qa' area of Sanaa is now largely populated by Taizis

18 Following a change in Saudi policy, between June 2013 and Jan 2014 some 270,000 Yemeni workers crossed one border crossing into Yemen, with many more returnees expected (H. Lackner, presentation at "Why Yemen Matters" conference, February 2014).

19 J. A. Allan discusses this issue in a number of different Middle Eastern contexts in *The Middle East Water Question: Hydropolitics and the Global Economy* (London: I. B. Tauris, 2001).

20 Handley, *Water Stress*.

21 Reproduced from the *Economist*, October 2, 2012.

22 McKinsey, "Yemen's Top Ten Priorities: Priority 6 Water" (presentation, 2010).

23 Fichtner made calculations which showed this could be delivered by a mix of fossil fuels and wind / solar renewables, see L. Theophil and T. Schmitt, "Renewable Energy Desalination: An Emerging Solution to Close MENA's Water Gap; The Case of Al Mokha, Yemen" (Fichtner GmbH, Stuttgart, Germany, 2012).

24 See Chapter 3 of Firebrace et al., "Reducing Conflict," contributed by Dr Richard Franceys.

References

Allan, J. A. *The Middle East Water Question: Hydropolitics and the Global Economy*. London: I. B. Tauris, 2001.

Breisinger, C., et al. "Climate Change, Agricultural Production and Food Security: Evidence from the Yemen." Kiel Working Paper No 1747, Kiel Institute for World Economy, Kiel, Germany, 2011.

Diamond, J. *Collapse: How Societies Choose to Fail or Survive*. London: Penguin Books, 2005.

Firebrace, J., et al. "Reducing Conflict through the Provision of Affordable Water and Increased Employment in Taiz." CPP Report. London and Sanaa, 2014.

Handley, C. *Water Stress: Some Symptoms and Causes; A Case Study of Ta'iz, Yemen*. London: Ashgate, 2000.

Hauck, L. "Water Markets: Alternative Water Networks in Sana'a, Yemen." Ruprecht-Karls-Universität Heidelberg, Germany, 2009.

Lackner, H., ed. *Why Yemen Matters: A Society in Transition*. London: Saqi Books, 2014.

McKinsey. "Yemen's Top Ten Priorities: Priority 6 Water." Presentation, Sanaa, 2010.

Theophil, L., and T. Schmitt. "Renewable Energy Desalination: An Emerging Solution to Close MENA's Water Gap; The Case of Al Mokha, Yemen." Fichtner GmbH, Stuttgart, Germany, 2012.

Ward, C. *The Water Crisis in Yemen: Managing Extreme Water Scarcity in the Middle East*. London: I. B. Tauris, 2014.

Weiss, M. "A Perfect Storm: The Causes and Consequences of Severe Water Scarcity, Institutional Breakdown and Conflict in Yemen." Water International Vol 40 Issue 2 pp 251-272, International Water Resources Association, 2015.

WFP. *The State of Food Security and Nutrition in Yemen 2012, Comprehensive Food Security Survey*. World Food Programme, Sanaa, 2012.

World Bank. "Yemen: Assessing the Impacts of Climate Change and Variability on the Water and Agriculture Sectors and the Policy Implications." Report No. 54196-YE. Washington, DC: World Bank, 2010.

7

"Our Main Concern is Security": Women's Political Participation, Engagement in the Security Sector, and Public Safety in Yemen

Joana Cook

Introduction

In 2011, following 32 years of autocratic rule, the Arab Spring initiated sweeping change across Yemen. Shifting from authoritarian to democratic leadership, a new political system and government accountable to their people are still being established. Since September 2014, it is also increasingly being challenged and the state's future is in a state of uncertainty. A critical component to state stability, security sector reform (SSR) has been key to transition where previous institutions had been largely built on nepotism and cronyism of the former regime. Furthermore, where women previously had limited political presence, during the Arab Spring they took to the streets by the thousands in protest and are now demanding constitutionally enshrined political quotas. In recent years (even prior to the Arab Spring), however, women have been slow to take on broader roles in the security sector where there was once little space for them. As public safety and political uncertainty become of growing concern, it is crucial to examine this topic. [1]

This chapter will discuss two recent and interconnected shifts in the public roles of women in Yemen: their increasing political participation, and their recruitment into the security sector. It will contextualize this current period with a brief review of the literature related to women and security, and a historical analysis of relevant factors that have excluded women from the political scene in the past, including government and political party structure, and issues related to development. It will set these amongst the growing security concerns that women currently face. This backdrop will clarify why women's participation in both politics and the security sector is critical and linked to wider public safety concerns. Finally, women's presence in both politics and the security sector will be considered in light of the increasing roles and priorities of foreign actors, in particular the US and EU, who have been supporting the Yemeni government. The chapter will conclude with suggestions for all actors involved.

This topic is particularly relevant for a number of reasons. At the time of writing, a draft constitution was ready for discussion, but the uncertain political and security situation currently threatens to derail these advances. Guarantees for women's roles in both politics and the security sector are currently included in this draft. Yemen's security situation is critical to both domestic and international actors and remains a focal point for donors and governments alike; women's political participation and presence in the security sector must remain a consideration in their strategies.

It is beyond the scope of this paper to address all aspects of women's political participation in Yemen, as well as their growing roles in the security sector. This paper does however, aim to highlight the importance and relationship between women's political participation and participation in the security sector, and show why it is vital to consider this in security sector reform in Yemen and the wider region.

The Inclusion of Women – What are the Benefits?

There is a substantial body of research that demonstrates the positive impacts which can result from the involvement of greater numbers of women in government, and protecting women's rights more broadly. A report by the World Bank showed that the higher the number of women in government, the lower the levels of corruption - thus improving investment potential and trust in the government.[2] There is also evidence that where women's economic and social human rights are restricted, there tend to be statistically higher levels of corruption.[3] Women are more likely to prioritize bills that focus on children, family and women,[4] health care and social services,[5] and are also more likely to introduce bills that would reduce gender discrimination.

From a security perspective, states with higher levels of social, economic, and political gender equality are less likely to rely on military force to settle disputes,[6] and states exhibiting high levels of gender equality demonstrate lower levels of violence in international crises and disputes.[7] There is a statistically significant relationship between the level of violence in a crisis and the percentage of female leaders.[8] Caprioli extends this analysis to militarized interstate disputes and finds a similar relationship: states with the highest levels of gender equality display lower levels of aggression in these disputes and are less likely to use force first.[9] Virtually the same pattern was found with respect to intrastate conflict.[10] United Nations Resolution 1325 is the most widely recognized document supporting the inclusion of women at all levels of decision-making in the security arena, but despite its international recognition, the United Nations Security Council cited "efforts [to increase women's role in global security] have lacked coordination and have been hampered by the lack of measurable results."[11]

While simply adding more women to a political or security structure is not a silver bullet, and caution must be paid to essentialist perceptions and stereotyping of gender roles in both the political and security spheres, there is significant evidence demonstrating the benefits that women's engagement can have. While many of these benefits also resonate with security sector reforms, how these become translated into practical initiatives on the ground is still unclear, inconsistent or overlooked.

Security: A Shifting Definition, a Change in Focus

Security is a contentious subject amongst academics, practitioners and populations. However, human security has taken on a greater importance in recent years, though can often appear in conflict with 'hard' security concerns. A number of these embody themselves in distinct ways in the case of Yemen.

In light of perceived grievances which drove the Arab Spring, human security also appears to have gained a renewed importance and relevance in the case of Yemen. Human security is defined by the UN as "freedom from fear and want,"[12] a concept which arose at the intersection of development and security literature.[13] George MacLean takes this further and defines human security as "security of the individual in his or her personal surroundings, community, and environment" which includes "protection from crime and terrorism, political corruption, forced migration, absence of human rights; freedom from violations based on gender; political, economic, and democratic development."[14] King points out that, "human security in the security literature captured the view that the focus of security studies should shift from the state to the individual and should encompass military as well as non-military threats."[15] How this shift is acknowledged in security sector reforms, in both practical terms and parties engaged, where actors may otherwise seem to prioritize more immediate security threats, remains crucial.

Traditional literature in the more niche field of women and security has often framed women as victims of conflict, in peacekeeping roles, as peacemakers in conflict, or in post-conflict situations. There is a glaring gap in examining how women as security practitioners emerge in security sector reforms, particularly in vulnerable societies. The topic of women in security most often revolves around the theme of 'soft' issues related to human security, as opposed to more 'hard' security issues that often (and increasingly) frame Yemen, such as terrorism. Such framing of roles can make women appear unsuited for non-traditional positions in institutions that are critical to the state, such as the police or military. This could have serious consequences in many areas. One rare report that examined gender broadly in counter-terrorism found that when gender was ignored, human rights and counter-terrorism initiatives suffered.[16] In some cases, counter-terrorism initiatives had direct negative impacts on gender equality in the broader society, in unique areas such as antiterrorism financing laws. It is of growing importance that the increased relevance of human security is reflected in strategies, programmes and initiatives. These must not only acknowledge differing gender impacts, but also involve diverse actors, and perspectives (including those of women) when planning, implementing and solidifying security reforms and programs.

One specific area worth analyzing in this context is women's participation at the security policy level. A special report on the role of women in global security analyzed the importance of women's political presence in relation to the construction of security-focused policies and concluded,

> "The number of women elected does not tell the full story – qualitative indicators could be used to supplement this data by examining, for example, the extent to which women in parliament contribute to policy discussions, whether their contributions are intended to further gender equality, and if their contributions impact on the outcomes of discussions."[17]

Other authors have stated that gender stereotyping continues to largely feed into perceptions of the competence of leaders to combat terrorism. In political contexts dominated by "fighting terrorism, deploying troops, protecting national security, and brokering peace agreements,"[18] such as in Yemen, this has specific relevance.

Women in political office also positively impact community engagement with law enforcement. Research has shown that having a larger proportion of women in political office resulted in an increase in willingness of female victims to report crimes, particularly at the local government level, as well as a determination by the police to intervene in such matters.[19] This was due in part to the perception that having women present in government would ensure a more responsive, accountable justice system. It is indeed critical to note how women in the political sphere are defining and translating their interests and concerns in relation to the security sector. These points demonstrate one area where gender, security and politics are directly linked. In the field of security, such benefits could have significant impact in new approaches and ideas in security policy and program formation.

It is against this wider backdrop that a closer examination of women's political participation and presence in Yemen's security infrastructure is required. While analysing the transitional security sector in Yemen in light of the constitutional reforms now at risk, the challenges the sector faces on the ground, and the roles women have begun to establish in it, this chapter will demonstrate why it is timely and critical to bring to the foreground the importance of including women in Yemen's security sector, while showing the benefits this can bring to a sector that has long lacked public trust, and how this is directly linked with political participation.

Women's Political Participation in Yemen

This section aims to analyse the most fundamental factors contributing to the current lack of political leadership by women in Yemen. It will show that a combination of factors are responsible for the historically poor representation of women in Yemen. It will suggest the main points that need to be addressed in order to effectively support an increase of women's political leadership. It will also show how this connects to women's integration into, and relationship with, the field of security.

Political Parties and Support

While historically women had significant rights and public roles in the PDRY, unification caused many of these to be essentially quashed by the more conservative policies of the Yemen Arab Republic (YAR). Between unification in 1990 and up to the Arab Spring, the political system in Yemen did not encourage or accommodate the establishment or growth of women's political leadership. Political parties in Yemen had been developing an increasingly narrow set of views of the role of women in their organisations and had been providing fewer and fewer resources to female party members. In fact, women tended to become more the objects of debate, while the occasions for them to shape Yemeni politics through political parties were becoming increasingly limited.[20] It is perhaps no surprise then that parties seemed to concentrate more on getting women to vote, than including them in any meaningful way within their parties. For example, the 2003 elections saw women turn out to vote at nearly the same rate as men and overall, 75% of the population voted.[21] Clearly there has been an effort by the parties to ensure that women are engaged enough in politics to vote, but not necessarily participate in any meaningful way beyond this. This was demonstrated by the 2003 elections, which saw fewer women in parliament than in 1993. At the time of writing, there was only one woman present in parliament and two in Majlis al-Shura (Shura Council).[22] Even following a recent push for a 30% quota, the most recent government only saw four women amongst the 36 new ministers. However, the current draft constitution notes, "Parties shall take care to ensure the representation of women and youth in their leadership bodies" (Article 13.4). It further notes, "To give effect to the principle of equal citizenship, the State shall enact legislation and take measures, to achieve effective political participation for women to ensure access to at least 30% in various authorities and bodies" (Article 76).[23] Given the risk that the draft constitution may not be ratified, the present crisis threatens to nullify the significant gains made by women in recent years.

Female membership of political parties and civic organizations has been extremely low in recent years. For example, less than one percent of Yemeni women were involved in a women's organization and only five percent claimed membership in a political party in 2009.[24] A 2007 study showed only two percent of Yemeni women had engaged in any type of activity to publicly express their views on social or political issues; Yemeni men are fifteen times more likely to have taken part in a public protest, march or demonstration.[25] Females in the 18 to 24 age group showed the highest rates of engagement, suggesting that support for young generations should be prioritized, particularly in light of increased engagement during the Arab Spring and National Dialogue Conference (NDC).

Women also face particular challenges within their political parties. For example, in 2003, Islah stated that, "women were unfit for election." Islah's political sector chairman, Muhammad Qahtan, justified this by saying, "Our society is still ignorant and there are still some social, cultural and ideological principles that women cannot stand against."[26] Islah spokeswoman, Amat al-Salam Raja even stated, "Women's contributions are unfit given current political conditions. So far the parties have not discussed the issue of areas closed to women, and it is still difficult for women to participate in the elections, as it would conclude with failure."[27] Sentiments such as these discouraged investment and effort in the political training of women. Perhaps this helps explain why Yemen did not have its first female minister until 2001, even though historically in the PDRY women had held positions such as in the Central Committee of the Yemen Socialist Party (YSP) and generally had some of the most advanced rights in the region. A 15 percent quota for women in 2007 was passed by parliament but was not approved by the key parliamentary committee.[28] Women made almost no progress under the Saleh regime where Saleh himself appears to have seen no political and personal interest in enhancing the role of women.

The Women's National Committee (WNC) in Yemen has pointed out two of the most critical reasons women were not significantly present in national political leadership. First, there was the minimal number of women participating in elections as candidates, holding leading positions in political parties, and leading public communities and civil society organisations. Second was the lack of women in decision making-positions such as parliament, consultative council, government and executing authorities, local governing, judiciary system, and as the countries' regional and international representatives.[29] Social, cultural and ideological factors have also been stated as reasons for women's lack of participation in these areas of governance.

Security can also be a key consideration in women's willingness to become involved in politics. Rashida al-Hamdani, the former Chairperson of the Women's National Committee (WNC), and former Yemeni delegate to the UN, highlighted the risks that are inherent for women wanting to participate in public life. For example, when the WNC pushed for a minimum age requirement for marriage, al-Hamdani stated, "The religious groups… demonstrated against [the] WNC and we were threatened. Our lives were in danger and the government did not do anything to secure [us]."[30] This also highlights how government and policing responsiveness can be linked to areas such as securing civil society and wider public safety.

With little support from the government itself, except to the minimal degree that would satisfy certain foreign donors' investment criteria, and even less support from the main political opposition group, Islah, there had been a significant lack of political will to change the corrupt, exclusionary, political system, let alone making concerted efforts to include more women. In cases where women attempted to participate, in some instances they faced security risks and a lack of support and protection from the security sector and government. Recent advancements in political and constitutional reforms offer an important turning point away from this. However, this will rest on the currently unfolding situation in the country.

Developmental and Social Hurdles of Political Participation

Women in Yemen are further burdened with a number of developmental and social hurdles to their political participation. A succinct summary can be seen in a 2010 Freedom House report, which states:

> "Yemen is a tribal and traditional country where prevailing cultural attitudes, patriarchal structures, and Islamic fundamentalism accord women low status in the family and community and limit their participation in society. Women are subjected to various forms of violence and discrimination, including domestic abuse, deprivation of education, early or forced marriage, restrictions on freedom of movement, exclusion from decision-making roles and processes, denial of inheritance, deprivation of health services, and female genital mutilation (FGM)."[31]

This statement, though dismal as it stands, does not fully capture the extent of challenges faced by women. The Gender Inequality Index produced by the World Economic Forum ranks Yemen 142 out of 142 countries.[32] These challenges will only be exacerbated by the current conflict.

While there have been improvements in certain areas, much work is still to be done. For example, while current levels of education among women in Yemen have been improving, they are still not equal to those of men. There is near equality in primary education with enrolment rates for girls and boys at 81% and 82% respectively, but this gap widens at secondary to 31% and 48.8% respectively.[33] The rural urban divide also contributes: whereas 24% of urban women are illiterate, this more than doubles to 60% of rural women.[34] The significance of this become clear when one considers that 68% of the population live in rural communities.[35]

Women in Yemen make up only 20.1% of the work force, compared to 74.3% of males.[36] Over one-third of this employment is in the agricultural sector, though this number is considered lower than actual figures.[37] Considering that women in paid employment are five times more likely to be engaged in civil activism,[38] the importance of education and employment for Yemeni women who may enter the political sphere cannot be underestimated. It would be worthwhile to note how the changing security situation also impacts upon this.

Broader humanitarian concerns are ever present in Yemen as well. 43% of Yemen's population is food insecure and almost half of Yemen's children under age five (two million children), are malnourished and 41% of these children are stunted.[39] 75% of Yemeni men chew qat, said to be "one of the primary causes of poverty in the country, decreasing productivity, depleting scarce resources, and consuming an increasingly larger portion of household budgets."[40] The annual population growth rate of the country is 2.3%, which is expected to see the current population of 26 million reach 31.2 million by 2025.[41] With no minimum age for marriage in the country, half of girls younger than 18 are married, a quarter of whom are married before they are 15.[42]

The negative stance taken towards the public mixing of men and women who are not related to each other has further restricted women's public engagement in critical ways. For younger Yemeni women, this has limited their mobility outside their homes. Opportunities for young women interacting in mixed-gender settings and learning from community leaders are severely limited. Limited mobility may also impact attendance in organizations or extracurricular programs (where available) where they could gain valuable leadership skills. This social taboo may also limit female participation in sports, another activity which can build critical skills such as self-confidence, leadership and teamwork.

Gender mixing has also been politicized by the leadership. President Saleh, in a 2011 speech held amid the growing protests to his rule, condemned women's public engagement in mixed gender settings. In response to popular demonstrations against him Saleh stated,

> "We call on [the crowds] and call on the Joint Meeting Parties to use their conscience and to join dialogue in order to agree on one decision for the sake of the security and stability of this nation. I call on them to reject the mixing of sexes as it is forbidden by Islam; the mixing of sexes is forbidden in the Al-Jami'ah Street."[43]

This was claimed by many to be an attempt by Saleh to appeal to Islamists for political support in a period where he was clearly being challenged by his people.[44] As a highly conservative country, religious justifications for actions have an additional degree of salience. This example also points to women's public roles and engagement as highly politicized. Furthermore, discussions of the status of the nation's security and stability pointedly attempted to exclude women.

While many of the concerns discussed appear to be humanitarian or developmental in nature, an increasing focus on human security emphasizes the link between security and the ability to participate in political life. Human security concerns have directly impacted women's ability to participate in significant political roles and other areas, such as employment and education in Yemen. As the general Yemeni population continue to struggle to survive, a policy environment which focuses not only on traditional (hard), but also human security interests, must emerge if recent political gains by Yemeni women are to be maintained and fostered.

After the Arab Spring

Many significant changes have been made since President Saleh left power, though are not yet solidified. Women's presence in the Arab Spring protests, subsequent participation in the NDC and call for a 30% political quota to be enshrined in the constitution are perhaps the most important among these. Women aim to advance their cause against a background of growing insecurity and competing priorities as Yemen debates its new constitution.

Though faced with opposition to their participation by some political parties in Yemen, women have had some support from the international community. "As the preparations for the NDC began, international countries that sponsored the GCC Initiative exerted pressure on both the political parties and the government to include women in the [NDC] conference."[45] Largely consisting of 'the Middle generation', that is, professional women and technocrats, the NDC was to consist of "565 delegates, 30% would be women. In addition, the women's issue as such would be represented by a group of 40 women."[46] However, the number of female ministers present at the time, only three out of thirty-four ministers in total at the time, was used by one author to show that "in terms of their participation in the transitional government, women did not make any significant inroads."[47] Women were, however, represented in all nine working groups and chaired at least one, and another sat on the committee supervising the NDC. Though there were complaints that certain groups and their interests were under-represented, such as rural women, this degree of representation itself represents a significant stride forward.

One succinct view of women's political progress since the departure of Ali Abdullah Saleh reflects many shared sentiments, and remaining challenges, present across the country:

> "Generally, the 2011 protests have not brought improvement to the living conditions of women in Yemen. The most significant effect of the upheaval is an increase in freedom of expression which enables women to express themselves politically. While the deteriorated security situation poses the greatest challenge for women, prevalent family values obstruct women from taking up a more active political role. While men agreed that the situation of women has improved, they did so only to the extent that it would enable women to better provide for their families. They continue to view political activism by women in a negative light. For that reason women depend on women's rights activists to speak for them at the national level."[48]

This suggests that more women should be present in significant political positions and secured through quotas, as either a percentage of candidates or legislators. At its earliest stage, this can begin with wider political expression, and engagement in the workforce, as well as increased public education on the benefits that women's representation brings to all members of society, supported by a wide variety of public actors (for example religious, political or tribal). Quotas have proved to be an important factor in increasing women's representation in countries such as Iraq, Afghanistan and Argentina.[49] Researchers at Harvard University concluded that quotas do increase female leadership in the political and corporate sphere (for example, in Norway); female leadership does influence policy outcome; and gender quotas do not cause sustained public backlash but instead update their views on how female leaders perform (for example in India).[50] Political parties should capitalize on the current political environment and show that they have an important place for women within their parties as Yemen goes through a period of parlous political change.

Women in Yemen's Security Sector

While there has been a fair degree of academic analysis on roles and agency of women in the Middle East, there has been a lack of similar concentration on women in the security context. Women in Yemen, for example, have garnered some niche academic focus in areas such as health and human rights, though attention to Yemen is often centred on security concerns revolving around state failure, Huthi rebels, southern secessionists and the terrorist threat presented by AQAP and its affiliates.[51] These security concerns have driven funding to Yemen from international actors. Investigation by the author has found only recent and limited research on women in the security sector in Yemen (often by NGOs) and only a handful of academic articles more broadly on the topic.[52] This research is marginally linked to female political participation. The period following the Arab Spring could not be a more critical period to examine and clarify the relationship between women's political participation, women in the security sector, and wider public safety concerns.

A number of initiatives have been taken by international actors to increase and broaden the roles of women in Yemen's security forces, in particular the police and counter-terrorism units.[53] There has also been increasing public support for their roles by authorities within Yemen's security forces.[54] While the future of these initiatives to recruit and maintain women in the security sector is still uncertain, what will be examined here is how this topic is integrally linked with public safety and women's political representation. It will also be suggested that unless these initiatives are seen as Yemeni policies, as opposed to externally imposed (for example linked to financial or developmental aid) or driven by external motivations, their chance of success may be significantly reduced.

Recent polls have indicated that the current security sector in Yemen is still not responsive to the needs of women. When (and if) laws are in place to protect the rights of women, they are still often not enforced adequately:

> "In part due to the lack of representation, women's rights violations were, and still are, common. Existing laws that supposedly protect women and girls are either inconsistently applied or lack enforcement. There are no laws to protect girls from early marriage—a persistent practice in the country—or to protect women from rape and harassment."[55]

Women's absence from the security forces, as well as a lack of gender awareness and training amongst security forces, risks leaving a gap in access to justice for women. As well, women's "asserted need for a full, equal and effective participation at all stages of peace-processes given their vital role in the prevention and resolution of conflict and peace building" remains unmet.[56] While this is the responsibility of actors that traverse the political, human rights, legal and security sectors, specifically increasing the number of women in security forces can help address one critical component of this challenge.

Drawing from, and expanding on a number of recent reports,[57] it can be argued that it is vital for women to become more involved in Yemen's security sector, in particular the police and military. This is based on a number of points. First, unless human rights and the rule of law are upheld and enforced for all members of society, including women, the government of Yemen will not achieve the accountability required for its population to distinguish it from the former regime. Second, including more women in the security sector also helps 'open it up' to women who may have been reluctant, or not allowed, to engage male officers when their rights are violated. Third, due to the highly disadvantaged and unequal position of women in Yemeni society, special attention needs to be paid to ensuring not only their political participation, but also to how their consultation and inclusion within the security sector itself can complement and support broader public engagement. Fourth, with the numerous security threats present in Yemen, coordination in these areas by Yemeni and international actors are tightly intertwined, and may see competition between national and international priorities. This risks politicizing or excluding the roles of women whose concerns may be overlooked by focus on specific objectives (e.g. dealing with AQAP). Fifth, if emphasis remains solely on women and political advancement, without consideration of how their involvement can be complementarily reflected in security practices, women risk being overlooked in larger security discussions and priorities. Finally, due to an increasing concentration on human security and a particular emphasis on the security of women (seen in examples like UNSC Resolution 1325), policies and engagement of this sector must reflect this concern.

Women have been largely excluded from the security sector due to many of the same factors that have kept them out of the political sphere: for example, social and cultural norms and little attention from political parties or security institutions themselves in advancing the position of women.

Institutions which enforce and embody the rule of law and protect the rights of citizens are an important component of reforms and future progress. Civil security, for example, is founded on the rule of law and encompasses "law enforcement, the prevention of crime, the protection of human rights in homes and public places, and the creation and maintenance of orderly communities. Civil security is needed to allow civil society to flourish."[58] Women can play an important role in this.

Current Perceived Security Threats

From a Western point of view, AQAP poses a major threat to Yemen -they also have the intent and capacity to launch attacks abroad. AQAP is the most capable of the al-Qaeda branches to carry out such an attack.[59] The risks that face ordinary Yemenis, however, are often quite different. Security engagement by external actors has tended to concentrate on terrorism, but also (arguably) has influenced Yemen's national security priorities by virtue of their significant financial and physical contribution in relation to support and training. This has created increased tension between the Yemeni population, national and international actors.

While there are very distinct roles for civil security and counterterrorism practitioners, there are important overlaps, for example between the criminal justice system and the military that have a direct impact on ordinary Yemenis. As one author states, "It is up to each country's citizenry, preferably acting through a fair process of representative government, to decide where it wishes to strike a balance between safety from terrorism and other issues and values."[60] Including women in both the formulation and execution of policy helps ensure that balance is also representative of the concerns of the population.

One survey of Yemeni attitudes that dealt with the 2014 situation in comparison to the 2011 Arab Spring highlights the different priorities between international and local security concerns, and reiterates the importance of local ownership in addressing them. Focus group participants have highlighted that "the rapidly deteriorating security situation after the 2011 protests negatively affected women the most."[61] Many of these same concerns did extend to the wider population with examples given including:

> "Shootings, random assassinations, the spread of arms, bandits on roads leading out of the cities, an increase of sexual harassment and robberies during blackouts, the absence of police protection in cities such as Al-Hudaida and Aden, and a general increase in common crime."

Women faced an additional burden "because of the conservative nature of Yemeni society" where "male and female relatives discouraged them from going to work, school, or other simple social activities because of security concerns." The same report pointed out that of the five most urgent priorities to improve women's status, security was the first concern. They explain that, "if a woman cannot go to work, school, or a hospital safely, then she would not have a chance to improve her living conditions."[62] These same factors, as noted above, also have a negative impact on the ability to engage in political activity.

For all focus groups across the country, "Security was the number one concern expressed... the most important indicator of the overall state of the country." All groups described the security situation in Yemen after 2011 as "the worst to date."[63] This insecurity was particularly present amongst the low status Akhdam community (already suffering from significant discrimination) who were most likely to "suffer the most from rape and sexual abuse" yet "least likely to find protection, compensation, or punishment for perpetrators within the legal system."[64] Alarmingly, some views suggest that up to 90% of Yemeni women are exposed to some form of sexual harassment.[65] Livelihoods, travel, and family care were also negatively affected by security concerns. For example, when midwives were unable to get to houses because of security concerns this impacts not only their income, but "the overall state of the family since women become unable to care for their families as they would if the situation was more stable."[66] Freedom to travel became impeded by increasing blackouts, further limiting ability to engage in work,[67] amid other prevalent concerns of sexual harassment.[68] 2015 has only seen this situation worsen.

Conflict furthermore threatens development, provides opportunities for terrorists, as well as affecting women's ability to participate in public life. Conflict damages the economy, which leads to negative consequences for a majority of society. It has direct repercussions on agriculture, commerce and trade, it leads to a reduction in earnings and impacts the supply of water and power. It deters foreign investment in the country, and with that the opportunity for local employment and economic benefits of investment in certain communities. On a more personal level, conflict can cause the displacement of people fleeing from areas of danger and disrupts families and livelihoods. At the governmental level, an increase of security concerns often means that resources are shifted from what author Amartya Sen refers to as 'entitlements'– such as health and education, key concerns for Yemeni women and the wider public.[69] When donors set their priorities, they might take into account that the inclusion of women in the security sector, as well as in politics, may lead to a greater support for women's concerns, while also positively impacting the security situation (including terrorist threat).

When women's health, access to education, ability to work, and basic freedom to travel are negatively impacted by security concerns, their opportunities to gain the skills and experience necessary to more actively engage in public life become greatly reduced. Therefore, even initiatives to create quotas for their participation may fall short if there is a limited pool of candidates to draw from, limited security support for those who do engage, or an unwillingness to concentrate on these concerns by leadership.

An important component of this, Security Sector Reforms (SSR) is essentially aimed at "the efficient and effective provision of state and human security within a framework of democratic governance."[70] SSR was at the forefront of priorities at the NDC and initial proposals discussed the objective of "Expansion and empowerment of women in the work of the security services and the military and intelligence."[71] This reflected the belief that:

> "In rebuilding security institutions, SSR should include a range of measures to increase the recruitment and retention of women and to create a work environment that is supportive of women not only in police and defense forces, but also in intelligence services, penal services, border authorities, the judiciary and the institutions that manage them."[72]

In the first draft of the new Yemeni constitution, Article 314 confirmed the aim to, "Empower and expand employment opportunities for women in the Armed Forces, Police and General Intelligence" as a key principle.[73] How the status of this constitution will evolve in the current political situation is presently unknown.

General challenges that face gender integration in SSR, are ones often cited more broadly to comprehensive reforms. For example SSR actors may have, "an impatience to complete programmes, leading to insufficient local ownership; and assumptions that models that have been used elsewhere can be replicated without due regard to context."[74] These have also impacted gender integration in SSR around the world. Considering the large number of national and international stakeholders that require consultation, commitment by a large number of individuals to engage these, and often long-term sustained financial resources required, it is no wonder that certain challenges may arise, particularly with currently niche subjects, such as increasing women's participation in the security sector. Furthermore, "Gender issues are often of great cultural sensitivity, so while external actors can encourage and support, initiatives must be led by local stakeholders."[75]

The benefits to directing attention on gender in the security sector are certainly worthwhile though. "By drawing on the full participation of both men and women [the security sector] can become more responsive to local needs, more legitimate and better able to address the range of security and justice priorities that coexist in communities."[76] It is important to emphasize the benefits of women's participation in the security sector in terms of the positive impacts it can have in many areas, including political, economic and social, for all Yemenis, both men and women.

Donor Priorities and Security

Foreign aid to Yemen has often been, and continues to be, framed largely in (oft controversial) security terms. Foreign donor concentration on their own national security interests may overlook, or compete with, local security concerns. For example, "Military actions and involvement, as well as weapons transfers, have provoked widespread mistrust of American motives and alienated some of the country's most articulate political activists."[77] This risks marginalizing local actors who may support security reforms in Yemen.

Yemen's military is furthermore the country's largest employer and contains, "60,000 active soldiers, 40,000 reservists and an additional 71,000 paramilitary forces.... constituting 40 per cent of the Yemeni government's total budget, or around 6 per cent of its GDP."[78] One of the concerns present in the military is the strong connection of some units to the regime patronage networks – a few of which are virtually tribal militias controlled by a sheikh, not a General representing the state. The consequences of this are apparent in the present situation, as it is clear that loyalties within the security institutions were to individual security actors, and not to the state or wider Yemeni population.

This has been a key point of concern in attempts to restructure the military and security sectors since 2011. The police forces employed 168,996 men in comparison to 2,868 women (or 1.7 %) in 2014.[79] While both police and military have distinct roles in relation to public security and protection, what these numbers indicate is that security provision is a significant source of employment, recipient of funding, and a critical representation of the Yemeni government to the Yemeni public. This also reflects on actors, such as foreign governments, who financially support and train these forces. In areas such as corruption, an issue that has in cases noted by the World Bank been positively impacted by increased membership of women,[80] glaring problems with the current military structures, such as the concern that up to one third of soldiers exists on paper only, demonstrate that there are wider benefits to be considered by engaging women.[81]

In relation to women and security, this can further point to two things: firstly, that these institutions are prioritized by the government, yet do not appear to be adequately responding to the security needs of the population, nor reflective of the demographics of the population. Secondly, the security sector itself could potentially act as an institution of employment and influence for Yemeni women. A more representative, responsive and accountable security sector could also help reinstate public trust in this system and the new government. Exploring the idea of meaningful engagement and recruitment of women in this area should be prioritized.

How this security sector reform may evolve in the unique Yemen context must also be considered. A seemingly emergent combination of:

> "A weak central government, military factionalization, empowerment of local tribal militias and increased external influence has the potential of transforming Yemeni civil-military relations into something akin to warlordism, in which military and/or tribal leaders exercise civil power at a local or regional level – either in support of or in opposition to the central government – through control of the militias." [82]

The critical impact this could have in areas such as national social and economic development, institution-building and political reform, and ultimately the position of women, is worrisome. This threatens to create "A state of perpetual crisis management and threat mitigation not only for the Yemeni central government, but also for regional and international stakeholders with a vested interest in the security and stability of the Yemeni state."[83] Such a state would not be conducive to maintaining the advances thus far achieved by all Yemenis, or addressing grievances which initially drove Arab Spring protests. Unless reforms that were the focus on the National Dialogue Conference are meaningfully addressed and implemented by all parties, also reflecting the increased inclusion of women in all areas, such a state of perpetual crisis management, and more recently a very real risk of state collapse, appears increasingly likely.

Women's Current Roles in Yemen's Security Sector

Women have historically had varied and senior roles in the justice and security sector in Yemen. For example, women in the PDRY were active in the judiciary, army and police force. Since the unification of Yemen, however, women have largely worked in less active positions in far fewer numbers. For example, in 2010 in the Yemeni Police Force, only 16 women had reached the rank of colonel, 17 had reached the rank of lieutenant colonel, three had reached the rank of captain and two were lieutenants.[84] Women's presence in the police force began to grow again in 2001 when the first class of female officers graduated from Yemen's Police Academy.[85] As noted above, women still account for less than 2% of the total police force. Female officers are not often found at police stations and this can prove challenging for officers who are dealing with female suspects, and female members of the public who may be seeking police assistance.

Women in policing fall under the reforms being led by the Ministry of Interior, largely in partnership with the EU. Noting some of the key challenges facing Yemen discussed above, and taking into account the comparable (though unique) case of Afghanistan, one report highlights the benefits that a greater emphasis on increasing the number of women in the security forces could provide. Discussing an increase in empowered, well-trained and experienced policewomen, it noted that benefits could include properly "react[ing] to violence against women, family violence, children in trouble, and kidnapping," as well as "Provid[ing] support to female victims of crime, and ensur[ing] the security of women in communities."[86] There are also important roles for women in the security forces to play, for example, in the prison system in relation to female inmates, or at border checkpoints.[87]

These are all critical components in creating a more secure environment for women in Yemen, and strengthening local ownership and response to security. By taking action in this area, the Yemeni government could show its strong support for improving the well-being of women and the wider population, and meet obligations to gender equality and reducing discrimination against women such as those in the United Nations Convention on the Elimination of All Forms of Discrimination against Women (CEDAW) as well as the NDC outcomes. However, if these initiatives remain unsupported and excluded from the discussions of SSR, they risk being viewed as "externally imposed, or unworthy of political attention and effort."[88]

This involvement could be led and supported by civil society organisations and female parliamentarians, particularly in the areas of oversight and gender sensitivity. At all times, this could emphasize the benefits it can bring to all Yemenis. It should also be borne in mind that,

> "In order to allow women parliamentarians, to be engaged in SSR there must of course be enhanced women's participation in parliament itself-an illustration of how SSR requirements go hand in hand with improving women's access to public decision making and policy formulation more generally."[89]

Considering that Yemen has a single female parliamentarian, and only two in the Shura Council, the impact that these politicians alone could have on SSR is minimal.

One case from Afghanistan demonstrates how not valuing and utilizing women in these positions can be detrimental: "It is evident that the return on present investment in recruitment, training and maintenance of policewomen is poor because of the failure to employ policewomen in value-producing work." This resulted in:

> "A waste of human capital, failure to protect the human rights of policewomen, and missed opportunities for using policewomen to advance government objectives for security and human rights, including the duty to provide the female half of the Afghan population with security services and access to justice."[90]

In the case of Afghanistan, the failure of the Ministry of Interior to recruit and advance women in the police force was attributed to (among other factors): organizational and leadership inertia, failure to finance gender priority, the absence of a gender policy and program, and a clear lack of recruitment plan."[91] The report pointed out that while there has seemingly been support for gender equity from other agencies and the international community, gender "frequently escapes attention when plans are developed and budgets allocated."[92] Similar statements could currently be applied to Yemen.

While 'cultural misperceptions' and religious misinterpretations of the role of women in this sector still exist in Yemen,[93] so too do negative perceptions of gendered traits associated with such roles. For example, positions in the security sector where displaying traits that are deemed to be masculine, such as aggression, toughness, or 'no-nonsense' attitudes are the norm, this may reflect negatively on traits deemed more feminine, or prompt women to be labelled as bossy, obnoxious or overbearing. Women also face a double burden as if they display traits that are perceived as feminine, such as passiveness, nurturing and cooperation, they may be labelled as weak and overly sensitive.[94]

In the context of Yemen, women face specific challenges in recruitment, in particular gaining family approval to enrol and battling social stigmas.[95] Women recruits may be viewed negatively as police and military roles are viewed as suitable for men only. To even sign up for the police college, women have to have written consent from their fathers.[96] Even with such restrictions, organizations like the Police Academy appear to be opening new, more specialized roles to women in the security forces.[97]

Yemenis themselves appear open to the idea of having female police officers: 51.64% of the population support this.[98] However, 75.3% of the population does not support the recruitment of women from their own family into the police.[99] This indicates that there is still a willingness to see female officers in the country and women should at least have the option to undertake this work if they so choose. As with political leadership, negative stereotypes can be dispelled when increasing examples of positive role models in this sector emerge.

Women have also been engaged in parts of the Yemeni Armed Forces, specifically counterterrorism unit, since 2006. This training has largely been led by the US. Though a relatively small unit, mostly limited to searching female suspects and site security in locations like airports and high-profile events, they are a unique example of women engaged in a predominantly male force and set to take on an increasing role in the sector.[100]

While the elite female counterterrorism unit, and establishing new police training programs could be viewed as a positive foundation for wider female engagement in the security sector, two points will impact these. First, the present security situation will significantly interrupt these advances and indeed likely halt them altogether. Second, any solution to the present situation in the country will likely have to be developed and supported internally. The status of Yemen's security forces will certainly be a part of any agreement, and it is important that the role of women in these is not forgotten. How women are being engaged in such efforts deserves further examination and support by all concerned actors.

Moving Forward

Since the 2011 Arab Spring, many significant changes have been made in Yemen, perhaps foremost amongst these being the political and security sector roles that women have carved out for themselves in this period and the opportunities available to create long-lasting change in both of these fields. The push for a political quota, and proposed minimum age for marriage and other suggested constitutional reforms are testaments to this. What cannot be neglected in this period, however, is the clear relationship between women's participation in both the political and security fields, and public safety more broadly.

The roles and support made available to women in the political and security spheres, as well as how they are engaged by all actors, must evolve in hard, measurable terms, regardless of what solution to the current crisis emerges. As pointed out by Gertrude Mongella, President of the Pan-African Parliament, 'the participation of women not only provides equal opportunity on a practical level, but also offers a new perspective and diversity of contributions to policy-making and priorities for development."[101] With a demonstrated relationship and significant overlap between competing political and security priorities and concerns of both national and international actors, addressing one cannot be 'siloed' from the other.

If meaningful and long-term change is to occur in Yemen, particularly in political, developmental and security terms, it is imperative that all actors sincerely and practically engage women in all steps of these efforts. This should be explicated in hard terms in constitutional reforms, as well as policy and programme development. Efforts should be made to introduce and support this idea through public education campaigns, as well as the recruitment and retention initiatives. Public spokespersons and endorsers of these efforts from various Yemeni backgrounds and sectors must be identified and engaged. This could include both politicians and other important public figures (for example religious or tribal) that support these efforts, as well as leaders and practitioners within the security sector itself. This will not be simple, quick or easy but short-term or sporadic remedies will not provide a lasting cure to the problem. How the present political situation unfolds will also be important. As a growing number of concerns related to development, security, terrorism and wider state stability emerge, it is important that, whatever solutions are considered and sought, the important roles women can, and should, play in these should not be neglected.

Notes

1 At the time of writing, Huthis had essentially taken over the government of Yemen, and Operation Decisive Storm was underway to remove them from power and re-establish the democratically elected government. The political outcome of this situation, the status of the January 2015 draft constitution, and the future of the state are currently unclear.
2 Andrew D Mason and Elizabeth M King, *Engendering Development through Gender Equality in Rights, Resources, and Voice* (Washington, DC: World Bank, 2001), 96.
3 Daniel Kaufmann, "Challenges in the Next Stage of Anti-Corruption," *New Perspectives on Combating Corruption* (1998): 144.
4 Sue Thomas, "The Impact of Women on State Legislative Policies," *The Journal of Politics* 53, no. 4 (1991), as cited in Pamela Paxton, Sheri Kunovich, and Melanie M Hughes, "Gender in Politics," *Annu. Rev. Sociol.* 33 (2007): 273.
5 Thomas H Little, Dana Dunn, and Rebecca E Deen, "A View from the Top: Gender Differences in Legislative Priorities among State Legislative Leaders," *Women & Politics* 22, no. 4 (2001), as cited in Paxton, Kunovich, and Hughes, "Gender in Politics," 273.
6 Mary Caprioli, "Gendered Conflict," *Journal of Peace Research* 37, no. 1 (2000).
7 Mary Caprioli and Mark A Boyer, "Gender, Violence, and International Crisis," *Journal of Conflict Resolution* 45, no. 4 (2001).
8 Ibid.
9 Mary Caprioli, "Gender Equality and State Aggression: The Impact of Domestic Gender Equality on State First Use of Force," *International Interactions* 29, no. 3 (2003).
10 "Primed for Violence: The Role of Gender Inequality in Predicting Internal Conflict," *International Studies Quarterly* 49, no. 2 (2005).
11 Valerie Norville, *The Role of Women in Global Security* (Washington, DC: United States Institute for Peace, 2010).
12 Lincoln C. Chen, "Human Security: Concepts and Approaches" in Tatsuro Matsumae et al., *Common Security in Asia: New Concepts of Human Security* (Strategic Peace and International Affairs Research Institute, Tokai University, 1995); United Nations Development Program (UNDP), *New Dimensions of Human Security* (New York: Oxford University Press, 1994); A Florini and PJ Simmons, *The New Security Thinking: A Review of the North American Literature* (New York: Carnegie Endowment for International Peace, 1998).
13 Gary King and Christopher JL Murray, "Rethinking Human Security," *Political Science Quarterly* 116, no. 4 (2001).
14 Ibid., 591.
15 Ibid., 589.
16 The Centre for Human Right and Global Justice, *A Decade Lost: Locating Gender in U.S. Counter-Terrorism* (New York: NYU School of Law, 2011).
17 Ibid.
18 Jennifer L Lawless, "Women, War, and Winning Elections: Gender Stereotyping in the Post-September 11th Era," *Political Research Quarterly* 57, no. 3 (2004): 479.
19 Anandi Mani, *The Power of Political Voice: How Women in Politics Can Help Tackle Gender Crime,* CAGE-Chatham House Series (London: Chatham House, 2014). Lakshmi Iyer et al., "The Power of Political Voice: Women's Political Representation and Crime in India," *American Economic Journal: Applied Economics* 4, no. 4 (2012).
20 Stacey Philbrick Yadav and Janine A Clark, "Disappointments and New Directions: Women, Partisanship, and the Regime in Yemen," *Hawwa* 8, no. 1 (2010).
21 International Institutue for Democracy and Electoral Assistance, "Voter Turnout Data for Yemen": http://www.idea.int/vt/countryview.cfm?CountryCode=YE
22 UNDP (2010)
23 Government of Yemen, "Draft Constitution English" (2015).

24 IFES (2009)
25 Ibid.
26 "Islah Deems Women Unfit for Election," *Yemen Today Magazine*, February 1, 2003.
27 Ibid.
28 IFES (2011)
29 Al-Salahi (2003)
30 Al-Hamdani, Rashida. Email to author, [online]. August 20, 2011. Available by e-mail: joana.cook@kcl.ac.uk
31 Freedom House Special Report: Yemen (2010).
32 World Economic Forum, "Global Gender Gap Report 2014" (2014).
33 UNICEF, "Info by Country - Yemen Statistics" (UN, 2014). The lower rates of female education in Yemen can be attributed to a number of factors, predominantly poverty, early marriage and a lack of female teachers and girls' schools. See World Bank (2009), 9.
34 Republic of Yemen (2006)
35 World Health Organization (WHO), "Yemen - Basic Country Data" (2015).
36 UNDP (2010)
37 Republic of Yemen (2007)
38 IFES (2009)
39 World Food Programme, "WFP Yemen: Situation report 16-31 December 2014" (United Nations World Food Programme, 2014).
40 World Bank (2007), as cited in Boucek and Ottaway (2010), 8.
41 Economic and Social Commission for Western Asia (ESCWA), "Demographic Profile of Yemen" (UN, 2015).
42 USAID (2007)
43 "Friday: Saleh Speech and Supporters," *Yemen Rights Monitor*, April 15, 2011.
44 "Yemen Women Lead Protests against Ali Abdullah Saleh's Regime," *The Telegraph*, April 17, 2011.
45 Sarah Ahmed, "Women's Voices in the 'New Yemen'," in *YPC Policy Report*, ed. Yemen Polling Center (Sanaa, Yemen Yemen Polling Center, 2014), 15.
46 Ibid.
47 Ibid.
48 Ibid., 21.
49 Paxton, Kunovich, and Hughes (2007), 269; Hunt (2007)
50 Rohini Pande and Deanna Ford, "Gender Quotas and Female Leadership," in *World Development Report 2012: Gender Equality and Development Background Paper* (World Bank, 2012), 3.
51 Christina Hellmich, "Fighting Al Qaeda in Yemen? Rethinking the Nature of the Islamist Threat and the Effectiveness of US Counterterrorism Strategy," *Studies in Conflict & Terrorism* 35, no. 9 (2012); Alexandra Lewis, "Violence in Yemen: Thinking About Violence in Fragile States Beyond the Confines of Conflict and Terrorism," *Stability: International Journal of Security and Development* 2, no. 1 (2013); Yezid Sayigh, "Fixing Broken Windows: Security Sector Reform in Palestine, Lebanon and Yemen," *Carnegie Papers* (October 2009); Adam C Seitz, "The 'Arab Spring' and Yemeni Civil-Military Relations," in *Why Yemen Matters: A Society in Transition*, ed. Helen Lackner (London: Saqi Books, 2014); Gregory D Johnsen, *The Last Refuge: Yemen, Al-Qaeda, and America's War in Arabia* (New York: WW Norton, 2013).
52 Mary Christine-Heinze and Sarah Ahmed, "Integrating Women's Security Interests into Police Reform in Yemen," in *A YPC Policy Report*, ed. Yemen Polling Center (June 2013); Joshua Rogers, Hannah Wright Saleem Haddad, Marwa Baabad, and Basma Gaber, "'It's Dangerous to Be the First': Security Barriers to Women's Public Participation in Egypt, Libya and Yemen," ed. Saferworld (October 2013).
53 Some of these include the International Women's Leadership Program run by the College of Policing in the UK, and the UNDP program on Leadership and Strategic Planning. Further information can be found at UNDP, "Police Female Leaders Further Develop Their Skills Attending a Leadership &

Strategic Planning Course," news release, September 8, 2013: http://www.ye.undp.org/content/yemen/en/home/presscenter/pressreleases/2013/09/08/police-female-leaders-further-develop-their-skills-attending-a-leadership-strategic-planning-course/; The College of Policing, "Breaking Down Barriers for Female Officers from Yemen to Bahrain" (April 2014): http://www.college.police.uk/en/21649.htm; see also Ginny Hill, "Yemeni Women Sign up to Fight Terror," *BBC News,* April 2, 2007.

54 See, for example, Abdulrahman Hussein, *Women and Security in Yemen* (film), ed. Saferworld (2014).

55 Jamila Ali Raja, "Yemeni Women in Transition: Challenges and Oppurtunities," *CDDRL Working Papers* 140 (2013): http://fsi.stanford.edu/publications/yemeni_women_in_transition_challenges_and_opportunities.

56 Ibid.

57 Mary Christine-Heinze and Sarah Ahmed, "Integrating Women's Security Interests into Police Reform in Yemen," in *A YPC Policy Report*, ed. Yemen Polling Center (June 2013); YPC, "Public Perceptions of the Security Sector and Police Work in Yemen: Major Survey Findings" (Sanaa: Yemen Polling Center, 2013); Ahmed, "Women's Voices in the 'New Yemen'"; Joshua Rogers et al., "'It's Dangerous to Be the First'."

58 Tonita Murray, "Police-Building in Afghanistan: A Case Study of Civil Security Reform," *International Peacekeeping* 14, no. 1 (2007): 108.

59 Subcommittee on counterterrorism and intelligence of the Committee of Homeland Security, House of Representatives, *Understanding the Threat to the Homeland from AQAP*, First Session, September 18, 2013.

60 Paul R Pillar, "Counterterrorism," *Security Studies: An Introduction* (London: Routledge, 2008), 470.

61 Ahmed, "Women's Voices in the 'New Yemen'," 19.

62 Ibid., 26.

63 Ibid.

64 Ibid.

65 Ashraf al-Muraqab, "Yemeni Women Subject to Frequent Sexual Harassment" *Yemen Times*, January 3, 2012: http://www.yementimes.com/en/1639/report/1814/Yemeni-women-subject-to-frequent-sexual-harassment.htm

66 Ahmed, "Women's Voices in the 'New Yemen'," 27.

67 Ibid., 30.

68 Ibid., 29.

69 Sen (1992)

70 Heiner Hänggi, "Conceptualising Security Sector Reform and Reconstruction," *in Reform and Reconstruction of the Security Sector*, ed. Alan Bryden and Heiner Hänggi (Geneva: DCAF, 2004), 1.

71 NDC, "Topic: Final Report of the First Period to Build the Foundations of the Army and Security and Their Role," ed. NDC working group (April 13, 2013).

72 Megan Bastick, *Integrating Gender in Post-Conflict Security Sector Reform* (Geneva: DCAF, 2008).

73 Government of Yemen, "Draft Constitution English."

74 Bastick, *Integrating Gender in Post-Conflict Security Sector Reform*, 21.

75 Ibid.

76 Ibid.

77 Sheila Carapico, "Yemen between Revolution and Counter-Terrorism," in *Why Yemen Matters,* ed. Lackner, 48.

78 Adam C. Seitz, "The 'Arab Spring' and Yemeni Civil-Military Relations," in *Why Yemen Matters,* ed. Lackner, 59.

79 Ahmed, "Integrating Women's Security Interests into Police Reform in Yemen," 28.

80 Mason and King, "Engendering Development through Gender Equality in Rights, Resources, and Voice."

81 Khaled Fattah, "Yemen's Insecurity Dilemma," *The Yemen Times*, February 11, 2014.

82 Seitz, "The 'Arab Spring' and Yemeni Civil-Military Relations," 66.

83 Ibid.

84 "Yemen: Female Police Surveillance of Terrorists in the Security Points and at the Entrances to Major Cities," *Al-Methaq*, October 14, 2010: http://www.almethaq.net/news/news-17831.htm
85 Faisal Darem, "Women Police in Yemen Fight Terrorism and Gain Acceptance," *Al-Shorfa*, July 7, 2010.
86 Tonita Murray, *Report on the Status of Women in the Afghan National Police* (Kabul: Afghanistan, Ministry of the Interior. Funded by the Canadian International Development Agency [CIDA], 2005).
87 Hussein, *Women and Security in Yemen.*
88 Murray, *Report on the Status of Women in the Afghan National Police*, 4.
89 Bastick, *Integrating Gender in Post-Conflict Security Sector Reform*, 9.
90 Murray, *Report on the Status of Women in the Afghan National Police*, 5.
91 Ibid., 6.
92 Ibid.
93 Hussein, *Women and Security in Yemen.*
94 Sandra Wells and Betty Sowers Alt, *Police Women: Life with the Badge* (Westport, CT: Greenwood Publishing Group, 2005), 40-41.
95 Hussein, *Women and Security in Yemen.*
96 Darem, "Women Police in Yemen Fight Terrorism and Gain Acceptance."
97 "Police College Announces 'Specialized' New Unit for Yemeni Women," *Yemeress*, August 19, 2014.
98 YPC, "Public Perceptions of the Security Sector and Police Work in Yemen. Major Survey Findings," 70.
99 Ibid., 72.
100 Ali Ibrahim Al-Moshki, "Women's Unit Prepares for Potentially More Active Role in Counterterrorism," *The Yemen Times*, May 15, 2014.
101 Bastick, *Integrating Gender in Post-Conflict Security Sector Reform*, 10.

References

Ahmed, Sarah. "Women's Voices in the 'New Yemen'." In: *YPC Policy Report*, edited by Yemen Polling Center. Sanaa, Yemen: Yemen Polling Center, 2014.

Bastick, Megan. *Integrating Gender in Post-Conflict Security Sector Reform.* Geneva: DCAF, 2008.

Boucek, Christopher, and Marina Ottaway. *Yemen on the Brink.* Carnegie Endowment, 2010.

Caprioli, Mary. "Gendered Conflict." *Journal of Peace Research* 37, no. 1 (2000): 51–68.

Caprioli, Mary, and Mark A Boyer. "Gender, Violence, and International Crisis." *Journal of Conflict Resolution* 45, no. 4 (2001): 503–18.

Caprioli, Mary. "Gender Equality and State Aggression: The Impact of Domestic Gender Equality on State First Use of Force." *International Interactions* 29, no. 3 (2003): 195–214.

Caprioli, Mary. "Primed for Violence: The Role of Gender Inequality in Predicting Internal Conflict." *International Studies Quarterly* 49, no. 2 (2005): 161–78.

Carapico, Sheila. "Yemen between Revolution and Counter-Terrorism." In: *Why Yemen Matters: A Society in Transition*, edited by Helen Lackner. London: Saqi Books, 2014.

College of Policing. "Breaking Down Barriers for Female Officers from Yemen to Bahrain." College of Policing, UK, April 2014: http://www.college.police.uk/en/21649.htm

Darem, Faisal. "Women Police in Yemen Fight Terrorism and Gain Acceptance." *Al-Shorfa*, July 7, 2010.

ESCWA (Economic and Social Commission for Western Asia). "Demographic Profile of Yemen." United Nations, 2015: http://www.escwa.un.org/popin/members/yemen.pdf

Fattah, Khaled. "Yemen's Insecurity Dilemma." *Yemen Times*, February 11, 2014.

Government of Yemen. "Draft Constitution English." Government of Yemen, 2015.

Hänggi, Heiner. "Conceptualising Security Sector Reform and Reconstruction." In *Reform and Reconstruction of the Security Sector*, edited by Alan Bryden and Heiner Hänggi. Geneva: DCAF, 2004.

Heinze, Marie-Christine, and Sarah Ahmed. *Integrating Women's Security Interests into Police Reform in Yemen.* Yemen Polling Center, June 2013.

Hellmich, Christina. "Fighting Al Qaeda in Yemen? Rethinking the Nature of the Islamist Threat and the Effectiveness of US Counterterrorism Strategy." *Studies in Conflict & Terrorism* 35, no. 9 (2012): 618–33.

Hill, Ginny. "Yemeni Women Sign up to Fight Terror." *BBC News*, April 2, 2007.

Hunt, Swanee. "Let Women Rule." *Foreign Affairs,* May/June 2007.

Hussein, Abdulrahman. *Women and Security in Yemen*. Edited by Saferworld. 2014. Film, 11:44.

IFES. "Focus on Yemen: Civic and Political Participation Brief." December 7, 2010. Available at http://moneyandpolitics.org/Content/Publications/Papers/2010/Focus-on-Yemen-Civic-and-Political-Participation-Topic-Brief.aspx

IFES. "Yemen Alters Electoral Law." Elections guide. January 1, 2011: http://www.electionguide.org/digest/post/16649/

International Institute for Democracy and Electoral Assistance. "Voter Turnout Data for Yemen": http://www.idea.int/vt/countryview.cfm?CountryCode=YE

Iyer, Lakshmi, Anandi Mani, Prachi Mishra, and Petia Topalova. "The Power of Political Voice: Women's Political Representation and Crime in India." *American Economic Journal: Applied Economics* 4, no. 4 (2012): 165–93.

Johnsen, Gregory D. *The Last Refuge: Yemen, Al-Qaeda, and America's War in Arabia*. New York: WW Norton, 2013.

Kaufmann, Daniel. "Challenges in the Next Stage of Anti-Corruption." *New Perspectives on Combating Corruption.* Washington, DC: World Bank (1998): 139–64.

King, Gary, and Christopher J Murray. "Rethinking Human Security." *Political Science Quarterly* 116, no. 4 (2001): 585–610.

Lawless, Jennifer L. "Women, War, and Winning Elections: Gender Stereotyping in the Post-September 11th Era." *Political Research Quarterly* 57, no. 3 (2004): 479–90.

Lewis, Alexandra. "Violence in Yemen: Thinking About Violence in Fragile States Beyond the Confines of Conflict and Terrorism." *Stability: International Journal of Security and Development* 2, no. 1 (2013): 1–22.

Little, Thomas H, Dana Dunn, and Rebecca E Deen. "A View from the Top: Gender Differences in Legislative Priorities among State Legislative Leaders." *Women & Politics* 22, no. 4 (2001): 29–50.

Mani, Anandi. *The Power of Political Voice: How Women in Politics Can Help Tackle Gender Crime.* CAGE-Chatham House Series. London, Chatham House: 2014.

Mason, Andrew D, and Elizabeth M. King. "Engendering Development through Gender Equality in Rights, Resources, and Voice." World Bank, 2001.

Matsumae, Tatsuro, Lincoln C Chen, Tōkai Daigaku, and Strategic Peace. *Common Security in Asia: New Concepts of Human Security*. Strategic Peace and International Affairs Research Institute, Tokai University, 1995.

Al-Moshki, Ali Ibrahim. "Women's Unit Prepares for Potentially More Active Role in Counterterrorism." *Yemen Times*, May 15, 2014.

Murray, Tonita. *Report on the Status of Women in the Afghan National Police*. Kabul: Afghanistan, Ministry of the Interior. Funded by the Canadian International Development Agency (CIDA), 2005.

Murray, Tonita. "Police-Building in Afghanistan: A Case Study of Civil Security Reform." *International Peacekeeping* 14, no. 1 (2007): 108–26.

NDC. "Topic: Final Report of the First Period to Build the Foundations of the Army and Security and Their Role." Edited by the NDC working group. Sanaa, Yemen: National Dialogue Conference, 2013. [online]

Norville, Valerie. *The Role of Women in Global Security.* Washington, DC: United States Institute for Peace 2010.

Pande, Rohini, and Deanna Ford. "Gender Quotas and Female Leadership." In *World Development Report 2012: Gender Equality and Development Background Paper.* World Bank, 2012.

Paxton, Pamela, Sheri Kunovich, and Melanie M Hughes. "Gender in Politics." *Annual Review of Sociology* 33 (2007): 263–84.

Pillar, Paul R. "Counterterrorism." In *Security Studies, An Introduction.* London: Routledge, 2008.
"Police College Announces 'Specialized' New Unit for Yemeni Women." *Yemeress*, August 19, 2014.
Raja, Jamila Ali. "Yemeni Women in Transition: Challenges and Oppurtunities." *CDDRL Working Papers* 140. Stanford: CDDRL, 2013: http://fsi.stanford.edu/publications/yemeni_women_in_transition_challenges_and_opportunities/
Republic of Yemen. *Report on the Situation of Women in Yemen 2007.* Women's National Committee, 2007.
Republic of Yemen. *Sixth National Report on the Implementation of the CEDAW.* December 2006.
Rogers, Joshua, Hannah Wright, Saleem Haddad, Marwa Baabad, and Basma Gaber. "'It's Dangerous to Be the First': Security Barriers to Women's Public Participation in Egypt, Libya and Yemen." Edited by Saferworld. October 2013.
Al-Salahi, Foad. "Yemeni Women's Political Participation." Women's National Committee working paper for the Second Yemeni Women National Conference, 8-10, 2003: http://www.yemeni-women.org.ye/Yemeni%20Women%92s%20Political%20participation.htm
Sayigh, Yezid. "Fixing Broken Windows: Security Sector Reform in Palestine, Lebanon and Yemen." Carnegie Papers. October 2009.
Seitz, Adam C. "The 'Arab Spring' and Yemeni Civil-Military Relations." In: *Why Yemen Matters: A Society in Transition*, edited by Helen Lackner. London: Saqi Books, 2014.
Thomas, Sue. "The Impact of Women on State Legislative Policies." *Journal of Politics* 53, no. 4 (1991): 958-76.
Subcommittee on Counterterrorism and Intelligence of the Committee of Homeland Security, House of Representatives. *Understanding the Threat to the Homeland from AQAP.* First Session, September 18, 2013.
UNDP. *Gender Inequality Report 2010.* Human Development Report. New York: UNDP, 2010.
UNDP. "Police Female Leaders Further Develop Their Skills Attending a Leadership & Strategic Planning Course." News release, September 8, 2013: http://www.ye.undp.org/content/yemen/en/home/presscenter/pressreleases/2013/09/08/police-female-leaders-further-develop-their-skills-attending-a-leadership-strategic-planning-course/
UNICEF. "Info by Country – Yemen Statistics." UNICEF, 2014: http://www.unicef.org/infobycountry/yemen_statistics.html
USAID. *New Insights on Preventing Child Marriage.* International Centre for Research on Women, April 2007: https://www.icrw.org/files/publications/New-Insights-on-Preventing-Child-Marriage.pdf
Wells, Sandra, and Betty Sowers Alt. *Police Women: Life with the Badge.* Westport, Connecticut: Greenwood Publishing Group, 2005.
World Bank. The Status of the Progress of Women in the Middle East & North Africa (2009): http://siteresources.worldbank.org/INTMENA/Resources/MENA_Gender_Compendium-2009-1.pdf
World Economic Forum. "Global Gender Gap Report 2014." Geneva: World Economic Forum, 2014: http://www3.weforum.org/docs/GGGR14/GGGR_CompleteReport_2014.pdf, http://www.unicef.org/infobycountry/yemen_statistics.html
World Food Programme. "WFP Situation Report 16–31 December 2014." United Nations World Food Programme, 2014: http://documents.wfp.org/stellent/groups/public/documents/ep/wfp271276.pdf
WHO (World Health Organization). "Yemen – Basic Country Data." WHO, 2015: http://www.who.int/leishmaniasis/resources/YEMEN.pdf
Yadav, Stacey Philbrick, and Janine A Clark. "Disappointments and New Directions: Women, Partisanship, and the Regime in Yemen." *Hawwa* 8, no. 1 (2010): 55–95.
YPC. "Public Perceptions of the Security Sector and Police Work in Yemen: Major Survey Findings." Sanaa: Yemen Polling Center, 2013.

About the Contributors

Noel Brehony is chair of Menas Associates, the British-Yemeni Society and the Council for British Research in the Levant; his PhD was on Libya. In his diplomatic career he served in Kuwait, Yemen, Jordan and Egypt. He was later Director of Middle East Affairs for Rolls-Royce plc. A former president of the British Society of Middle East Studies, he is on the Advisory Board of the London Middle East Institute at SOAS. He co-edited *British and Egyptian Relations from Suez to the Present Day* (Saqi 2007). His book *Yemen Divided,* the Story of a Failed State in South Arabia was published by I B Tauris in 2011.

Joana Cook is a PhD Candidate in the Department of War Studies at King's College London where her research focuses on women in security practices in Yemen. She has previously worked at the International Centre for the Study of Radicalisation (ICSR) at King's College London, and as a journalist throughout Canada and Africa. She is a Research Affiliate with both the Canadian Network for Research on Terrorism, Security and Society (TSAS), and Public Safety Canada (Kanishka Program) where she focuses on women and extremism.

Stephen W. Day is a professor of Middle East politics. He received his PhD from Georgetown University in Washington, DC in 2001. Since then, he has taught at Indiana University, St. Lawrence University, and Stetson University and Rollins College (currently) in Florida. He was recently named a Fulbright specialist in diplomacy, peace-making, and conflict resolution. His book, *Regionalism and Rebellion in Yemen: A Troubled National Union*, was published in 2012 by Cambridge University Press. He has authored numerous articles in Middle East Journal, Middle East Policy, Foreign Policy, and online sites. He uses Twitter @ DaySWTweet.

James Firebrace graduated from Cambridge University with a BA and MA in Social and Political Science, and later gained an MSc with distinction at the London Business School. His early career focused on the development challenges of the Middle East and Sahelian Africa, setting up and running a number of consortia. A spell as Director General of Consumers International led to extensive consulting and advisory work in the energy and water sectors. He set up James Firebrace Associates Ltd (www.firebrace.com) in 1998, specializing in the analysis and management of longer-term strategic issues, particularly in relation to water, economic revitalization, sustainable livelihoods, innovation and the private sector, and conflict prevention.

Helen Lackner has worked in Yemen for over 15 years in the past half century. Her long practical experience of rural development issues in over 30 countries has informed her analyses and writing. She is currently emphasizing research on a range of aspects of Yemen's social and political development and has a particular interest in water management. She is the author of *PDR Yemen: Outpost of Socialist Development in Arabia*, and most recently edited *Why Yemen Matters* (Saqi, 2014). She occasionally contributes to Open Democracy and other publications.

Martha Mundy is professor Emerita of Anthropology at the London School of Economics and Research Associate in the Interdisciplinary Graduate Environmental Science Program at the American University of

Beirut. She has published: *Domestic Government: Kinship, Community and Polity in North Yemen* (1995) and with R. Saumarez Smith, *Governing Property, Making the Modern State: Law, Administration and Production in Ottoman Syria* (2007). As these titles suggest, her enduring concerns have been with agrarian relations and the changing nature of work in the Arab East, with property and legal form, and with Islamic jurisprudence as a tradition of debate.

Frédéric Pelat studied tropical agronomy in Toulouse and Montpellier. He lived in Yemen from 1998 to 2011, working through the NGO that he created (Iddeales) on small development projects aiming at enhancing local resources and farmers' knowledge. He holds a MSc in social anthropology from the London School of Economics and is currently a PhD student in the anthropology and sociology of development at IHEID Geneva. Recent publications include, 'Neither security nor sovereignty: the political economy of food in Yemen' in *Food Security and Food Sovereignty in the Arab World*, edited by M. Kamrava and Z. Babar, (Hurst 2014), co-authored with M. Mundy and A. al-Hakimi.

Peter Salisbury is a freelance journalist and analyst who has worked on Yemen for six years. The former energy editor at MEED, the Middle East Economic Digest, he has contributed regularly to Businessweek Middle East, the Economist, the Financial Times and Foreign Policy, among others. Peter enjoyed a close association with Chatham House's Yemen Forum between 2011 and 2013, working as a project consultant and co-authoring a major new study on the effect of corruption and capital flight on political stability. He has also consulted to the UK government's Department of International Development, the UN and the World Bank on political economy issues in Yemen.

Saud Al-Sarhan, PhD, is the Director of Research, and Head of the Contemporary Political Thought Unit at King Faisal Centre for Research and Islamic Studies. He is also a visiting fellow at the "Legitimate and Illegitimate Violence in Islamic Thought" (LIVIT) project at Exeter University in the United Kingdom, and a Distinguished International Affairs Fellow, the National Council on U.S.-Arab Relations, USA.

Charles Schmitz is professor of Geography at Towson University in Baltimore, Maryland, an affiliated scholar with the Middle East Institute in Washington, DC, and a board member of the American Institute for Yemeni Studies. Recent publications include a chapter on Yemen's geography and another on the economy in *Yemen: Nations in Focus* by Steven Caton, a series of short articles with the Middle East Institute on the rise of Ansar Allah, and "Yemen: Failing State or Failing Politics" in *Fragile Politics: Weak States in the Greater Middle East*, edited by Mehran Kamrava.

Iain Walker is Senior Researcher at the Max Planck Institute for Social Anthropology in Halle. Following his master's fieldwork in Mauritius, he carried out doctoral research in the Comoros, and has subsequently worked on issues of mobilities and identities in East Africa, as well as in Yemen, the UAE and Saudi Arabia. He has held an ARC Postdoctoral Fellowship at Macquarie University, Sydney, and an ESRC Fellowship at Oxford. His current project, 'Converging cultures: the Hadrami diaspora in the Indian Ocean', is part of the Leverhulme-funded Oxford Diasporas Programme (2011-2015). He is the author of *Becoming the Other, Being Oneself: Constructing Identities in a Connected World.*

Abbreviations

AQAP	Al Qaeda in the Arabian Peninsula
CIARC	Consortium of International Agricultural Research Center
COCA	Central Organization for Control and Auditing
CPO	Central Planning Office (CPO),
DFID	Department for International Development
DPA	Document of Pledge and Accord
EITI	Extractive Industries Transparency Initiative
FAO	Food and Agriculture Organisation
GAFSP	Global Agriculture and Food Security Program
GCC	Gulf Cooperation Council
GDP	Gross Domestic Product
GPC	General People's Congress
GTZ	Deutsche Gesellschaft für Technische Zusammenarbeit
IFAD	International Fund for Agricultural Development
IMF	International Monetary Fund
ISIS	Islamic State of Iraq and Levant
IWRM	Integrated Water Resource Management
JMP	Joint Meeting Parties
LNG	Liquefied Natural Gas
MAI	Ministry of Agriculture and Irrigation
MoPIC	Ministry of Planning and International Cooperation
MWE	Ministry of Water and Environment
NASS	National Agricultural Sector Strategy
NDC	National Dialogue Conference
NFSS	National Food Security Strategy
NLF	National Liberation Front
NWRA	National Water Resources Agency
NWSSIP	National Water Sector Strategy and Investment Programme
OECD	Organization for Economic Co-operation and Development
PDRY	People's Democratic Republic of Yemen
PNPA	Peace and National Partnership Agreement

RALP	Rainfed Agriculture and Livestock Project
RWWSSP	Rural Water Supply and Sanitation Project
SFD	Social Fund for Development
SNACC	Supreme National Authority for Combatting Corruption
SSR	Security Sector Reform
TFR	Total Fertility Rate
TWSLC	Taiz Water and Sanitation Local Corporation
UNDP	United National Development Programme
UNSC	United Nations Security Council
USAID	United States Agency for International Development
WNC	Women's National Committee
WHO	World Health Organization
WPF	World Food Programme
YAR	Yemen Arab Republic
YECO	Yemen Economic Corporation
YLNG	Yemen Liquefied Natural Gas
YSP	Yemeni Socialist Party

Chronology

1904/05	Border between British Protectorates and Ottoman controlled area established.
1934	Britain and Imamate agree on border. Treaty of Taif.
1962	Overthrow of the Imamate. Formation of the Yemen Arab Republic.
1962-70	Civil War in YAR.
1963	The National Liberation Front set up and start campaign to end British control of South Arabia.
1967	The People's Republic of South Yemen (PRSY) established.
1970	PRSY becomes the People's Democratic Republic of Yemen.
1978	Ali Abdullah Saleh becomes President of YAR.
1986	January: civil war in the PDRY.
1990	Unification of YAR and PDRY to create Republic of Yemen; Ali Abdullah Saleh President and Ali Salem al-Bayd as Vice President.
	Iraq invades Kuwait. Expulsion of 800,000 Yemenis from Saudi Arabia.
1990s	Emergence of Believing Youth, later became known as the Huthi Movement.
1994	Civil War between north and south during which southern leaders set up the Democratic Republic of Yemen. War ends with defeat of south in July.
1995	Regime accepts IMF advice and Structural Adjustment.
1999	Presidential election: Ali Abdullah Saleh elected President.
2000	Saudi Arabia and Yemen agree on Jeddah border treaty. USS Cole attacked in Aden port.
2004	Hussein Badr al-Din al-Huthi killed by government forces, during first Huthi War.
2005	Second Huthi war.
	Joint Meeting Parties formed.
2006	Ali Abdullah Saleh re-elected. 23 AQAP suspects escape from prison.
2007	Third Huthi war.
	Emergence of Southern Movement (Hirak).
2008	Fourth Huthi war.
2009	Fifth and sixth Huthi war. Saudi military support Yemeni armed forces.
	Formation of Al-Qaeda in the Arabian Peninsula (AQAP).
2010	January: Friends of Yemen set up in London.

2011	February: the anti- regime movement develops and expands throughout the country after the downfall of Tunisian and Egyptian rulers. 18 March: over 50 peaceful demonstrators killed in Sana'a by snipers suspected of being regime supporters. 3 June: Saleh seriously wounded and many of his close allies killed and wounded in bomb explosion at the Presidency's mosque during Friday prayers. May-June: AQAP seizes territory and sets up Islamic emirates in Abyan. October: UN Security Council adopts Resolution 2014 supporting GCC initiative on transfer of power, need for humanitarian assistance and concern over activities of al Qaeda. November: Ali Abdullah Saleh signs GCC transfer of power agreement on 23 November. December: Government of National Unity formed.
2012	February: Abd Rabbuh Mansour Hadi elected President of Yemen for 2 year Transitional period. Start of reforms of security/military institutions. May: AQAP attack on Sanaa parade; 120 young security graduates dead. June: army re-takes lands in Abyan from AQAP. September: Riyadh Donor Conference pledge $7.9 billion in economic assistance.
2013	March: National Dialogue Conference starts. April: Major changes in the military and security forces. August: Government apologizes to South and Huthis for their treatment by former governments. December: AQAP kill 65 at the military hospital in Sanaa.
2014	January: NDC ends. Proposals for a federal structure are agreed by special committee. Huthi military activity in Saada, al-Jawf and Amran. Huthis drive Salafis out of Dammaj. February: Committee to draft new constitution is appointed. April: Army launched major offensive against AQAP. June: Huthi forces capture Amran July: Fuel subsidies cut. Huthis move into Sanaa and demand reversal of subsidy cuts. September: Signing of the Peace and National Partnership Agreement. October-December: Huthis increase pressure on government in Sanaa and move into other governorates, including Hodeida and Ibb. Fighting involving Huthis and anti-Huthi tribes and AQAP in al-Bayda. November: Government under Khaled Bahah appointed.
2015	January Draft constitution is published. President Hadi and Bahah government resign and are put under house arrest by Huthis. February: Huthis set up Revolutionary Council which issues a Constitutional Declaration. February: Hadi escapes to Aden and withdraws his resignation. March Launch of Operation Decisive Storm.

Maps

Yemen – Physical Map

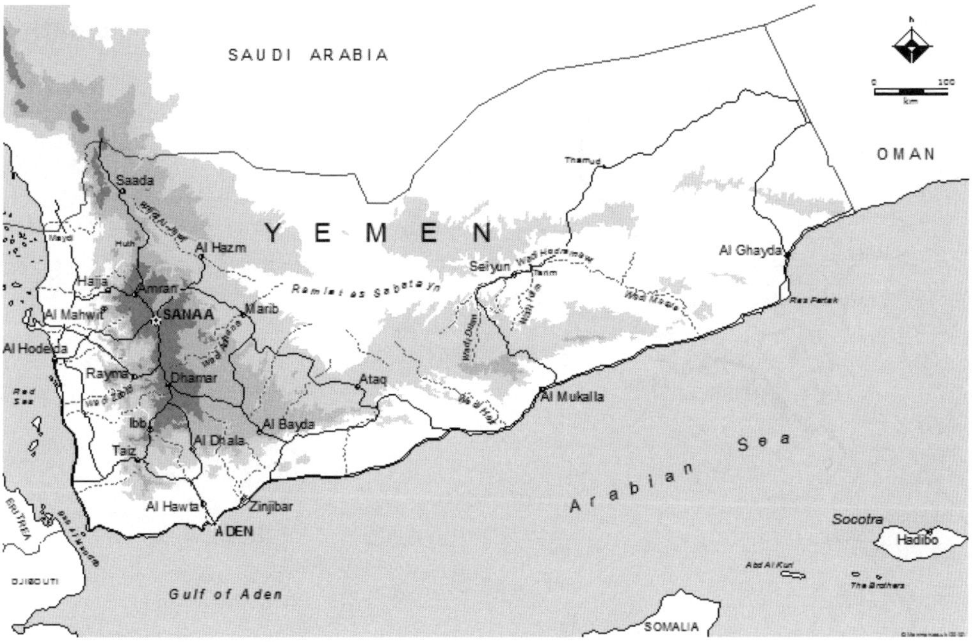

Map by Sebastian Ballard (Mapman)

Yemen – Political Map

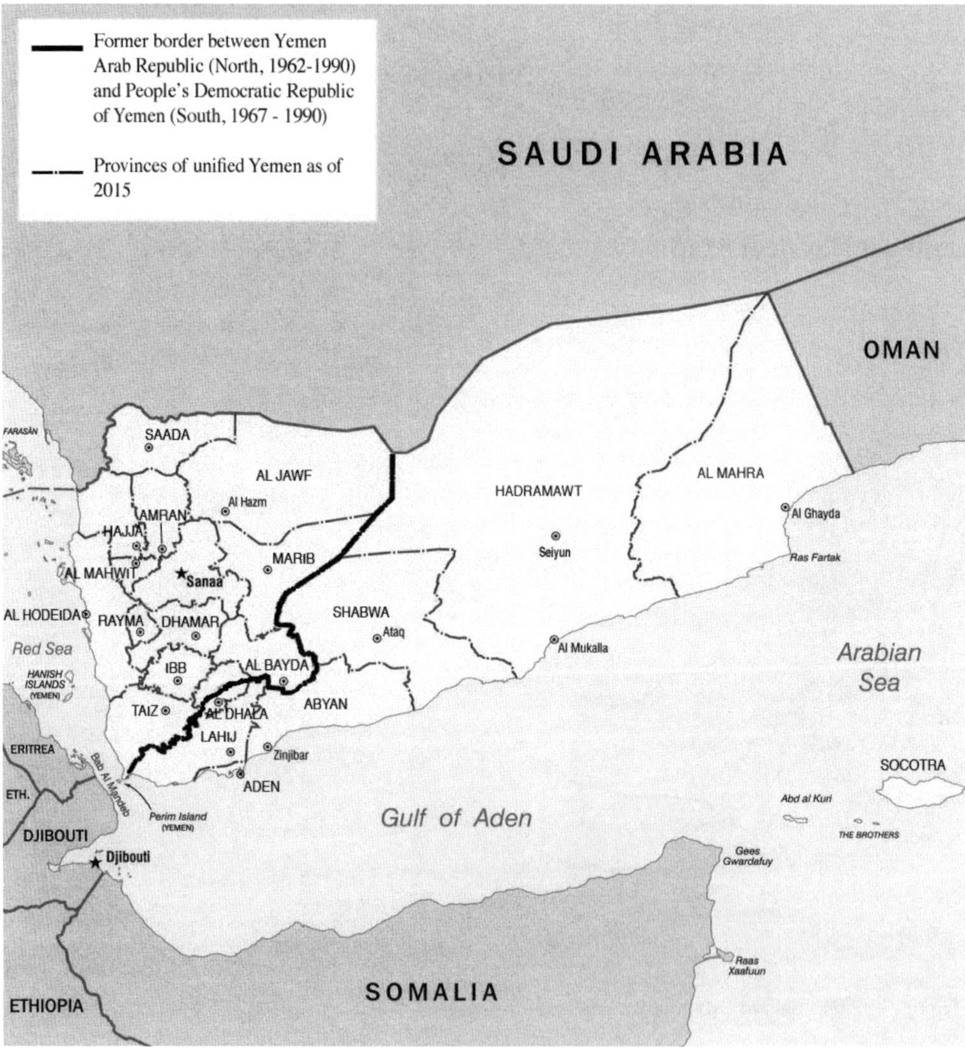

Political Map of Yemen Map by Azhrai Elneiri (KFCRIS)

Yemen – Federal Map

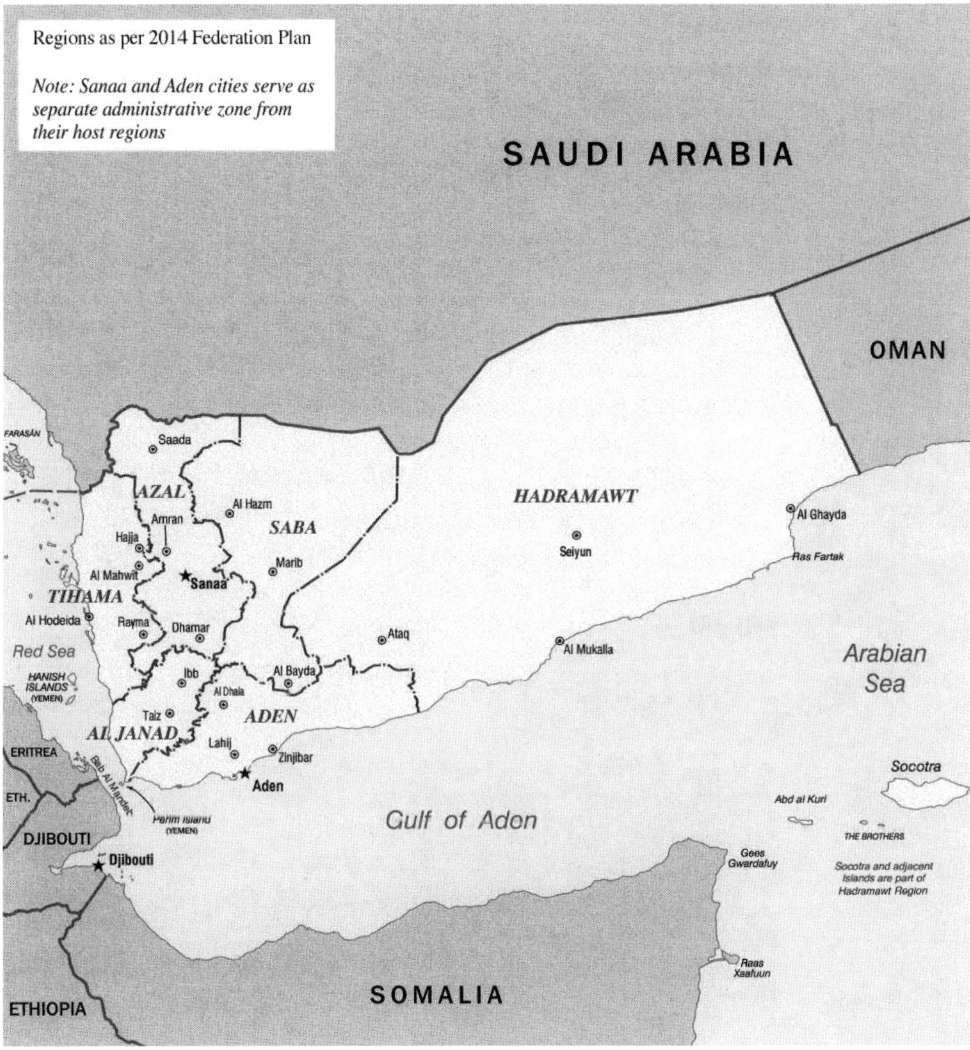

Yemen Federal Regions Map by Azhrai Elneiri (KFCRIS)